The GIANT Bathroom Book of DUMBOLOGY

Geoff Tibballs

Magpie Books, London

Constable & Robinson Ltd
3 The Lanchesters
162 Fulham Palace Road
London W6 9ER
www.constablerobinson.com

First published in the UK as *Dumbology* by Magpie Books,
an imprint of Constable & Robinson Ltd, 2005

This edition published by Magpie Books, 2008

Illustrations by Duncan Proudfoot

A copy of the British Library Cataloguing in Publication Data
is available from the British Library

ISBN 978-1-84529-950-7

Printed and bound in the European Union

3 5 7 9 10 8 6 4 2

Contents

Military Errors

2

The Spy who Came in from the Litter Tray

At the height of the Cold War, in what must have been a truly surreal planning meeting, the CIA came up with the inspired idea of wiring an ordinary domestic cat to obtain covert information about the Russians. It was hoped that the animal, which was surgically altered to accommodate transmitting and control devices, could eavesdrop on conversations from such vantage points as window sills, park benches, or dustbins.

The clandestine project, codenamed Acoustic Kitty, took five years to design and cost over $15 million. The patriotic pussy experienced no little discomfort in the course of its contribution towards national security. In a delicate operation, its stomach was opened up so that batteries and wires could be inserted. Its tail was used as an antenna. When the cat surrendered to natural hunger cravings and displayed a tendency to abandon its surveillance mission, surgeons simply put in another wire to override the desire for food.

Finally in 1966, after exhaustive testing, Acoustic Kitty was ready to be released on its first live trial at a top secret location. Nothing, it seemed, had been left to chance. The CIA surveillance van was driven to a park and, as agents and scientists sat in the vehicle twiddling hi-tech dials, congratulating each other on their expertise, the cat was set free. Seconds later it walked across a road and was run over by a taxi.

Military Magoos

For sheer short-sightedness, the achievements of Prussian Army lookouts under Prince Augustus William were hard to beat.

In 1757 the Prussian forces were locked in bitter conflict with Austria. In the face of an Austrian offensive, the Prussians found themselves in a tight corner. They harboured hope that a nearby road would offer a safe escape route until the lookouts reported that the road in question was blocked by batteries of Austrian artillery. It was only after the Prussians had sustained heavy casualties in selecting an alternative means of escape that they learned that the Austrian guns were, in truth, nothing more deadly than a herd of cattle.

Having clearly learned little from their folly, the lookouts proceeded to cause further panic after spotting what they believed to be more

Austrian guns. This time the Prussians burned all their own transport and pontoon bridges before realizing that these "guns" were really tree trunks.

Regiment of firs

Prussian commanders of the eighteenth century obviously suffered from appalling eyesight. In 1757 the Prussian army was forced to abandon a safe escape route when its leaders saw the road blocked by what they thought were batteries of Austrian artillery . . . but which turned out to be a herd of cattle. In the same year, the Prussians failed to press home their advantage against the French when they mistook young fir trees for French infantry marching to the rescue.

The Pig War: A Ham-fisted Approach

For thirteen years in the mid-nineteenth century, Britain and the United States hovered on the brink of all-out war as a ruthless invasion force sparked a bitter territorial dispute. The force in question was neither a well-drilled army nor a flotilla of warships . . . just a solitary wandering pig.

The pig was a none-too-innocent pawn in a game that had been played out for over forty years. Both the British and the Americans had long laid claims to the Oregon Country, a vast expanse of land consisting of the present-day states of Washington, Oregon and Idaho, parts of Montana and Wyoming, and the Canadian province of British Columbia. The Anglo-American agreement of 1818 had provided for joint occupation of the Oregon Country but by 1845 both sides had grown dissatisfied with this arrangement. The British were alarmed at the hordes of Americans swarming over the Rocky Mountains to settle on the west coast and argued that, in doing so, they were trespassing on land promised to Britain by earlier treaties and agreements and through the trading activities of the Hudson's Bay Company. This estimable company had been formed by the British back in 1670 primarily to trade in furs with North American Indians. For their part, the Americans considered the British presence an affront to their "manifest destiny" and firmly rejected the idea that the great land west of the Rockies should remain under foreign influence. Threats and counter-threats ensued, but common sense ultimately prevailed and in June 1846 the dispute was resolved peacefully with the signing of the Oregon Treaty.

Or so it seemed. The wording of the treaty was decidedly ambiguous. It awarded the United States undisputed possession of the Pacific Northwest south of the 49th parallel, extending the boundary to "the middle of the channel which separates the continent from Vancouver's Island; and thence southerly through the middle of the said channel, and of Fuca's straits to the Pacific Ocean." The problem was that there were two channels between Vancouver's Island and the mainland – Haro Strait, nearest to Vancouver's Island, and Rosario Strait, nearest to the mainland. And separating these two channels was a small, sparsely-inhabited outcrop called San Juan Island. Naturally enough, Britain insisted that the boundary should run through Rosario Strait; equally predictably, the Americans said that it should pass through Haro Strait. In short, both sides considered that the treaty had awarded them possession of San Juan Island.

The Hudson's Bay Company had posted a notice of possession on San Juan Island even before the Oregon Treaty. In 1850 it set up a salmon-curing station there and three years later a sheep ranch known as Belle Vue Farm. Meanwhile the Americans went about pressing their own claims to the island and when Washington Territory was created in 1853, San Juan Island was attached to Whatcom, its northernmost county.

By 1859 there were some 25 Americans on San Juan Island. They eyed the British residents with deep suspicion. The feeling was mutual. Amid such an atmosphere of tension and hostility, even the most trivial incident would send either side running to their respective government. Such an incident occurred on 15 June of that year when a pig owned by Englishman Charles Griffin strayed onto the potato patch of his American neighbour, Lyman Cutler. Reacting angrily to the pig poking its snout in where it didn't belong, Cutler fetched his rifle and shot the animal dead. Griffin responded to this act of aggression by protesting to the British government who threatened to have Cutler arrested. This gesture brought a swift reprisal from the American citizens on the island in the form of a petition requesting US military protection. The Commander of the Department of Oregon, Brigadier General William S. Harney, hated the British anyway, and needed little excuse to intervene. Thus on 27 July, 66 US soldiers of the 9th Infantry under the leadership of Captain George E. Pickett landed on San Juan Island. The Pig War was up and trotting.

The British were not prepared to take this lying down and James Douglas, Governor of British Columbia, ordered three warships under Captain Geoffrey Hornby to be sent to remove Pickett and his troops – by peaceful means if at all possible. Although heavily outnumbered, Pickett refused to withdraw. Mindful of his orders, Hornby was reluctant to attack and so the situation drifted into stalemate. For the next couple of months the two sides kept a respectful distance from each other at opposite ends of the island, all the while building up their forces. Each new contingent of British sailors arriving in San Juan harbour was matched by a fresh influx of American troops. By the end of August the number of American soldiers on the island had risen to 461 (guarded by 14 cannon) but they were still no match for the British who now had five warships in the vicinity, carrying a total of 2,140 troops and 167 guns.

When word of the stand-off reached Washington, officials there were horrified to learn that the simple action of an irate farmer had escalated into an international crisis. In the hope of averting conflict between the world's two great powers, US President James Buchanan sent General Winfield Scott, Commanding General of the US Army, to try to keep a lid on the confrontation. Rear Admiral Robert Baynes, commander of British naval forces in the Pacific, was also alarmed at the prospect of military action and told Governor Douglas that he had no intention of involving "two great nations in a war over a squabble about a pig."

After the ham-fisted over-reaction to a local dispute, at last common sense began to prevail. General Scott and Governor Douglas put their heads together and agreed that each nation should withdraw the vast majority of its reinforcements, leaving San Juan Island with a single company of US soldiers and a British warship anchored in the harbour.

San Juan Island remained under joint military occupation until 1872. No shots were fired, the only casualty (apart from the unfortunate pig) being Brigadier General Harney, who was officially rebuked and subsequently reassigned for allowing the situation to deteriorate to the brink of war. Eventually it was Kaiser Wilhelm I of Germany who was called in to act as arbitrator and, following a year-long deliberation, his three-man commission ruled in favour of the United States, establishing the boundary line through Haro Strait. Thus San Juan Island became an American possession and the final frontier between the United States and Canada was set. On 25 November 1872 the British Royal Marines withdrew from the island and by July 1874 the last of the US troops had also departed. As far as the senseless Pig War was concerned, the Kaiser had saved America's bacon.

8

Invasion Farce

The most inept invasion of recent times was carried out in 2002 by the Royal Marine Commandos on a highly realistic exercise designed to practise beach landings. The twenty men, bristling with assault rifles and mortars, stormed ashore from their amphibious landing craft. In a well-rehearsed manoeuvre, they fanned out across the sand to take up firing positions and search out the troops playing the role of defenders. It was all hugely impressive – until two passing policemen politely asked them why they were invading Spain.

The red-faced Marines apologized profusely, explaining that they thought they were in Gibraltar. "Ah, señores," replied the policemen, "that is a few miles to the south."

While the Marines clambered back into their craft to carry on their war elsewhere, British defence chiefs tried to play down the map-reading blunder. At a time of delicate negotiations with Spain over the future of Gibraltar, a sudden act of war by Britain was deemed far from helpful. Luckily the mayor of La Línea de la Concepción, Juan Carlos Juarez, dismissed the invasion as "trivial".

He added proudly: "They landed on our coast with typical commando tactics. But we managed to hold them on the beach."

Siesta slip-up

On the baking hot afternoon of 20 April 1836, while his Mexican troops were engaged in frequent border skirmishes with Texan soldiers, General Antonio Lopez de Santa Anna ordered his troops to take a much-needed siesta. While the Mexicans dozed, the Texans struck and routed the enemy in just 18 minutes.

The K-Boats of the First World War: Sub-Standard

In response to erroneous intelligence reports during the First World War that the Germans were building a new submarine capable of speeds of up to 22 knots, Britain came up with its own monster craft – a cross between a submarine and a battleship which the Allies fully expected would give them control of the seas both above and below water. As it turned out these K-boats, as they were called, came nowhere near to achieving either goal. On the contrary they were such a disaster, killing almost as many British sailors as German submarines could manage, that one wonders whether the Hun deliberately planted the misinformation which led to their construction.

Weighing 1,883 tons and with a length of 338 feet, the steam-powered K-boats were three times the size of any other contemporary British submarine. But, at least where submarines are concerned, size isn't everything. Their sheer bulk rendered the K-boats clumsy on the surface, ponderous when diving and, once eventually underwater, difficult to raise to the surface again. It took the K-boats an eternal 11 minutes to dive, but this excessive time did not seem to perturb the naval planners who assumed that submarine crews would see the masts of approaching ships long before the enemy could spot them. In reaching this conclusion, the planners appeared to forget that the Germans were equipped with such items as aeroplanes and airships which would have no trouble in detecting a cumbersome, slow-diving submarine. To get the K-boats' two small funnels folded down into their watertight wells took just thirty seconds, but there were also a series of ventilators that had to be shut before diving and the most trivial obstruction – such as a piece of wayward wire – was sufficient to jam these ventilators open. On other occasions the K-boats inexplicably dived too fast, making them liable to exceed the safe diving depth. All things considered, some sceptics thought the K-boats were simply an accident waiting to happen. They didn't have to wait long.

The first two flotillas of K-boats were ready for testing at the start of 1917. K2 promptly caught fire on its inaugural test dive, and on 29 January, K13 sank during trials in Gare Loch off the Firth of Clyde in Scotland. Meanwhile K3, with the future King George VI aboard, mysteriously dived to the sea bed on its first test but fortunately resurfaced with its VIP unharmed. K4 ran aground, K5 sank, K6 got stuck on the sea bed and K7 was written off after accidentally ramming K17 on exercise. But the worst in this dreadful series of accidents occurred on the night of 31 January 1918 as a large force of warships were leaving the Firth of Forth on exercise. Two flotillas of K-boats were travelling a distance ahead of the cruiser squadron when a jammed helm on K22 (which was the hapless K13, renumbered) caused two K-boats to collide and veer alarmingly out of control. In the ensuing confusion, one of the cruisers rammed and sank K17 and K6 crashed into K4, cutting her in half. When K22 was damaged irreparably following a disagreement with another cruiser, it was decided to put the K-boats – and the submariners who had the misfortune to serve on them – out of their misery. As the war came to an end, they were consigned to their rightful place – the scrapheap – having claimed 250 British lives but not one German.

General Chaos

"Biscuit" Brandon

The 1824 war between Britain and the Ashanti (part of present-day Ghana) witnessed a display of supreme incompetence by Charles Brandon, the British army's stores manager. Surrounded by 10,000 warriors and running low on ammunition, the British redcoats ordered Brandon to break open the reserve ammunition he had brought from the coast. As the Ashanti forces closed in, Brandon unscrewed the ammunition boxes, only to find that they were full of biscuits instead. He had brought the wrong supplies.

Mink manoeuvres

In February 1995 Sweden's defence minister sheepishly admitted that the supposed Russian submarine intrusions into Sweden's waters that had greatly concerned the nation's security forces for the past three years, were really just frolicking minks. The Minister blamed the confusion on hi-tech hydrophonic equipment installed in 1992.

Unleash the dogs of war

During the Second World War, the Russians invented a unique device called the "dog mine". The idea was to train dogs with food to run beneath tanks and thus, with bombs strapped to their backs, to wreak havoc on the German Panzer divisions. Alas, the dogs proved unexpectedly true to their training, associating food with only Russian tanks, and forcing an entire Soviet division into retreat. The plan was quickly scrapped.

Never on a Sunday

Confederate General Thomas "Stonewall" Jackson was a devoutly religious man who considered fighting on a Sunday to be sinful. He adhered to this principle at the American Civil War battle of Mechanicsville in 1862 where he stood alone praying on an adjacent hill, steadfastly refusing to speak to anyone all afternoon. Suffering from a distinct lack of leadership, his troops sustained heavy losses.

Scraper capers

A paint scraper worth 50 cents was accidentally dropped into a torpedo launcher of the US nuclear submarine *Swordfish* in 1978, thereby jamming the loading piston in the submarine's cylinder. After divers toiled in vain for a week trying to free the piston, it was eventually decided to put the *Swordfish* into dry-dock where her repair bill came to $171,000.

No enemy needed

After years of living in the shadow of the Prussian ruler Frederick the Great, Austrian Emperor Joseph II set his heart on a military triumph of his own. Declaring that he was going to rid the world of barbarians, Joseph marched into Transylvania in 1788 and prepared to attack the infidel Turks. Ignoring local advice, he camped his army in marshland outside Belgrade and watched helplessly as 172,000 of his troops promptly went down with malaria, 33,000 fatally. When he heard that the Turkish Grand Vizier was on his way, Joseph took the remains of his army to do battle with the Turks. A long march saw the Austrians reach a bridge near the town of Karansebes by nightfall. There, some of the Austrian hussars bought a heady local brew from roadside peasants, but when a number of infantrymen tried to share the experience, the hussars forced them back. Instant dissent broke out in the Austrian ranks with the irate footsoldiers firing shots into the air and attempting to frighten the hussars by shouting "Turci! Turci!" as if the enemy were upon them. The drunken hussars joined the call, also yelling "Turci!" and firing indiscriminately. By now the rear columns of the Austrian army were approaching the bridge and, hearing the pandemonium and shooting, they panicked and started firing at each other in the darkness. In an effort to calm the situation, officers raced up and down the lines calling "Halt!", but to the hysterical soldiers it sounded like "Allah!" Certain that the Turks were about to slaughter them, the baggage handlers and transport workers at the rear endeavoured to drive their wagons through the mass of troops ahead, but merely succeeded in creating a terrible stampede and sending soldiers plunging into the river. Those who didn't drown were crushed underfoot. It was not until daybreak that it became apparent that the Austrians had killed or injured 10,000 of their own number. The Turks still hadn't arrived.

Fortunately not a twenty-one gun salute

Presiding at the funeral of a Korean War veteran in Champion, Ohio in 1994, Rev. Thomas Gillum was accidentally shot in the face when the local guard of honour fired a four-gun salute.

Wresting defeat from the jaws of victory

When British General Sir George Colley invaded the Transvaal in 1881, his outnumbered troops suffered an immediate setback at the hands of the Boers. He thought he could turn things around by attacking the enemy from the 6,000-foot high Majuba Hill, but, instead of digging in at the summit, the British began arrogantly jeering at the Boer garrison at the foot of the hill.

Meanwhile Colley himself was so confident of success that he decided to take a nap. Stung into action, a few hundred Boers started to climb the hill under cover of fire from their colleagues on the ground. The news was relayed to Colley, but he thought it of little consequence and went back to sleep. When the gravity of the situation finally dawned on him, he attempted to launch a counter attack, only to be shot through the head by a twelve-year-old boy. From their vastly superior vantage position, the British lost 93 men that day; the Boers lost one.

Child's play

A child pulled the wrong lever at a Dutch army show and destroyed the £115,000 engine of a brand new armoured vehicle. The army had opened up the vehicle at the show in Hoogeveen to allow the public to see its interior and to let children play on it. But when one boy fiddled with the automatic fire extinguisher lever, with a loud bang he released a cloud of nitrogen, which caused panic in the crowd and immobilized the vehicle. "Nobody had thought that a child would even find the handle," said the driver ruefully. Unable to be repaired in Holland, the armoured truck had to be sent back to its manufacturers in Finland.

Error-prone Erskine

When considering their losses in the Peninsular War, the British had little doubt as to their greatest liability – Sir William Erskine. The appointment of the accident-prone Erskine as a senior commander already seemed a bad idea after he had contrived to lead a cavalry charge away from the enemy at the Battle of Sabugal in 1811. Then, when the Duke of Wellington ordered him to guard a vital bridge to prevent the French escaping at Almeida, Erskine wrote down the command, put it in his pocket and forgot all about it. So when the French forces retreated, they were able to free themselves from the Iron Duke's iron grip by fleeing unchallenged across the unguarded bridge. Wellington subsequently described it as, "the most disgraceful military event that has yet occurred to us." The only thing Erskine managed to do properly, was commit suicide shortly afterwards.

York and Lancaster vs Wales

The combined armies of York and Lancaster were routed by a single drunken Welshman at a Wars of the Roses re-enactment society battle in 1997. The mock battle, staged at Kidwelly Castle, Llanelli, was totally authentic until onlooker Leighton Thomas, a 24-year-old unemployed butcher, decided that neither army was trying hard enough. With a beer can in one hand and yelling "I'm a Viking butcher, I'll cut you all into little pieces," Thomas set about both sides, sending axemen, pikemen, cavalry and artillery fleeing for the safety of the castle, hastily pulling up the drawbridge behind them. Unable to find a battering ram, Thomas proceeded to head-butt the heavy wooden drawbridge before a Lancastrian soldier used his mobile phone to summon reinforcements. Thomas, who admitted punching a minstrel, was jailed for six weeks for assault. "I must have blacked out," he said. "I was uptight after an argument with my girlfriend."

Onoda's War, 1939–1974

In 1944, Hiroo Onoda, a twenty-three-year-old lieutenant in the Japanese army, was posted to Lubang Island, 75 miles south of Manila, to perform guerrilla and intelligence duties. His orders were to continue fighting even if his unit was wiped out. Onoda obeyed the orders to the letter – and continued to fight the Second World War for the next thirty years. During that time he resisted all attempts to make him surrender because he was convinced that stories that the war was over were nothing more than US propaganda. Leaflets dropped on the island signed by Onoda's chief of staff and announcing Japan's surrender were dismissed along with loudspeaker appeals by friends, relatives and former comrades for him to come out of hiding. Search parties and Japanese police were greeted with a hail of bullets. While fighting the world war single-handed, Onoda took care to conserve his ammunition although he would occasionally snipe at islanders or take pot shots at an imaginary enemy. This went on until 1974 when, following a chance encounter with a holidaying Japanese student who relayed the emperor's concern for Onoda's plight, the solitary soldier finally agreed to lay down his arms if ordered to do so by his commanding officer. Thus, retired Major Yoshimi Taniguchi temporarily left his job as a bookseller to fly to Lubang where, at 3 p.m. on 10 March 1974, Onoda was persuaded to stop fighting and thereby bring an overdue conclusion to the Second World War.

Legal Goofs

20

Crazy Criminals

MacMuffin muppet

A man wandered into a McDonald's in Sydney, Australia, at 8.50 one morning in 2000, produced a gun and demanded cash. However the cashier said she couldn't open the till without a food order. So the robber ordered a Big Mac, but was told by the cashier that they weren't available until 10.30 because only the breakfast menu was on offer at that time. Frustrated, the gunman gave up and walked out.

"When I said 'nobody' . . ."

A pair of Michigan robbers entered a record store, nervously waving revolvers. The first one shouted, "Nobody move!" When his accomplice moved, the first bandit shot him.

Invisibility juice

McArthur Wheeler robbed two Pittsburgh banks in broad daylight in 1995, making no attempt to disguise himself. He was arrested that night after videotapes of him taken from the bank's surveillance cameras were shown on TV news. When police officers showed him the tapes, Wheeler wailed, "But I wore the juice!" Apparently he thought that smearing his face with lemon juice would render it invisible to security cameras.

Coke pants

Leonard Hodge, 22, of Madison, Wisconsin, was arrested in 1996 for failing to carry a driver's licence. During a routine search, police officers found cocaine in his underwear. In his defence, Hodge claimed that the underpants he was wearing weren't his.

The patient bomber

Adelio Vazquez, 50, was arrested in Chicago in March 1994 and charged with attempting to rob a branch of the Liberty Bank. According to a teller, Vazquez handed over a note threatening that a bomb would explode unless he was given $45,000. The teller pointed out that such a large withdrawal would require a manager's authorization, and asked Vazquez to take a seat while the money was fetched. Instead the teller called the police who arrived a few minutes later to find Vazquez still sitting in the waiting area, chatting to one of the bank's managers.

Fecal felon

A would-be petrol thief got more than he bargained for when he attempted to siphon fuel from a motor home parked on a street in Port Macquarie, Australia. He decided to siphon the fuel by sucking it through a hose but inadvertently inserted the hose into the motor home's sewage tank instead. The police arrived to see him throwing up by the side of the road next to a pool of sewage. The vehicle owner declined to press charges, saying it was the best laugh he'd had in ages.

Toy thief

A man who twice tried to rob a petrol station in Port Elizabeth, South Africa, with a toy gun suffered the ignominy of being beaten up during both attempts. On the first occasion a station attendant refused the robber's demands for money and attacked him, forcing him to flee. Undeterred, the robber returned shortly afterwards, this time crawling through an open window and demanding money from the attendant who responded by hitting him again and this time holding him until the police arrived.

Dead driver

In 1991 Sacramento funeral director Melvin Lincoln was found guilty of defrauding an insurance company by trying to fake his own death and that of his wife. The deception was discovered when the supposedly deceased Mr Lincoln tried to renew his driver's licence.

Eleven years and eight months

The world's least successful attempt at avoiding a prison sentence belonged to Romanian fugitive Ioan Stoica who hid in a basement for eight years in order to miss out on a three-and-a-half year jail term. Thirty-four-year-old Stoica was sentenced for fraud by a court in his absence in 1994. Police officers eventually found him eight years later hiding in the basement of his parents' home at Avrig. He said that during that period he had left the basement very occasionally and only ever by night. He was immediately sent to jail to serve the three-and-a-half years plus an additional two months for trying to cheat the judicial system.

Teamwork

A gunman who tried to steal £20,000 from a security van in Torquay, Devon, in 1997 was knocked down by the motorcycle he was planning to use for his getaway. As the robber struggled with a security guard, his accomplice roared up on a motorbike but merely succeeded in sending the gunman flying, enabling him to be overpowered by a Methodist minister until the police arrived.

Salamied

A criminal mastermind lurched from one blunder to another while trying to rob a Miami delicatessen. First he forgot to check that the store owner wasn't armed and ended up having his nose broken when the owner whacked him with a giant salami. Fleeing heavy-headed and empty-handed, he then decided that the best place to lie low for a couple of hours was in the boot of a parked car. Not only did he manage to get himself locked in, but the vehicle in question belonged to an undercover police team who were pursuing another criminal. It was not until five days later that they heard a whimpering sound from the boot and promptly arrested the unfortunate delicatessen raider.

$5, $10 . . . $16?

In 1997 police in Wichita, Kansas, arrested a 22-year-old man at an airport hotel after he tried to pass two counterfeit $16 bills.

Lobster love

Intent on stealing a live lobster from a restaurant, a Bristol man stuffed it down his pants and made a hasty exit. His progress was slowed a few yards down the road when the lobster clamped its powerful claw on its abductor's penis, landing him in hospital for four weeks.

Short-sighted shootout

Two old-timers from Cleveland, Ohio, who decided to settle a long-standing feud with a gun duel, both survived the experience without so much as a graze. The 1981 shoot-out took place in the hallway which separated their apartments. Armed with antique pistols, the pair stood five feet apart and each fired twelve bullets. Every one missed. The police said afterwards: "There were bullet holes above, bullet holes down, and bullet holes all over the hallway." Officers speculated that the lack of accuracy may have had something to do with the fact that one antagonist needed a stick to prop himself up while firing and the other had trouble seeing because of glaucoma.

Self-harm in Salford

Wearing balaclavas and carrying a shotgun and a sledgehammer, armed robber John Lawrence and an accomplice burst into a Salford, Manchester, post office in July 1999. But then it all went horribly wrong for 24-year-old Lawrence. For no sooner had he yelled "Give us your money" than he slipped on a loose carpet tile, fell flat on his face and accidentally shot himself in the leg. Bleeding heavily, he limped away empty-handed but was arrested later in hospital.

Mug

Bank robber Anthony Colella got away with $1,300 from a New York hold-up, but was then mugged of his ill-gotten gains. In an inspired move, Colella went straight to the police to report the mugging – and was promptly arrested for the original robbery.

French farce

An armed raider in Bordeaux, France, burst into a post office and demanded £8,000. The female cashier said there wasn't that much money on the premises so the robber lowered the demand to £4,000. When told that wasn't available either, the robber ordered her to withdraw the money from his own account and duly handed over his ID card.

Fire!

When Dwayne Rice spotted a man acting suspiciously outside the door of his fourth-floor Philadelphia apartment, his actions sparked a bizarre chain of events. In his wisdom, 39-year-old Rice decided to get rid of the unwelcome visitor by setting off the fire alarm. So he stuffed some paper in a paper bag, set it alight and held it up to the smoke detector in his apartment. But he was taken aback by the ferocity with which the bag burned and, panicking, threw it onto his bed. In a matter of seconds, the whole room caught fire and Rice ran to the window screaming for help. Fearing he was about to be engulfed by flames, he had the bright idea of hanging from the window ledge, kicking in the window of the floor below and swinging into that apartment. It may have looked easy in the movies, but it was beyond Rice who, unable to kick in the window, lost his grip and fell four storeys, landing in the parking lot. He ended up in hospital where he was charged with arson, 73 counts of reckless endangerment – one for each person in the building – risking a catastrophe and endangering the welfare of children. Still, there was one consolation. As the fire raged through two floors of the apartment block, the sinister stranger disappeared.

Jittery in Jordan

A nervous thief in Amman, Jordan, took three sleeping tablets from a large batch of medication he had stolen during a raid on a hospital pharmacy. But the pills he took to calm his nerves were so strong that he fell asleep. He was found by hospital staff who alerted the police.

What's going on ear?

James Cottrell of Runcorn, Cheshire, left behind incriminating evidence when he snatched a woman motorist's bag – his false ear. He grabbed the bag while she sat in her car, but when a plastic ear was found at the crime scene, police quickly arrested Cottrell who, they said, was known to them. They added that his ear would be returned to him when it was no longer needed as evidence.

Blackbacks

An unemployed American printer who turned to counterfeiting was caught because he used black ink instead of bright green on his phoney bills. It turned out that he was colour-blind.

Fargo farrago

A robber who escaped with cash from the First Community Bank in Fargo, North Dakota, was surprised when police officers came to his home to arrest him an hour later. They told him that they knew his identity because he had written the note demanding money from the cashier on the back of his bank deposit slip.

The RTS bomber

Iraqi terrorist Khay Rahnajet didn't pay enough postage on a letter bomb he sent in 1999 and so it came back to him marked "return to sender". Forgetting it was a bomb, he opened it and was killed in the explosion.

Go straight to prison

After robbing a Massachusetts bakery, Vincent McKenzie was chased by police all the way to Connecticut. There he decided to ditch his getaway car and escape on foot by hiding in what he believed to be a shopping mall. It turned out to be a newly-built state prison.

Pigeon-pilfering pillocks

Thieves who stole fifteen homing pigeons from bird fancier Peter Ball of Langley, Berkshire, tried them out – and watched in despair as they flew straight back to his loft.

Nudist nabbed

In February 2001, Kurt Briel insisted on stripping naked at a store in Stuttgart to prove that he wasn't shoplifting . . . and was arrested for indecent exposure.

Pickup blowback

A petrol thief got more than he bargained for when he went on a midnight raid at a golf club in Jackson County, Illinois. While pumping the stolen gas into his pickup truck, he dropped the petrol cap on the ground, and, in order to provide some light by which to find it, foolishly lit his cigarette lighter. The resultant explosion destroyed the club house, half a million dollars worth of equipment and his pickup truck.

Dim dialling

An arsonist who set fire to a shop in Hamburg, New York, phoned a friend to boast about it . . . but dialled the wrong number and called the local fire chief instead. The call was quickly traced.

Drug depository

James Bridgewater was arrested in Kankakee, Illinois, in 1992 following a mix-up at the drive-in window of the First America Bank. He was carrying two white sacks – one containing money to be deposited, the other containing two grams of marijuana and rolling papers. Unfortunately for 32-year-old Bridgewater, he put the wrong bag into the pneumatic tube.

Early release

Seeing an opportunity that was too good to miss, prisoner Sherman Lee Parks of Arkansas decided to escape from jail . . . on the very day he was due to be released. He was quickly re-captured to start another stint behind bars.

Gossipy goon

While waiting for the cashier to hand over the money, Texas bank robber Natalie Copeland couldn't resist telling the people behind her in the queue that there was a car at a local dealership which she had been coveting for months. After carrying out the robbery, she compounded the error by heading straight to the showroom and using the stolen cash as a down payment on the car. Alerted to her intentions, police officers got her address from the dealer.

Tough nut

Ram raider Roland Tough was branded "Britain's dimmest burglar" in 1999. Tough took photos of himself modelling designer clothes stolen in the raid on a Tesco's store in Manchester, and then sent the film to the same supermarket for processing. Staff there immediately recognized the clothing and electrical goods that had been snatched in the raid two weeks previously. Police swooped when Tough went to collect the photos.

Balaclava? Check. Name tag? Check.

A would-be Texas grocery-store robber went to the trouble of disguising his face with a balaclava but forgot to remove from his breast pocket a laminated badge that bore his name, place of employment and position within the company – an oversight spotted by at least a dozen witnesses.

Butterfingers

After ransacking a house in Malaysia, a burglar ran to his getaway car, only to discover that he had dropped his car keys in the house. So he returned to the building he had just robbed, knocked on the door and, explaining what had happened, politely asked for his keys back. He begged the victims not to call the police but they refused, so he ripped off the car's license plates in an attempt to avoid detection and made a hurried escape on foot.

Cowboy

An Irishman left his old trainers behind in a Bedford shoe shop and exited wearing an expensive pair of cowboy boots for which he hadn't paid. He didn't get far, however, as he limped down the road in two right boots, one a size 9, the other a size 11.

Well matched

A prisoner escaped from a Washington, DC, jail in 1997 so that he could secretly attend his girlfriend's robbery trial. During the adjournment for lunch he went out for a sandwich, but she needed to see him and so had him paged. The police recognized his name immediately and arrested him when he returned to the courthouse in a car that he had just stolen.

Perfect timing

Having cased a Boston, Massachusetts, bank for several days waiting for the perfect moment to strike, a gunman marched up to the cashier's window and yelled: "This is a hold-up, nobody move!" Alas, the next five customers in line were armed FBI agents, waiting to cash cheques in their lunch break.

High five!

A bank robber in Evansville, Indiana, went to great lengths to conceal his identity during a raid until, on the way out of the door and buoyed by his success, he jumped up and high-fived the window, leaving a nice incriminating palm print.

Colander cretin

Police in Radnor, Pennsylvania, interrogated a none-too-bright suspect by putting a metal colander on his head and connecting it with wires to a photocopying machine. The message "He's lying" was placed in the copier, and whenever they thought the suspect wasn't telling the truth, they pressed the copy button. Convinced that the "lie detector" was working, the gullible suspect eventually confessed.

Big Ears in Ukraine

A disguised criminal's hopes of entering Slovakia from Ukraine in 2000 using someone else's papers ended abruptly at the customs post when his artificial ears fell off.

Balaclava malfunction

Absent-minded robber Barry George Paquette was swiftly arrested after making off with cash from a convenience store in Edmonton, Alberta, in 1997. Paquette was half-way through the raid when he realized he had forgotten to pull down his balaclava. He stopped the robbery momentarily while he remedied the oversight but by then the store's surveillance camera had already captured a perfect close-up of his face.

Doddering deadbeats

A pair of 78-year-old burglars were caught red-handed in São Paulo, Brazil, when the homeowners returned unexpectedly. The one inside the house was too deaf to hear the warning of his accomplice outside, and the lookout wasn't fit enough to escape.

Limited ladder length

A daring jailbreak from Fresnes high-security prison near Paris in May 2001 fell apart in mid-air. An executive helicopter was hijacked by gunmen outside a luxury hotel and the pilot was forced to fly to Fresnes and hover over the prison. But the rope ladder which was dangled from the helicopter was too short for the two would-be escapees to reach. The helicopter had to abandon the mission, leaving the prisoners with their feet still firmly on the ground.

Broiled burglar

A burglar decided to break into a pizza parlour at Rockford, Illinois, through an air duct on the roof. Unfortunately he selected the wrong air duct – the one which led directly to the oven. When the oven didn't work the following morning, the manager called a repairman who found the burglar dead in the duct. He had suffocated.

Perfect timing II

Deciding to pocket a few items from the Barnsley branch of British Home Stores in 1979, a shoplifter was horrified to find himself apprehended by eight pairs of hands. The shop was holding a convention of store detectives at the time.

Lost in France

After being refused asylum in Britain, a Kosovan refugee tried to flee to France by hiding in a lorry leaving Folkestone, only to end up in Winchester. His flawed flight came to light when he was discovered in a lorry full of paper at a Hampshire County Council supplies depot. A depot worker said: "He was a bit confused when we started speaking English to him because he thought he was in France."

Garrett the goon

Driving a stolen car in a strange neighbourhood, Larico Garrett of Manchester, Connecticut, made the mistake of asking a police officer for directions. As Garrett drove off, the officer became suspicious and checked the licence plates. Garrett was arrested shortly afterwards.

Self-apprehending

A car thief in Ensley, Alabama, had the bright idea of using the stolen vehicle to drive his girlfriend to the local police station to report a burglary. "It's a whole lot easier when they bring the cars to you," smiled Sgt David Smith of the Birmingham Police auto division who quickly spotted the car as one that had recently featured on a theft report.

Prominent probationer

The most hapless attempt to blend in with a crowd was made by an American ex-convict who came up with the inspired idea of wearing a stolen bright orange prison uniform at a Florida rock festival – an event that was swarming with police officers. The twenty-five-year-old from Lakeland had stolen the uniform when released from prison in January 2002. Pasco County officers said that he should have been at home under a curfew when they arrested him three months later at the festival.

Keen-eyed sheriff's detective Mark Morrison said he first became suspicious when he saw the words "Polk County Jail" written on the man's shirt and trousers. The suspect told officers he was dressed in a Hallowe'en costume but was arrested for violating his parole. A baffled sheriff's spokesman commented: "He stood out in the crowd. If you're violating your probation, the last thing you want to do is draw attention to yourself."

"Hands up! This is a donation!"

A man came up with what he thought was a foolproof way of snatching the contents of a till from a store in Louisiana. He walked into the store, put a $20 bill on the counter and asked for change. When the store clerk opened the cash drawer, the man pulled a gun and grabbed all of the money – $15. He then ran out, leaving his $20 bill on the counter, and thus finished the raid $5 out of pocket.

Paper tiger

Not wishing to look conspicuous, a bank robber in Portland, Oregon, handed the cashier a note ordering her to put all the money in a paper bag. She read the note, wrote on the bottom, "I don't have a paper bag" and handed it back to the raider. His masterplan foiled, he fled empty-handed.

"Here I am!"

A policeman on patrol duty in Bristol was stunned to see a thief waving to him from a shop he had broken into. The burglar had mistaken the officer for his accomplice.

Phoney policeman

A man who enjoyed dressing up as a policeman to stop motorists in Taiwan was arrested when he made the fairly basic mistake of pulling over a real officer. Lin Shang-teh had bought the police badge at a souvenir shop and became addicted to wearing the uniform, but when he stopped the officer, the cop noticed immediately that he had no weapon, no radio and no serial number on his fake badge.

Slaton spliff

A man was detained overnight at a police station in Slaton, Texas, on a minor charge. While in his cell he smoked marijuana, given to him by a visitor, as a result of which he found himself facing a jail sentence of up to twenty years. To compound his folly, the original charge was dropped.

Slow-speed chase

An Illinois gas station robber had clearly given insufficient thought to his getaway. For not only did he choose an extremely slow 18-wheel tractor-trailer but the vehicle also had his name on the door. He drove off at such a snail's pace that the manager had time to call the police, get into her own car and tail him for several miles before the cops arrived. So leisurely was his progress that she even had to slow down at times to avoid bumping into him.

ID(iot) parade

As a woman left her local convenience store in New York, a thief snatched her purse. However, she was able to give officers a detailed description of the culprit and a suspect was swiftly apprehended. Officers then took him back to the store and told him to stand there for a positive ID. The man quietly did as he was told and when the victim appeared, he said: "Yes, officer, that's the woman I stole the purse from."

Bad day

Canadian Timothy Carney blew his top when, heading back to his car, he saw a police officer writing out a parking ticket. In a violent rage, he kicked the officer's car, causing $1,000 worth of damage. As a result Carney was arrested and, on being searched, was found to be carrying marijuana. So he was charged with that offence too. To round off his day, it turned out that the ticket wasn't even for his car!

Getaway gone awry

Paco Bocconini snatched £3,000 from a post office at Cariato, Italy, in 1997 and ran outside to find that his getaway car had been stolen. Unwisely, he had left the engine running.

Fake "roobels"

A gang of Russian counterfeiters produced a near-perfect set of 50,000-rouble bank notes which would have made them a fortune once in circulation but for one tiny error. They had mis-spelt "Russia".

New York Prostitute Department

New Yorker Scott Bernstein got his wires badly crossed when he tried to phone for a prostitute. Five times he got through to the Colonie Police Department where each time an officer politely informed him that he had the wrong number. But Bernstein didn't believe him, and rang the same number again. On the sixth call, the police arranged to meet him at a local hotel where they then arrested him.

Hook crook

A 36-year-old man who robbed an Ontario discount centre in 1996 was quickly apprehended, principally because he had made no attempt to disguise the metal hook which he used in place of a hand. The case brought a new meaning to the phrase “by hook or by crook.”

Hard worker

A North Carolina lawyer was charged with fraud in 1994 after billing clients for over 1,200 hours a month when a 31-day month contains only 744 hours.

Three blind mice

Three armed robbers who targeted a South Shields travel agent’s in 1997 accidentally burst into the shop next door. Appropriately, it was an optician’s.

In vino veritas

A Brazilian thief who broke into a church to steal a projector and a vacuum cleaner was arrested when he fell asleep after drinking two bottles of communion wine.

Alabama asshole

An escapee from an Alabama jail was dismayed at the speed with which police tracked him down. He had overlooked the fact that left behind in his cell was a detailed map of his hideout.

Lucky Las Vegas

After a 1962 Long Island safe robbery had netted a cool $105,000, one of the raiders was anxious to get rid of part of his one-third share because he thought that much money would draw attention to himself. So he went to Las Vegas and gambled heavily in a dice game. But despite his best efforts, he couldn't lose and came away with another $10,000 in his pocket.

Robbery receipt

After breaking into a woman's home in 2000, a burglar in Japan felt so sorry for his victim that he gave her a receipt for the theft so that she could claim on insurance. On it he obligingly included his name and address.

Keystone criminals

A 1975 raid on the Royal Bank of Scotland in Rothesay degenerated into farce when, on the way in, the three would-be raiders got stuck in the bank's revolving doors and had to be helped free by the staff. Undaunted, they returned a few minutes later and announced that it was a robbery, but the staff thought it was a practical joke and refused to pay up. While one of the men vaulted the counter and twisted his ankle on landing, the other two made their escape, only to get trapped in the revolving doors again.

Follow the money

Police at Inman, South Carolina, had little difficulty picking up a suspected bank robber. Having forgotten to ask the cashier for a bag, the hapless crook was reduced to stuffing the money into his trousers and socks. As he ran out of the bank, the notes flew everywhere and he was quickly arrested.

Dumb drug runners

A bungling cocaine-smuggling ring which started off with a ton of the drug in Colombia managed to lose over two-thirds of it on the way to Europe – and then got caught. The gang took a fishing boat across the Atlantic to collect the tonne of cocaine from South America, but the dilapidated vessel was not in a fit state to carry all of it. So the captain loaded just 650 kilograms on board, sealed in concrete, and sailed back to Europe. Arriving in Portugal, the captain had to hack away at the concrete with a pick-axe in order to get at the drug, but the operation was so noisy that he feared capture and gave up after retrieving a mere 300 kilos. An accomplice then turned up in a rented removal van, loaded the cocaine into packing boxes and set off for Berlin. However the gang forgot to contact him with further instructions. After a few weeks he tired of waiting, decided to sell 2 kilograms himself and was immediately arrested by police. He wasted no time in giving German officers details about his clueless colleagues.

From the frying pan . . .

Over a period of several weeks Arnold Ancheta, an inmate at the Elmwood Correctional Facility, California, hatched an ingenious escape plan. He carefully hacked out holes in the cell wall to use as foot holds and then, using a mop handle to bend back the steel bars, squeezed his body through an overhead skylight. Once through the skylight, he jumped to the ground and scaled the fence which he thought would take him to freedom. Unwisely he chose the fence that led him straight into the adjacent women's jail.

Careful planning

A man planning to rob a Yorkshire village store reckoned he had left nothing to chance. Armed with an imitation revolver, he had his motorcycle parked outside for a quick getaway and wore a full-face crash helmet to mask his identity. Sadly he had forgotten that painted in inch-high letters around the helmet was his name. His arrest was swift.

Unmugged mug

Some weeks after the incident, a Cape Town businessman reported to police that two men had mugged him and robbed him of his $4,500 Rolex watch in January 2001. To prove his loss to the insurance company, he provided two witnesses to the mugging. But the suspicious insurance company wanted further evidence of the missing watch, so he helpfully sent them a photograph of the watch on his desk at work. On the desk was a calendar. The date on the calendar was February 2001.

April Fool's Day

A man was arrested for attempting to rob the Sussex County State Bank in Vernon Township, New Jersey, in 1995. It was felt that he had drawn attention to himself by banging on the bank's doors while wearing a ski mask, a few minutes after the bank had closed for the day. Appropriately, it was 1 April.

Milwaukee moron

Michael Cooper of Germantown, Wisconsin, was stopped by police for doing 85 mph in a 65 mph zone. He told the officers that he was in a hurry because he had to drive to Milwaukee to pay a traffic ticket.

Doggy-do desperadoes

Two teenage muggers attacked a woman near Huddersfield and snatched her plastic shopping bag . . . which contained the dog mess she had recently cleared up.

Nude nut

Melvin Weaver of Hawaii came up with what he thought was a foolproof way of burgling an apartment. He elected to carry out the robbery in the nude, reasoning that the occupants would be so shocked as to be unable to give the police an accurate description. Caught in the act, he fled the scene of the crime but the police had no trouble tracking him because neighbours kept calling in to report a naked man running down the street.

Lucky day

While waiting for her boyfriend to grab the money from a US convenience store, a woman spotted a competition entry form on the counter. Thinking it might be her lucky day, she filled out the form, complete with her name, address and phone number. She realized it wasn't when she was arrested a few hours later, having left the form behind in the store.

Keystone Cops

High tide

After chasing an erratically-driven car onto a beach, officers in New Zealand got out to talk to the occupants, but when they tried to return to their patrol car they found that it had been cut off by the tide. To the acute embarrassment of the officers, the police vehicle had to remain on the beach overnight because tow trucks were unable to move it.

Right number, wrong road

Police on a dawn drugs raid smashed down the front door of a house and pinned a middle-aged couple to the wall, only to discover that they had got the wrong address. Hearing the commotion at his Gosport, Hampshire, home in 1993, 51-year-old Brian Palliser thought he was being burgled and ran downstairs to challenge the intruders. Instead he was confronted by a dozen police officers who dragged his wife Jean from bed and searched the house for 15 minutes. It was only then that the police realized that although they had got the right house number, they had got the wrong road! Their superintendent returned later to apologize to the couple.

Right road, wrong man

A team of private detectives hired to gather evidence against a Yorkshire man spent four years and £50,000 monitoring and videoing the daily movements of a neighbour by mistake. They had been sent to record the activities of a man who was suing for industrial injury, and it was only when they presented the company concerned with videos apparently showing him in good health that they were told they had been following and filming the wrong man. One villager who had observed the clandestine surveillance operation with bewilderment said: "I can't see how anybody can be so incompetent."

"I'm hit!"

Approaching a group of suspects in a stolen car, a New Jersey police officer pulled his gun, but in transferring the weapon from his right to his left hand, he succeeded in shooting himself in the thigh and shattering the front passenger side window of the patrol car. He immediately yelled to his two colleagues: "I'm hit." Thinking he had been shot by the occupants of the stolen car, the confused cops pumped 38 bullets into the vehicle. Amazingly the suspects survived.

Illegible, illegal

A man accused of attempted poaching walked free from court after lawyers were unable to read a policeman's handwritten report on the case. Terry Button, allegedly trespassed on private land in search of game, but neither defence lawyer Derek Johashen nor the prosecutor could read PC Richard Edmonson's notes. Bedford magistrates accepted Mr Johashen's claim that to try Mr Button would be in breach of the Human Rights Act, which states that all defendants have the right to know the case against them.

Do as I say, not as I do

A British detective training South African police officers to fight crime was himself tricked out of over £1,000. Frank Waghorn from Avon and Somerset police was fooled by two people pretending to help him as he withdrew money from a cash machine in Port Elizabeth.

Balloon bedlam

In June 1998, police launched an armed raid on a house in Hartlepool, north-east England, sealed off the street, evacuated neighbouring homes and deployed a spotter plane to circle overhead . . . all because the householder, 45-year-old Tommy Dixon, decided to burst a balloon. Mistaking the popping of the balloon for the sound of gunshot, a passer-by contacted the police, and the next thing Mr Dixon heard was a voice through a loudhailer telling him to come out with his hands up. He said afterwards: "I wandered into the street and all I could see was guns pointing at me and neighbours watching me. I was petrified. It doesn't help that I'm Irish!"

Mulligan mix-up

A man was arrested, held for 20 hours and driven 150 miles to court . . . to face someone else's driving charge. Brian Mulligan from Manchester appeared in court in Pwllheli, North Wales, after police officers mistook him for another man with the same name. It wasn't until magistrates checked the arrest warrant that they realized the police had the wrong man. For although Mr Mulligan's name matched the warrant, his address and date of birth were different. Mr Mulligan, who had to make his own way home, said, "I knew I had done nothing wrong, but nobody was taking any notice."

Pier pressure

Two New York officers drove at speed to a pier to investigate a gang of suspicious youths. When they arrived the youths dispersed and the officers headed back to their squad car . . . just in time to see it sliding down the gravel beach and into the water. They had forgotten to put the hand-brake on. Red-faced, they had to catch a bus back to the station house.

Patrol car panic

Nottinghamshire police sparked a nationwide hunt when one of their patrol cars went missing. The vehicle had been taken in for a service but when officers went to collect it from the depot, there was no sign of it. A national alert was issued amid fears that the car had been stolen, but it was called off the following day after the county council contractors realized that it had been sent to a different garage.

Brown-eyed handsome man

Armed police swooped on a gun-toting gang in Acton, London, in October 1999, only to find that it was part of a video shoot for Sir Paul McCartney. To promote his single *Brown-Eyed Handsome Man*, the former Beatle had hired actors dressed as American police officers and equipped them with imitation firearms. But when the Metropolitan Police were tipped off that four men were pointing guns at cars, they swung into action, sealing off the street and threatening the perpetrators with CS gas. It was then that McCartney emerged from his trailer to calm the situation and explain what was going on.

Michigan mistake

When police in Saginaw, Michigan, pulled over a motorist on a traffic violation, they found that the man was carrying a pistol in his car. Despite his protestations that he had never seen the weapon before, the officers duly arrested him. But the red-faced law enforcers had to release the suspect the following day with a grovelling apology because it emerged that the gun had fallen into the car from the holster of one of the officers while they were questioning the motorist.

Up on a roof

A group of policemen who arrested a burglar on the roof of a bank in Rainham, Kent, had to be rescued by firefighters after they became stuck.

Fax and phone solo

Minutes after being radioed about the theft of a saxophone, North Yorkshire policewoman Vicky Lacey arrested a man who fitted the description. But the musical instrument case wasn't as open and shut as it appeared. For she then learned that the theft report had been misheard. It wasn't a saxophone that had been taken . . . but a fax and phone. "Vicky will never live this down," said a colleague. "She has been the talk of the station."

Cheque? Check.

Police in Indianapolis naïvely allowed a woman accused of passing $100,000 worth of dud cheques to post bail with a cheque. Not surprisingly, it bounced.

Sheet stealers

After staying at the Roadchef Lodge at Watford Gap services on the M1 in February 2000, a couple were accused of taking a sheet from the motel. Kevin and Katherine Mulgrew were tracked 150 miles to their home in Oldham, Lancashire, and arrested when a search failed to find the sheet. They then spent seven hours in a police cell. The next morning the missing sheet was discovered by staff in the laundry bag outside the motel room.

Defective detectives

An alert, thoroughbred police officer is never truly off duty, and rarely was this better illustrated than by the deeds of two of Hampshire's finest, Police Constables Mick Cotterill and Grant Darbey. Guests at a party at Botleigh Grange Hotel near Southampton in 1998, the two off-duty officers sprang into action on discovering a man's body in the foyer. Keeping cool in an emergency and remembering their training, the dynamic duo urgently tried to revive the victim by checking his airways and starting to remove his clothing. At this point their doubts as to whether or not they were dealing with a fatality were dispelled when the corpse leaped to his feet and demanded to know what they thought they were doing. He was, he added curtly, an actor taking part in a murder mystery weekend. While the two defective detectives slunk away sheepishly and later became the butt of station jokes, a Hampshire police spokesman explained with commendable understatement: "It was a bit of a surprise when the man made a full recovery so quickly in front of them."

Courtroom Calamities

Smart

Chaos reigned at Bulawayo Magistrates Court in 2001 when Smart Ngwenya faced a charge of tampering with cars. His name was called, but a different Smart Ngwenya, a witness waiting to give evidence in another case, was brought into the courtroom instead. The mistake was discovered when the charges were read, and officials hustled him out and brought in another Smart Ngwenya . . . who also turned out to be the wrong man. At the third attempt the “right” Smart Ngwenya was brought in, but he denied the charge, claiming mistaken identity.

Overwhelmed

The US Court of Appeals in San Francisco granted Brent Paul Swanson a new trial after he had been convicted of robbing a bank in Phoenix, Arizona. The court ruled that his lawyer, David Ochoa, should not have addressed the jury by saying: “The evidence [against Swanson] is overwhelming, and I’m not going to sit here and insult your intelligence.” Ochoa explained that he felt he had so few options in his closing argument that he felt an unorthodox approach might just have saved his client.

Rogozensky in the rafters

In the act of trying to escape from a courthouse in Decatur, Georgia, in 2003, a prisoner fell through the roof and landed in the judge’s chambers. Ben N. Rogozensky was one of a group of inmates awaiting hearings when he was taken to an empty jury room to speak with his attorney. There, Rogozensky hatched his cunning plan. Asking to go to the adjacent toilet, he managed to climb into the ceiling crawl space from where he planned to make his daring bid for freedom. Unfortunately, the ceiling gave way beneath his weight and he plunged barefoot into the chambers of State Court Judge J. Antonio DelCampo. A startled technician who was fixing the judge’s computer promptly alerted security, ensuring that Rogozensky would be given plenty of time to think up a more practical escape plan.

Witten bitten

After defendant Bill Witten had sworn at him for refusing to reduce his bail on a charge of grand larceny, Judge Joseph Troisi of St Mary's, West Virginia, took off his robes, stepped down from the bench and bit him on the nose. Judge Troisi resigned from the bench shortly after the 1997 incident. He was said to have had a history of courtroom outbursts.

Foolish foreman

A 1998 trial at Lewes Crown Court in East Sussex was held up after the foreman of the jury managed to get his hand stuck in one of the exhibits – a pair of handcuffs. With no key to free him, the local fire brigade had to be summoned with bolt-cutters.

Junior juror

A computer error resulted in an eight-year-old boy from New Jersey being summoned for jury service in 2001. It was the second time Kyle Connor had been summoned to serve on a jury, the first being when he was five. Kyle said he was perfectly happy to try it, as long as the judge didn't mind.

Previous convictions?

The world's least convincing bogus lawyers were the pair who represented an assault suspect at Kathlehong magistrates' court, South Africa, in January 2002. They first aroused suspicion by addressing the magistrate as "Your majesty" instead of "Your honour". Then during proceedings one of them rather gave the game away by asking aloud what "previous convictions" meant. Facing charges of impersonation, the two men were obliged to hire genuine lawyers to represent them in their own cases.

[Cough] guilty

A defendant at Cardiff Crown Court was mistakenly sentenced to two years in prison in April 1999 . . . simply because a juror happened to cough at an inopportune moment. Unable to stifle a tickle at the back of his throat any longer, the juror coughed just as the foreman was announcing a verdict of "not guilty" . . . with the result that the noise drowned out the word "not". Judge Michael Gibbon, thinking that defendant Alan Rashid had been found guilty on the charge of making a threat to kill, promptly jailed him for two years, thanked the jurors for their efforts during the two-day trial and released them. The puzzled jurors assumed that Mr Rashid was being sentenced for other offences of which they were unaware until, on the way out of the building, one juror asked an usher why the defendant had been sent down after being found not guilty. The official realized there had been a blunder and called everyone back into court. A confused Mr Rashid, who, minutes earlier was being consoled in the cells, was led back to the dock and told by the judge that he was free to go after all. His lawyer, Penri Desscan, said, “It was pretty bizarre. One moment my client was facing two years’ imprisonment, the next he was going home on the bus.”

Unlucky seven

Sentenced to seven years’ imprisonment, Frank Green of San Antonio, Texas, begged the judge not to give him seven years because seven was his unlucky number. So the judge gave him eight years instead.

Political Gaffes

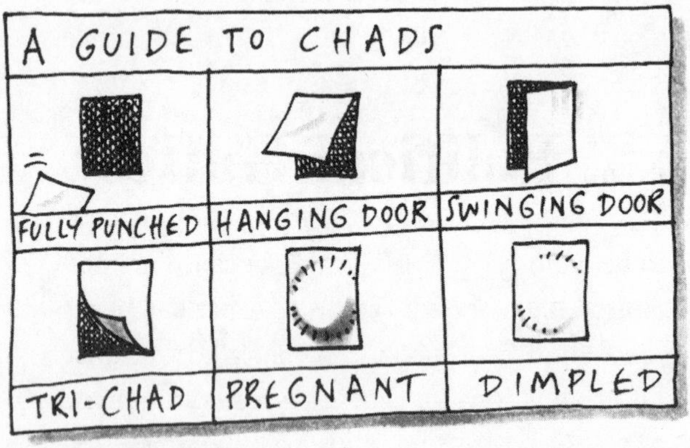

Bush vs Gore: The 36-Day Election Night

It was the longest election night in US presidential history, a seemingly never-ending saga that was in danger of running longer than *Peyton Place*. For 36 days it dragged on, each new day bringing a new recount, a new challenge, a new court ruling and, inevitably, a new batch of lawyers eager to pick over the sorry carcass of the American electoral system. In the annals of US elections, the chaotic November 2000 contest between George W. Bush and Al Gore will undoubtedly go down as the *tour de farce*.

While the rest of the world watched and listened in bewilderment as Democrat Gore, the man who had been on the point of conceding defeat on 8 November, was still frantically pulling rabbits out of the hat in mid-December in his desperate bid to get into the White House by any door that was slightly ajar, the impenetrable American judicial process came into its own. With both parties launching more appeals than Amnesty International, the question of who had actually won no longer rested with the American voters but with an array of District

Courts, Federal Courts and Supreme Courts, each of which appeared to have an uncanny knack of reversing the previous decision. The Supreme Court was rumoured to have the final say, and so the world eagerly awaited the verdict of Diana Ross.

Yet it had all started like any other US Presidential election – big hair, cheesy grins, wives with silly names, cheerleaders, gaffes, accusations, counter-accusations and dirty tricks campaigns. It was expected to be a close run thing if only because neither candidate exactly captured the imagination of the American public. George W. Bush was best known for having a father who was once president, a drink-driving conviction, for sending a record number of Texan prisoners to the electric chair, and for having no obvious grasp either of the English language or of world affairs. Al Gore's sole claim to fame was having a wife called Tipper whom he once kissed in public. So amazed and impressed were Americans by this display of genuine marital affection after the Bill and Hillary show that the kiss was calculated to be a real vote-winner. Indeed Gore's advisers urged him to repeat the performance in the belief that another kiss meant another state (two states if tongues were brought into play). If only he and Tipper had engaged in a steamy sex session on the podium, Al Gore would now be sitting in the White House.

One of the many confusing things about US Presidential elections is that the winner is not the one with the most votes, or even with the most states. It is the one with the most electoral college votes. Each state has a certain number of electoral college votes (distributed on the basis of population), ranging from Alaska, Vermont, Delaware, Wyoming, Montana, the Dakotas and District of Columbia with only three apiece to the likes of Ohio (21) Illinois (22), Pennsylvania (23), Florida (25), Texas (32), New York (33) and, the biggest prize of all, California (54). So whilst Bush and the Republicans were leading on states won – mainly in the nation's conservative heartland and the South – Gore was dominating the big industrial states with the greater

The Swiss Navy
Among those invited by the US State Department to a special display to mark the completion of the Panama Canal in 1914, was a representative of the non-existent Swiss Navy. The American ambassador to Switzerland, Pleasant A. Stovall, duly issued the invitation to the Swiss Foreign Office, but when it was pointed out that landlocked Switzerland had no navy, the offer was quickly withdrawn.

number of electoral college votes. As the night wore on, with the battle neck and neck, it seemed increasingly certain that the identity of the new President would be decided by the key state of Florida, where Britons go to holiday and Americans go to die.

Just as the race for the White House was a close-fought affair, so was the race among the TV networks to be the first to announce the winner. Predictions were based principally upon exit polls, conducted on a sample of voters as they cast their ballots. Exit polls are notoriously unreliable except, of course, in countries where the army tells the electorate who to vote for. Nevertheless in the early evening CNN felt sufficiently confident to predict a win for Gore in Florida. At the time, Al and his running mate, Joe Lieberman, were at dinner and whoops of delight were their response to the news that the White House was now within touching distance.

But within 90 minutes Bush had hit back, snatching the 21 electoral college votes of Ohio plus Gore's home state of Tennessee which yielded another 11. Overall Bush was now three ahead. Two hours after its original prediction, CNN backtracked and announced that Florida was "undecided". Suddenly Bush was in the ascendancy with the Gore camp clinging defiantly to the belief that Florida might still

Packer the cannibal

Seeking a name for a new staff canteen in 1977, the US Department of Agriculture decided to commemorate a renowned nineteenth-century Colorado pioneer, Alfred Packer. In a wave of publicity, Agriculture Secretary Robert Bergland duly opened the Alfred Packer Memorial Dining Facility with the words: "Alfred Packer exemplifies the spirit and care that this agriculture department cafeteria will provide." A few months later the building was hastily renamed when it was discovered that Packer had been convicted of murdering and eating five prospectors in 1874.

be theirs. Then came the California result. A win for Gore and fifty-four crucial votes. He was back in front and Bush's face began to tell the strain. Not for long. More victories in the South propelled Son of George back into the lead. With just four states to go, Bush was ahead by five. All eyes turned to Florida.

Twenty minutes later and a new poll suggested that Florida was leaning towards Bush, but then Gore captured Iowa to edge ahead once again. CBS now took it upon itself to defy the latest poll and declare that Al Gore would be the next President of the United States. CBS had won the race with the news. It was just a shame the news was wrong. For at the very moment that CBS was making its grand announcement, CNN, NBC and many of the nation's newspapers were declaring Bush to be the winner, some having changed their front pages four times in the course of the night. Ten minutes later, CBS felt obliged to swap sides again and go for Bush. "If you're disgusted with us," said CBS anchorman Dan Rather, "frankly, I don't blame you." At least he was honest – a quality not normally associated with

American politics. His sentiments were echoed over at CNN by presenter Judy Woodruff, "We've been saying all night we didn't know what was going to happen," she said, "and we've just proved it. If you'd like to pass the humble pie, I'll eat it."

With the networks declaring Bush the victor in Florida, Gore telephoned his rival to congratulate him and prepared to make a public speech conceding defeat. No sooner had he stepped into his car en route to concession than the networks changed their minds again, suggesting that the result in Florida was so close that, under state law, an automatic recount would be declared. Gore immediately ordered his convoy to do a U-turn and, 50 minutes after congratulating Bush, he called him back to retract everything.

As scorn was poured on the multi-million dollar exit polls which had got it so disastrously wrong, one commentator admitted: "The networks don't just have egg on their faces – we have whole omelettes."

The first count in Florida put Bush ahead by 1,655 votes (out of nearly 6,000,000 cast), thereby necessitating the recount. It was announced that the result of the recount was expected on 9 November but, in another twist, it emerged that there were some 2,300 postal votes still due to be received in Florida from American citizens living overseas. These were valid provided they were postmarked 7 November (polling day) or earlier and received by 17 November, meaning that there was every chance that the outright winner of the election would not be known for a further week or so.

America also had to brace itself for the prospect of having a President who was not elected by the majority of the voters. Gore had won the popular vote – albeit by some 300,000 out of nearly 100,000,000 people who went to the polls – but Bush, if he picked up Florida as anticipated, would secure the all-important electoral college vote. Unlike America itself, this was not without precedent. In 1888 Grover Cleveland had narrowly won the popular vote but had finished

65 college votes behind Benjamin Harrison. And 12 years earlier, Sam Tilden had received 51 per cent of the popular vote compared to 48 per cent for Rutherford Hayes – but had lost the election by a single college vote. That particular election went on for six months. America was warned.

Bush despatched former Secretary of State James Baker to observe the recount while Gore sent one of Baker's successors, Warren Christopher. Little did they know that they would soon be joined by an entire circus. Amidst all the chaos and confusion, Bush remained upbeat, assuring supporters that he had won even if the sparkling mineral water would have to be put on ice. Speaking from his mansion in Austin, Texas, he said of the Florida recount: "If that result is confirmed in an automatic recount as we expect it will be, then we have won the election." He just didn't know that it would take another five weeks.

With the recount barely under way, events took a more sinister turn. Democrats accused Republicans of dirty tricks in Florida, a state whose governor, as they were quick to remind everybody, was George W. Bush's younger brother Jeb. It was widely known that Jeb was expected to deliver Florida for his big brother. Now, as the whispering campaign gathered momentum, some Democrats were beginning to wonder just how far he had been prepared to go to fulfil that promise. At the heart of Democrat discontent was Palm Beach County where election officials had insisted on sticking to old-fashioned IBM punch-cards to count votes. In theory it was a straightforward procedure. Voters simply used a special pen to punch the hole next to the name of their chosen candidate, but Democrats claimed that voters were confused by the huge number of candidates – 13 in total – who were listed on the punch cards. More specifically, the design of the cards appeared to baffle voters. With candidates' names arranged opposite each other, hundreds of voters said that they had accidentally voted for Reform Party candidate Pat Buchanan instead of Al Gore. Buchanan

Not dead yet

On 22 March 1979, Indian Prime Minister Morarji Desai solemnly announced to Parliament that the country's elder statesman, Jayaprakash Narayan, had died earlier that day in a Bombay hospital. The nation was plunged into mourning. Parliament was suspended for the remainder of the day, schools and shops were closed, flags were flown at half-mast and funereal music was played on the principal radio station. It was upon hearing this music that a perfectly healthy Mr Narayan realized he was listening to his own obituary. The Prime Minister was forced to make a grovelling apology, revealing that he had been given the duff information by the National Intelligence Bureau.

himself admitted that most of the 3,407 votes he received in Palm Beach were probably intended for Gore. One voter said: "It was so hard to tell who and what you were voting for. I couldn't figure it out – and I have a doctorate."

Some voters said that when they realized their error they tried to rectify it by then punching the correct Gore hole. However, two holes meant that officials discarded the ballots as spoiled. As many as 19,000 Palm Beach ballot papers were rejected from the count because they had been completed incorrectly. Democrats maintained that the vast majority of these were intended for Gore – enough to sweep him to victory in Florida and to the White House.

In another Florida county, Pinellas, it emerged during the recount that 400 Gore votes had not been included in the original count. The National Association for the Advancement of Colored People then joined the controversy by claiming that some African Americans had

Litterasy

The British Department of Education had to pulp 48,000 copies of a pamphlet designed to improve literacy in the year 2000 . . . because of a spelling mistake. The word "vocabulary" had been spelt incorrectly.

been unfairly turned away from polling stations in Florida and intimidated. It said that some were handed damaged ballot papers, disqualified for dubious reasons and handed a pencil rather than a pen to fill in their ballot cards.

The lawyers smelled blood. As the Democrats set up an "assault squad" of lawyers to take statements from those who said they had voted the wrong way, Florida congressman Bob Wexler commented: "There has been amazing confusion at the ballot box. It appears 3,500 voters have been disenfranchized. The result is we are electing the wrong man as President."

Gore campaign manager William Daley added: "Because this disenfranchisement of these Floridians is so much larger than the reported gap between Governor Bush and Vice-President Gore, we believe this requires the full attention of the courts in Florida and concerned citizens around our country."

The Democrats were now threatening legal action to demand a re-run of the Palm Beach election, bringing a predictably angry response from the Republicans. James Baker, Bush's appointed overseer at the recount, insisted that anyone in the county unhappy with the ballot paper should have made their complaint before election day. "There were no complaints until after the election," he said. "It is a ballot paper that has been used before in the county, it was approved by an elected Democratic official, and printed in the local press before polling day."

As calls of foul play grew louder, Jeb Bush tried to distance himself from the furore by stepping down from the three-strong certification board which would eventually announce the Florida result.

While there was a degree of sympathy for the Democrats from independent observers, it was also felt that an unprecedented legal challenge which could drag out the election for months could only serve to damage America's reputation abroad. A nation which sees itself as a bastion of democracy and fairness was feeling distinctly uneasy about being held up to charges of voting irregularities. And how could it claim to be at the forefront of world technology when it couldn't even design a readable ballot paper?

Even the *New York Times* and the *Washington Post*, both of which endorsed Gore's candidacy, urged him to forget legal action for the sake of the country. Although agreeing that there was concern over the 19,000 discarded ballots in Palm Beach, the *New York Times* stated: "It does not, however, seal the case that such lapses should be a reason for a protracted legal challenge that paralyses the succession process, undermines the finality of presidential elections and makes nervous a world that looks to the United States as a model of political stability."

The *Washington Post* said that Gore's threat of legal action risked "a political war that could spread far beyond Florida, one that would be far harder to stop than to begin."

Although the Bush camp loftily continued to insist that victory was theirs, Gore was clearly not going to give in without a fight. As the war of words escalated, William Daley affirmed: "Contrary to claims being made by the Bush campaign, this election is not over."

Apart from the legions of lawyers descending on Florida, the other people to profit from the situation were the country's comedians and talk show hosts. The likes of Jay Leno and David Letterman came out with a string of one-liners on the constitutional crisis.

"George W. Bush is not President of the United States. Al Gore is not President of the United States. What do you say we just leave it that way?"

"They told George W. Bush that votes by the Floridians would decide the election. He said now was not the time to bring foreigners into it."

"They called in the head of Russia's election commission to help out with the Florida vote recount. Vladimir Putin won."

"I'm not saying Bush is getting confident that he is going to win but he spent all day trying to pronounce the word 'inaugural'."

"Both candidates are feeling the pressure. Al Gore has been testy with his staff. And late today George W. Bush broke down and yelled at his parents: 'You promised!'"

Even outgoing President Bill Clinton got in on the act. "The American people have spoken," he told reporters, "but it's going to take a little while to determine exactly what they said!"

It was then that the humble chad entered American popular consciousness. Mistrusting the automatic recount, the Gore camp pushed for votes in Palm Beach to be recounted by hand, their stance hardened by a sample hand recount in Palm Beach (representing around 1 per cent of the vote) which produced an additional 19 votes for Al Gore. If applied to the whole county, that would have been sufficient for Gore to carry the decisive state of Florida. Checking by hand required poll officials to hold the hole-punched ballot papers up to the light to determine whether or not they had been perforated properly. The lack of a proper hole – or "under-votes" as they became known – would have caused the machine to reject the vote rather than count it. The object of the exercise was to decide which candidate voters had been trying to indicate on papers in which the tiny squares of paper – or "chads" – had not been fully punched out. After lengthy deliberation, officials concluded that they would count as votes any papers in which the chad was left swinging. This included "hanging-door chads" (hinged at the top), "swinging-door chads" (swinging from the side) and "tri-chads" (in which three of its four corners were

Stiff opposition

In Oklahoma in 1990 Frank Ogden III enjoyed a landslide local election victory over Josh Evans . . . despite the fact that he had been dead for three months. It appears that Evans' campaign, which made great play of the point that he was still alive, did not go down well with voters, and in the end he couldn't cope with the stiff opposition.

hanging on grimly). However "pregnant chads" and "dimple chads" (which simply bulged and let no light through) were not to be counted as votes.

But just when that all seemed clear, Gore camp lawyer Leon St John pointed out a flaw with the "sunlight test", as it had been christened. He argued that even if one corner of a paper was punched, sometimes the light still wouldn't shine through. So the Palm Beach canvassing board agreed to reconsider and finally decided that a vote counted if any corner of the paper was punched, regardless of whether it passed the sunlight test!

An editorial in the *St Petersburg Times* said scathingly: "Welcome to Electoral Land, Florida's latest theme park sensation."

While three other mainly Democratic counties in Florida – Volusia, Broward, and Miami-Dade – also prepared to recount votes by hand, the Republicans vowed to fight the manual recounts in the courts. And in a tit-for-tat measure, they threatened to call for recounts in Iowa and Wisconsin, both of which had been declared as narrow victories for the Democrats. The Gore camp responded by instigating an FBI investigation in Miami over allegations of "a huge number" of spoiled voting cards in three counties. Miami Democrats said that 17,000 papers had been spoiled in the predominantly black areas of Liberty City, Opalocka and north-west Miami because voters appeared to have

Disappearing Dartford

Although it was mentioned in the Domesday Book and is the home of Europe's largest shopping mall, the historic market town of Dartford was mistakenly omitted from a new tourism map produced by Kent County Council. The map showed neighbouring villages, but where Dartford should have been, there was just a green space. The town's MP, Dr Howard Stoate, commented: "The omission is especially disappointing given that Dartford is trying hard to boost its profile as a tourism destination." The council replied: "We regret that Dartford was left off the map. It was a genuine mistake."

chosen two candidates. "This is just too many spoiled votes to be human error," said a senior Democrat hinting none too subtly at a conspiracy theory. Black Democrats went on to claim that they had been barred from voting or had been given ballot papers which had already been punched for Bush.

Arizona's Republican senator John McCain, who lost the party nomination to Bush, voiced the fears of many Americans who feared that the deadlock could paralyse the country and that the ongoing dispute was doing neither candidate any favours. "I think the nation is growing a little weary of this," he said. "And whoever wins is having a rapidly diminishing mandate."

New Jersey's Democrat senator, Robert Torricelli, agreed. "My fear was that we would head to a downward spiral of retribution with lawsuits in different states. Unfortunately we have now entered that spiral."

James Baker offered a Republican-coated olive branch, promising

Green

An Ohio council candidate missed out on a vital election press conference in March 2001 . . . because he didn't know the way to City Hall. Green Party candidate Greg Richey mistakenly went to the Statehouse in Columbus and stood outside for ten long minutes wondering why nobody else had turned up. Eventually he accosted a passer-by who told him he was waiting outside the wrong building and gave him directions to City Hall.

to drop the court action on condition that the Democrats stopped all hand recounts and respected the result of the automatic Florida recount, due later that week. "Whoever wins then, wins," he told NBC. "We will accept that result." It was an offer the Gore camp found easy to refuse.

So Bush, Baker and Co. went to US District Judge Donald Middlebrooks to order the cessation of the hand recounts which were now under way in the heavily Democratic counties of Palm Beach, Broward, and Miami-Dade. Middlebrooks, who just happened to be a staunch Democrat, dismissed the application. The Republicans immediately announced their intention to appeal.

Gore then came up with his own solution. He was prepared to accept the result if the Republicans would allow the new totals from the hand recounts in those three counties to be added to the certified results from the other 64 Florida counties plus the overseas absentee ballots which were due in on 17 November. Failing that, he suggested a hand recount in all 67 Florida counties. For once, Bush understood the question, but that didn't mean he liked it. He rejected hand recounts as chaotic and arbitrary, claiming that the process was

Mayor mayhem

Acting on a whim, Mayor Jim Baca of Albuquerque, New Mexico, decided to test the panic button which, he had been assured, would bring security guards rushing to his office within a matter of seconds. Having pressed the button, he waited . . . and waited. After fifteen minutes and no sign of anyone racing to his aid, he gave up and prepared to go home. As he stepped out into the corridor he bumped into the security staff, all of whom were frantically searching for the key to his office.

"unfair, gives rise to human error and the potential for great mischief." Surely such a thought was inconceivable in the land of the free . . .

Six days after non-election night, by which time Bush's lead in Florida had been reduced to about 300 according to unofficial counts, a new name entered the cast – Florida Secretary of State Katherine Harris, a woman nicknamed "Cruella De Vil" by the Democrats. She announced that the state's vote count would become official at midnight on 17 November when the overseas absentee ballots would be added to the totals. In doing so, she rejected requests from four counties – the aforementioned three and Republican-leaning Collier – to submit hand recounts after that deadline, claiming that it was her duty under Florida law. "The reasons given in the requests are insufficient to warrant waiver of the unambiguous filing deadline imposed by the Florida Legislature," she said. In simple language – and this was in short supply – she wanted to declare Bush the winner on 17 November. End of story.

But not quite. For the formidable Mrs Harris was not exactly the most impartial observer according to Democrats. She actively campaigned for Bush and was a close friend of his brother Jeb. She was almost family, they wailed, so they challenged her ruling in court.

Then a very strange event occurred, quite out of keeping with the accepted order of things. Circuit court judge Terry Lewis, a Democrat appointment, ruled in favour of the Republicans. Contrary to Democrat expectations, Judge Lewis upheld Katherine Harris's imposition of a 17 November deadline – one which effectively excluded the laborious hand recounts as they were not likely to be completed for a further seven days. But in American politics when one door closes another can be battered open and the Democrats were confident of finding a court which would take their side. They didn't have to look far since the Florida Supreme Court in Tallahassee possessed a predominantly Democrat-appointed bench.

The Bush camp protested that all 6,000,000 votes in Florida had already been counted twice by machine – three times in some counties. With the inclusion of the overseas ballots, he now had a lead of 927. That, he said, should be the final result, adding that any hand count in random counties was unfair and unconstitutional as it meant that not all votes were being treated equally. However Gore was willing to stand by the result if the entire state was recounted by hand, but Bush didn't want that either. A hand count to him was like a red rag to that big animal with horns he could never remember the name of.

The Florida Supreme Court restored the Democrats' faith in partisanship. It refused to allow Harris "to summarily disenfranchize innocent electors in an effort to punish dilatory board members" and ruled that the manual recount was permissible. Imposing a deadline of 26 November for the completion of all recounts, the court added that it considered the right of people to cast their votes was of overriding and "paramount concern". Welcoming the 43-page ruling as a "get out of jail" card, Gore proclaimed: "We will move forward now with a full,

St. Chad.
Patron
saint of
disputed
elections?

fair and accurate count of the ballots in question. I don't know what those ballots will show. I don't know whether Governor Bush or I will prevail. We do know our democracy is the winner tonight."

James Baker threw the rattle out of the pram. "It is simply not fair . . . to change the rules either in the middle of the game or after the game is played. The Supreme Court has pretty well rewritten the Florida electoral code." He said the Republicans planned to appeal.

There was a further blow for Bush when running-mate Dick Cheney suffered a heart attack. The stress and strain of this messy, protracted affair was starting to become unbearable for those closest to the two candidates. It was British Prime Minister Harold Wilson who once remarked that a week was a long time in politics. That was nothing compared to two weeks of American politics.

There was no easing of the tension over the next seven days which produced the by now familiar round of court rulings and appeals. Bit by bit Bush's lead was whittled away as the results of the recounts filtered through, but Gore suffered a major setback when election officials in Miami-Dade County stopped their hand count on the basis that it would be impossible to finish in time for the 26 November deadline. Gore turned to the Florida Supreme Court to force Miami-Dade to resume the count but this time the judges let him down. When the count was halted, Gore had picked up only 157 extra votes in Miami-Dade. If the count had been allowed to continue, his campaigners calculated that he could have picked up as many as 800. He was hanging on by the slenderest of threads – not unlike some of the chads which continued to exercise the sharpest legal minds of both camps. Republican sources accused the Democrats of exerting pressure on the counters to include ballots that would normally be rejected. Local judge Charles Burton conceded: "We are dealing with marks that are barely discernible to the human eye."

On 26 November – 19 days after the election – the world waited anxiously to find out who would be the 43rd President of the United

States. The official result in Florida was announced as a victory for George W. Bush by the margin of 537 votes. The Republicans celebrated; the Democrats said they would appeal.

Al Gore was not a happy man. He was furious that Katherine Harris had refused to include his 180-vote gain from the Palm Beach recount because it had missed the latest deadline by just two hours. In refusing the county's appeal for an extension of the deadline on the grounds that it did not comply with state law, she had, according to the Democrats, once again shown herself in her true colours. She even discounted the partial hand recount submitted by Palm Beach and instead certified the result of the machine recount. Democrat senator Jack Reed snarled, "This just goes to prove her position throughout: 'Don't bother me with the votes, I know who won'."

As well as Palm Beach, Gore contested the results in two other counties – Nassau and that old battleground, Miami-Dade – claiming that both had acted illegally. He maintained that Nassau contravened the law by ignoring the results of the state-ordered recount and submitting the original election-night results, and that Miami-Dade should not have refused to recount ballots by hand. By his calculations, he had actually won Florida by nine votes, having arrived at this figure by discounting some of the overseas ballots which his team insisted were included illegally and by adding on the rejected 180 votes from Palm Beach. Even some Democrats began to scratch their hands in bewilderment.

While a nationwide poll revealed that six out of ten Americans, including a quarter of his own supporters, thought he should concede, Gore announced his intention to fight on through the courts. Perhaps, harking back to election night, he knew how reliable polls were! "I believe very strongly that every vote has to be counted," he said. "What we're talking about is many thousands of votes that have never been counted at all. How can we tell our children that every vote counts if we don't count every vote?" The speech-writers were working overtime.

Cannabis cabinet

A matter of days after Prime Minister Tony Blair had declared that drunks should be marched by police to cashpoints to pay on-the-spot fines, his teenage son Euan was found drunk in London's Leicester Square. Shadow Home Secretary Ann Widdecombe also put her foot in it in 2000. Shortly after she announced that her party would impose a zero-tolerance policy for soft-drug users, seven of her Shadow Cabinet colleagues admitted they had once smoked cannabis.

In the meantime Bush emerged from his ranch retreat to appear on TV, neatly positioned between two United States flags, and told the nation: "The election was close, but tonight, after a count, a recount and yet another manual recount, Secretary Cheney and I are honoured and humbled to have won the state of Florida." Wisely, he stopped short of declaring himself President. In the prevailing climate, with further legal battles imminent, that might have been tempting fate.

There appeared to be no end in sight to the conflict, and political commentators took the long-term view and discussed what would happen if Clinton's successor had still not been chosen by Inauguration Day, 20 January 2001. In that event, the presidency could have passed to the most senior member of the Senate, 97-year-old Strom Thurmond. Now that would have been a novelty.

With Mickey Mouse and Pluto ruling themselves out as a stop-gap dream team, attention re-focused on Bush and Gore, and the former thought he had received a timely boost when the US Supreme Court over-ruled the Florida Supreme Court's decision to extend the election

Biyaga betrayal

In July 1991, five hundred anti-government protesters carried the supposedly dead body of martyr Abel Biyaga through the streets of Douala, Cameroon, and screamed at soldiers: "You shot him; shoot us too." As the soldiers obliged by firing into the air, Biyaga suddenly jumped from the funeral cart and ran off. Bewildered and betrayed, the protesters quietly drifted away.

deadline in order to allow the hand counting of ballots. However the judges also noted that if the Florida court wished to clarify its decision and explain what authority it was using, the case would be reconsidered. Basically the Supreme Court ruling was so confusing and complicated that nobody was any the wiser. Sources close to Gore said afterwards that his team was still "trying to figure out" exactly what the decision meant. But they would probably appeal anyway.

Although the outcome of the election remained as elusive as ever, there was no stopping the rise and rise of the chad. It became the most talked-about word in the United States. TV stations ran specials on the African country of Chad and newspapers suggested that the seventh-century English bishop St Chad should become the patron saint of disputed elections. There was even a nice little line in chad jewellery, brought out just in time for the Christmas market. Internet company Enjewel.com incorporated the chads into sterling silver earrings, cufflinks and necklaces, retailing from around $50. Company president Sheldon Ginsberg offered Florida residents a 15 per cent discount . . ."if they fill out the order form right the first time."

By 8 December the deadline for all states to submit their representatives to the electoral college was just four days away. The college would then formally select the President six days later. Sensing the need for urgency, both sides went to court.

The day started badly for the Gore camp when two Florida circuit court judges dismissed his pleas for another recount of excluded ballots. Bush now stood on the very brink of victory, but two hours later the situation was plunged into chaos again when, by a split four to three decision, the Florida Supreme Court ordered an immediate recount of 9,000 disputed votes in Miami-Dade. The court also ruled that 215 votes for Gore in Palm Beach and another 168 in Miami-Dade must be added to the final tally, thus reducing Bush's lead in Florida to just 154. Furthermore, it ordered an immediate manual recount of all under-votes (some 43,000 in total) in any Florida county where such a recount had yet to take place, decreeing that a ballot should be considered legal if a "clear intention" of voter intent is determined. So no room for ambiguity there then?

Predictably the Gore camp welcomed the decision. A senior adviser to the Vice-President enthused: "Finally someone is going to open the ballot box and see how people voted. I think they are going to find that the people of Florida elected Al Gore." The Republicans muttered that the ruling "sets a dangerous precedent, which places Gore's recount obsession over the rule of law." They said they would appeal.

Bush took his case to the largely Republican US Supreme Court who, by a five to four split, immediately issued an emergency order to stop the counting pending its hearing. That hearing took place on 11 December, both sides putting their arguments to the court in 45-minute sessions. After 34 hours of deliberation, the nine highest judges in the land produced a muddled and divided 65-page ruling. With all but two of the nine being Republican appointments, it was scarcely surprising that they voted seven to two to reverse the Florida Supreme Court's decision to order recounts, arguing that the move would be unconstitutional. Then the court split five to four in deciding that new recounts should not be ordered because there was insufficient time. Gore aides spent hours poring over the ruling to see if they had any further recourse before finally declaring: "The race is over." For once there would be no appeal. George W. Bush had taken Florida by 537 votes.

Bush quickly tried to unite the nation behind him, but there was more chance of Elmer Fudd and Bugs Bunny calling a truce. Gore remained bitter in the knowledge that he had won more individual votes – 50,158,094 to 49,820,518 – than his opponent and at the wholly unsatisfactory outcome of the saga. His feelings were echoed by non-Republicans everywhere. Eighty-year-old John Paul Stevens, one of the US Supreme Court judges who dissented from the majority decision, dealt his colleagues a stinging rebuke saying that their ruling would undermine public confidence in the rule of law.

He wrote: "Although we may never know with complete certainty the identity of the winner of this year's presidential election, the identity of the loser is perfectly clear. It is the nation's confidence in the judge as an impartial guardian of the law." Outside protesters waved placards proclaiming: "President Bush, hail to the thief."

And so it was all over. The most undignified scrap in the history of American politics was finally at an end. While the Bush Baby prepared for office, Al Gore the sore loser retreated to lick his wounds, and the scores of lawyers went back to bleeding the public dry. It is difficult to think of anything positive to have come from the 2000 presidential election . . . except that at least everyone in the western world now knows what a "chad" is.

Prohibition: The Noble Experiment

When the United States government introduced prohibition in 1920, the intention was to improve society by outlawing alcohol. However the initiative had precisely the opposite effect over the next 13 years, creating the most alcoholic and lawless period in American history. Seeing the new law as an affront to civil liberties, ordinary citizens hit the bottle with a vengeance while organized crime blossomed as machine-gun-toting mobsters battled for control of the illicit liquor industry. Prohibition proved so unpopular that, with the exception of the vocal lobbying groups, almost the whole of America raised a glass to its eventual demise.

There was nothing new about the concept of prohibition in America. As far back as the colonial days upper- and middle-class citizens had tried to limit the consumption of alcohol to what they called "responsible and respectable persons." Drunkards were punished by being put in the stocks but, despite repeated local legislation, the nation remained an alcoholic stronghold. The anti-drink movement derived much of its support from the rural communities of the south where alcohol was seen as the root of all evil, responsible for everything from industrial inefficiency to wife-beating. Organizations such as the Women's Christian Temperance Union and the Anti-Saloon League championed the cause, the latter in particular regarding the saloon as a den of iniquity, inhabited by undesirable German and Irish immigrants. The single event which hastened the onset of prohibition was the United States' entry into the First World War in 1917. "Drys", as those in favour of prohibition became known, argued that a government that called for maximum agricultural production as part of the war effort, could not justify wasting vast quantities of grain for the manufacture of alcohol. By that same year 18 states in the south, midwest and west had passed anti-drink laws while numerous other states had individual counties where alcohol was prohibited.

Thanks to the indefatigable efforts of campaigning evangelists such as Billy Sunday, the move towards national legislation gathered pace until the National Prohibition Act – or Volstead Act – became law at one minute past midnight on 17 January 1920. It was named after its author, Andrew Volstead, a Republican Congressman from Yellow Medicine County, Minnesota. On the eve of its introduction, jubilant temperance leaders gathered in churches and auditoriums across the United States. The Anti-Saloon League of New York declared: "At one minute past twelve tomorrow morning a new nation will be born . . . Tonight John Barleycorn makes his last will and testament. Now for an era of clear thinking and clean living!" Over in San Francisco, Christine Tilling, a leading light in the local Women's Christian Temperance Union, welcomed prohibition as "God's present to the nation" while in Norfolk, Virginia, twenty pallbearers escorted a horse-drawn hearse containing an effigy of John Barleycorn through the streets. In the same town, Billy Sunday promised a 10,000-strong congregation: "The reign of tears is over. The slums will soon be a memory. We will turn our prisons into factories and our jails into storehouses and corncribs. Men will walk upright now, women will smile and the children will laugh."

There was more intoxicating rhetoric in Chicago from the "White Ribboners", as female temperance crusaders were known. Not content with cleaning up their city, they vowed to dry up the rest of the world. Amidst the euphoria of that night, there appeared to be no bar to their progress.

Under the Volstead Act, the maximum penalties for manufacturing or selling liquor were a $1,000 fine or six months in prison for a first offence, and a $2,000 fine or five years in jail for a second offence. To facilitate enforcement, the United States was divided into ten administrative departments, each headed by an Assistant Commissioner. Additionally, each state had a Federal Prohibition Director, supported by an Assistant and a Legal Advisor. And at the sharp end were 1,500 armed Revenue Agents whose task it was to weed out those who sought to defy the new law by selling or manufacturing alcohol. John F. Kramer, the head of the Prohibition Commission, vowed that no stone would be left unturned, promising: "The law will be obeyed in cities, large and small, and in villages, and where it is not obeyed it will be enforced. The law says that liquor to be used as a beverage must not be manufactured. Nor sold, nor given away, nor hauled in anything on the surface of the earth or under the earth or in the air." Even more confident was New York's chief revenue agent, Colonel Daniel Porter, who maintained: "The penalties for violation are so drastic that the people of New York will not attempt to violate it. There will be no violations to speak of." And Josephus Daniels, the Secretary of the Navy, announced boldly: "The saloon is as dead as slavery!"

To put it mildly, these predictions were a shade premature. Within an hour of the Volstead Act taking effect, six armed bandits raided a Chicago railroad switching yard and, after tying up the watchman, made off with $100,000 worth of whisky which had been reserved for medicinal use. The die was cast.

Far from forsaking alcohol in favour of more innocent pleasures, the American nation developed a collective thirst. Hardened drinkers had little difficulty in finding watering holes as illegal drinking houses – or speakeasies – sprang up everywhere, operating behind the façade of legal establishments such as ice cream parlours or cleaners. Even the dry cleaners weren't dry. By 1922 there were already some 5,000 speakeasies in New York, the figure consequently rising to an estimated 32,000 – more than twice as many as the number of legal drinking houses in the city before prohibition. Meanwhile ordinary respectable citizens – those who were supposed to be protected by the act – turned to drink as a protest against the draconian measures. Libraries had record numbers of visitors – not as part of the envisaged moral crusade, but so that people could read up on home-brewing. Recipes also appeared in newspapers and magazines and even in leaflets produced by the Department of Agriculture which thus succeeded in scoring a spectacular own goal on behalf of the US government. With home-brewing equipment available from local hardware stores for less than $10, a cottage industry started up overnight, the family bathtub being requisitioned for the concoction of such dubious products as bathtub gin. Figures showed that nearly 15,000,000 gallons of wine were being made in Chicago homes each year at the height of prohibition. On a more organized scale, as the mash vat and the three-spout copper still became the mainstay of sweatshop labour, some 200 gallons of alcohol a day could be produced by a single moonshining operation. The illegal manufacture of alcohol rapidly became America's biggest – and most profitable – industry.

One of the major problems facing the enforcement agents was the widespread availability of alcohol, which could be distilled from hundreds of legal products ranging from perfume to antifreeze. Agents in Detroit seized a liquor called Pebble Ford which they discovered had been distilled from "Parisienne Solution for Perspiring Feet, 90 per cent Alcohol." Another significant source of alcohol was the medicine cabinet. The first five months of prohibition saw a staggering increase in the amount of liquor prescribed as medicine, with over 15,000 doctors and 57,000 retail chemists suddenly applying for licences to dispense intoxicants. The medical profession was quick to take advantage of the situation and prove itself as corrupt as the rest of the nation, with doctors readily selling prescription books to patients desperate for alcohol.

The side-effects of this illicit distillation were often tragic, some 35,000 Americans dying from poisonous liquor during the 13 years of prohibition. Over a four-day period in New York in 1928, a total of 34 people died from wood-alcohol poisoning. And by 1930 1 per cent of the adult population of Wichita, Kansas, was affected by jake foot – an incurable and painful limb disease caused by drinking bootlegged Jamaica Ginger. Victims lost control of their hands and feet, and were unable to perform simple tasks like holding a knife and fork or striking a match. Up to 15,000 cases were reported nationwide between March and June 1930. People didn't care what they were drinking . . . just as long as it was alcoholic. When one suspicious drinker asked a chemist to test the bootlegged liquor which he had just bought, he received the somewhat worrying reply: "Your horse has diabetes." The initiative which was intended to be so beneficial to America's health was having precisely the opposite effect.

Despite figures which showed record levels of liquor consumption in the first year of prohibition, officials did their best to put a brave face on it. However it was already apparent to all but the most committed tub-thumper that the Volstead Act was unworkable. John Kramer's pledge that his agents would eliminate the import of liquor into the United States turned out to be wishful thinking. The long US coastline made it all too easy for smugglers, and it was estimated that 2,000 cases of liquor per day entered the coves and bays of Long Island Sound alone. Rum came from Cuba, whisky from Canada, and tequila from Mexico – with such regularity that in 1925 Treasury officials admitted that agents probably only seized about 5 per cent of all the liquor smuggled into the country that year.

Faced with an impossible job, many enforcement agents succumbed to temptation. The general feeling became one of: "If you can't beat 'em, join 'em." In return for a share in the lucrative profits, officials great and small turned a blind eye to the bootleggers and speakeasies. Any liquor operator worth his salt had the local lawmen on his payroll. It made sound business sense. The amount of cash needed to buy off the state and federal enforcement officers hardly made a dent in the profits. It was just a drop in the ocean of liquor. Prohibition agents were each being paid just $2,500 a year to risk their lives in trying to close down an industry whose income reached over $2 billion a year. In these circumstances, widespread corruption became inevitable. Among the plethora of wildly optimistic predictions regarding the success of prohibition, one was to prove uncannily accurate. At the outset of the noble experiment, Congressman Fiorello La Guardia, a confirmed "wet", said of New York: "In order to enforce prohibition it will require a police force of 250,000 men . . . and a force of 250,000 men to police the police."

A mere ten days after the Volstead Act became law, three Chicago agents were charged – two for accepting a bootlegger's bribe, the other for selling confiscated liquor. In December 1921, the Prohibition Bureau launched a blitz on corruption by sacking 100 agents in New York. But this was merely the tip of the iceberg, and over the next decade some 12 per cent of Bureau employees were dismissed for various misdemeanours. Theoretically the agents could call on the assistance of the Coast Guard, customs and immigration officials in their bid to fight crime, but corruption was rife there too. A crackdown on corrupt enforcement officials in one Indiana city resulted in the arrest of the mayor, the sheriff, a judge, a city prosecutor, and several police officers. In Leavenworth, Kansas, the chief of police was indicted for violating the Volstead Act, and in neighbouring Wichita it emerged that the county attorney and sheriff had been bought off by liquor racketeers. Some politicians were more open in their opposition to prohibition. The colourful Mayor of Chicago, William Hale Thompson (known to all as Big Bill the Builder), was proud to proclaim that he was, "as wet as the middle of the Atlantic Ocean." In the light of such statements, it was hardly surprising that Chicago became the bootleggers' capital.

Those agents who were above corruption faced a thankless task in trying to enforce prohibition. Congress gave the Enforcement division of the Treasury Department just $2 million to make America dry, and, with such limited resources, in 1920 only 1,500 agents were employed to ensure that the laws were obeyed. The Prohibition Bureau was woefully under-staffed and under-funded.

Despite Daniel Porter's assertion that the Volstead Act would not be violated in New York, an average of 50,000 alleged violators were arraigned each year during prohibition. Having helped bring cases to court, the agents faced further frustration as they quickly found that obtaining a conviction was nearly impossible. Of 6,904 cases heard by the grand jury between 1921 and 1924, 6,074 were dismissed; of those that went to trial during that period, only 20 ended in convictions. Judge Alfred J. Tolley of the Court of General Sessions, who believed that prohibition had made the United States "the most lawless country on the face of the earth," was so concerned by these statistics that he summoned grand jurors to his chambers to ask why they so rarely returned an indictment. The foreman replied: "The men tell me that they will not indict men for offences which they are committing themselves." The number of cases brought to court also had the effect of clogging up the US legal system. Consequently courts set aside special "bargain days" where cases were quickly disposed of without a jury by promising defendants reduced sentences if they would plead guilty. Seeing known felons escape lightly hardly boosted the morale of the agents.

In 1928 a federal grand jury delivered indictments against 167 people for their part in a major Pittsburgh liquor ring. Among the accused were the usual suspects – a county judge, two magistrates, a superintendent of police, the chief county detective, a special county detective, three police inspectors, eight lower-ranking police officers, five Republican ward chairmen, and a former deputy collector for Internal Revenue. However all the charges were dropped when the assistant attorney handling the case decided he would be unable to mount a successful prosecution because witnesses were reluctant to testify for fear of reprisals from those in high places. On some occasions prohibition agents were their own worst enemies in the courtroom, their behaviour, or at least their image, alienating jurors. Due to the widespread opposition to prohibition, the man in the street viewed agents not as noble officials trying to uphold the law for the good of America, but as brutal killjoys out to wreck a harmless pleasure. Agents were social lepers. When Colonel Ira L. Reeves resigned as prohibition administrator for New Jersey because he thought the Volstead Act was unenforceable, he wrote: "I do not know of a single agent on my force who was accepted by the community in which he lived as a welcome neighbour and citizen in whom people could place confidence." So low was the esteem in which agents were held by the public, that a federal jury acquitted Helen Morgan of serving liquor in her New York nightclub because, as one of the jurors later confessed: "We couldn't take the word of two prohibition agents against Miss Morgan."

Agents and police alike were also accused of being trigger-happy. Between 1920 and 1929 they shot dead 2,000 alleged violators of the Volstead Act. Homes, garages and workplaces of ordinary citizens were ransacked on the strength of nothing more than anonymous tip-offs. In one instance a housewife was shot dead and her husband clubbed unconscious by a federal agent who thought he could smell alcohol. America became the land of the gun and the land of the lawless. Under prohibition, crime syndicates prospered in every major city as gangsters quickly discovered that there was more money to be made from the manufacture and distribution of alcohol than from ventures such as prostitution and gambling. A legitimate liquor industry which lined the pockets of honest businessmen had been replaced by an illegal one which lined only the pockets of the mob. A further irony was that the immigrant population whose activities the temperance crusaders had sought to discourage by closing down their bars were the very ones to reap the benefit of the new wave of organized crime. Second-generation Italian and Irish immigrants dominated the underworld, none more so than the legendary Al Capone whose army of 1,000 gunmen killed as many as 250 people while trying to gain control of the Chicago liquor racket between 1920 and 1927. His organization boasted an annual income of $70,000,000 and naturally enough he did not exactly welcome challengers to his supremacy. When the O'Banion gang tried to muscle in on Capone's territory, the man who gave his occupation as "furniture dealer" retaliated by having seven of the O'Banion mob machine-gunned to death. The St Valentine's Day Massacre, as it became known, confirmed Capone as top dog. Yet the authorities seemed powerless to touch him (when he was finally nailed in 1931, it was on the relatively trivial charge of tax evasion) and he himself endeavoured to maintain an air of respectability by claiming that he was performing a public service by breaking the Volstead Act. "I've always regarded it as a public benefaction," he said, "if people were given decent liquor."

A rhyme in the editorial column of the *New York World* summed up the prevailing attitude in the country:

> Prohibition is an awful flop.
> We like it.
> It can't stop what it's meant to stop.
> We like it.
> It's left a trail of graft and slime,

It's filled our land with vice and crime,
It can't prohibit worth a dime . . .

With it now patently obvious that prohibition wasn't working, a panel of experts led by former attorney general George Wickersham told President Hoover in 1931 that any benefits of prohibition were far outweighed by the social and political costs. The report warned that the Volstead Act promoted disrespect for the law from ordinary citizens, lawlessness by the police, and it also demoralized the federal judiciary. Furthermore the Great Depression, heralded by the stock market crash of 1929, brought calls for the money spent on enforcing prohibition to be used to provide unemployment relief instead. Those in favour of repealing the Volstead Act also made the point that reinstating a legitimate liquor industry would create hundreds of thousands of much-needed jobs. The "drys" were reeling. The likes of Rev. Billy Sunday refused to give up without a fight. He continued to describe liquor as "God's worst enemy; Hell's best friend," but most people had now come to the conclusion that the Capone mob represented a far greater menace to society than an open saloon.

The 1932 presidential election was fought between Hoover and Franklin D. Roosevelt. Whoever was the victor, prohibition was dead. Even Hoover, the erstwhile champion of prohibition, which he had called "a great social and economic experiment, noble in motive and far-reaching in purpose," conceded defeat on the issue, his U-turn and promise to repeal the Volstead Act dismaying the "drys." Roosevelt also promised repeal, along with "a New Deal and a pot of beer for everyone." It proved to be a winning slogan.

Although Billy Sunday maintained that repeal would be "an insult to America," no sooner had Roosevelt been elected than prohibition was scrapped. But its mark would be left on Americans for generations to come. The middle-classes, who had previously frowned on drinking, now considered it a respectable pleasure; the rebellious youths of the Jazz Age, for whom the hip flask had become a token of sophistication, had taken to drinking big time, fuelled by the excitement that they had been breaking the law; and for the first time women were seen drinking in public. Liquor became the number one social recreation. Now that it was once again legal to do so, the only ones left drowning their sorrows were Capone and his henchmen.

Dead mayor

In 1974 a town in Western Australia managed to re-elect a mayor whose death had caused the election in the first place. The red-faced town clerk had to admit that this had been "a bad mistake," one apparently caused by confusion on the part of those preparing the ballot sheet.

States of Confusion

The reluctant defector

A Yugoslav seaman was the reluctant recipient of political asylum in the United States in 1970, simply because of his limited command of English. Siatki Sili, a greaser on a Liberian tanker which had docked at Connecticut, called in to a bar in New London and, eyeing up the local girls, uttered the only word of English he knew: "immigration." His remark set off a chain of confusion which spiralled up through the United States Immigration Service, the State Department, a Senator's office and finally to the White House. As a result, the bemused Sili was granted temporary asylum and taken into custody by American officials. By the time the misunderstanding had been resolved, the unwilling defector had missed his boat which was on its way back across the Atlantic.

Carter's carnal desire for the Poles

President Carter's December 1977 visit to Poland remains fondly remembered for the efforts of the State Department translator, one Stephen Seymour. Stepping from his plane at Warsaw Airport, the President spoke innocently of his "desires for the future" but Seymour's warped translation meant that the crowds were told instead that the President had "lusts for the future." Worse was to follow when Carter's casual remark that he wished the Polish people well was translated by Seymour into an assertion that the President "desires the Poles carnally." Scarcely had they recovered from that shock than the good people of Warsaw were informed, rather than the innocuous comment intended regarding his flight from Washington, that the President had “left America never to return.” Seymour was not finished yet. When the President sought to praise the Polish constitution of 1791 as one of the three great documents in the eighteenth-century struggle for human rights, his words came out as ridicule. At first the Poles laughed at the gaffes, but soon they became angry. Seeking to defuse a potential diplomatic row, a member of the President’s party remarked wryly that Seymour was a great translator of written Polish. Not surprisingly, Seymour was replaced within a matter of hours by someone who could actually speak the language.

The lopsided peace

An omission from the Paris Peace Treaty at the end of the Crimean War left the small English border town of Berwick-upon-Tweed officially at war with the might of Russia for 110 years. Having changed hands between Scotland and England 13 times over the years, Berwick was referred to as a separate entity in all State documents. At the outbreak of the Crimean War, Britain declared war on Czarist Russia in the name of Victoria, Queen of Great Britain, Ireland, Berwick-upon-Tweed and all British Dominions. But when the war ended two years later in 1856, the Paris Peace Treaty forgot to mention Berwick, and therefore, technically, the town remained at war with Russia. It was not until 1966 when a Soviet official, realizing the gravity of the situation, visited Berwick to negotiate a peace settlement. The Mayor of Berwick, Councillor Robert Knox, replied: “Please tell the Russian people that at last they can sleep peacefully in their beds!”

Pulvapies for mayor

Voters in an Ecuadorian village once accidentally voted a foot deodorant as mayor. With election posters beginning to appear in the area, the enterprising manufacturer of foot deodorant Pulvapies added one of his own: "Vote for any candidate, but if you want well-being and hygiene, vote for Pulvapies." Clearly the phrase was a winner with the Ecuadorian electorate – they were so impressed with the slogan that they duly voted Pulvapies into office.

"Mrs Who?"

In 1965 a number of top-level international calls intended for the White House went instead to a New York housewife whose phone number happened to differ by one digit from the Presidential seat. In fact the actual number for Mrs Rose Brown's home in Queen's was the same as that of the White House and her area code for long-distance dialling was almost identical – 202 for Washington, 212 for New York. When he learned that his calls had been going astray, President Lyndon B. Johnson wrote to Mrs Brown saying: "I couldn't be more gratified to know that you are handling these calls with all the diplomacy of an ambassador." In return, the President promised to be equally tactful when receiving any calls meant for the Brown family.

White House Wisdom

About to give an important speech during the 2000 Presidential campaign, George W. Bush spotted in the crowd Adam Clymer, a reporter on the *New York Times*. Unaware that someone had just switched on his microphone, "Dubya" confided to his running mate: "There's Adam Clymer, a major league asshole from the *New York Times*." The gaffe was broadcast to a world overjoyed to know that, in the event of a Bush victory, the Presidency would once again be in safe hands.

Bush has already proved to be the master of the inane with insights such as this incontrovertible view on the oil crisis: "More and more of our imports come from overseas." He followed this up with a true Bush philosophy: "I hope the ambitious realize that they are more likely to succeed with success as opposed to failure." Small wonder that he has been accused of taking a "Texas chainsaw to the English language." On a live radio show he demonstrated his grasp of foreign affairs by declaring: "I think there is a Trojan horse lurking in the weeds trying to pull a fast one on the American people." Er, yes, George . . .

Rather like a Demolition Derby race, his sentences start off promisingly before disintegrating into a crumbling wreckage of syntax. Then again, he probably thinks "syntax" is a vice measure Bill Clinton tried to scrap. Campaigning in Wisconsin, he explained his belief in family values: "Families is where our nation takes hope, where wings take dream," before adding: "I know how hard it is to put food on your family." A two-year-old couldn't have put it better.

When he and Senator John McCain were competing for the Republican nomination, Bush said of his opponent: "Senator McCain takes the high horse and claims the low road." He got in one of his biggest muddles on the issue of affirmative action and racial quotas, explaining his position thus: "Quotas are bad for America. It's not the way America is all about. So let's be clear then: If affirmative action means what I just described, what I'm for, then I'm for it." On the subject of abortion, he once pronounced: "I would have said yes to abortion if only it was right. I mean, yeah, it's right. Well no, it's not right. That's why I said 'no' to it." And in a talk delivered from the White House rose garden the next day, he gushed: "This is our first event in this beautiful spot, it's such a beautiful, beautiful part of our national – really, our national park system, my guess is you would want to call it." He gets very upset when people pick up on his eccentric and highly inventive use of language and barked at one reporter: "I think if you know what you believe, it makes it a lot easier to answer the questions. I can't answer your question."

There have also been unfortunate slips of the tongue including: "If the terriers and bariffs are torn down, this economy will grow." More often than not, however, he shows himself to be a direct descendant of Mrs Malaprop with such gems as, "A tax cut is really one of the anecdotes to coming out of an economic illness." Asked about his proposed missile defence system, Bush declared: "I don't want nations feeling like that they can bully ourselves and our allies. At the same time I want to reduce our own nuclear capacities to the level commiserate with keeping the peace." Regarding the nation's security "Little Georgie," as his mother calls him, vowed: "We cannot let terrorists and rogue-nations hold this nation hostile."

Echoing how Ronald Reagan had inadvertently sent the world's money markets into a frenzy in 1987 after suggesting the dollar could weaken when he meant he wanted a stable dollar, Bush struck in 2002 by mixing up "deflation" and "devaluation" when discussing the Japanese economy. His comments that Prime Minister Junichiro Koizumi had talked about "the devaluation issue" panicked dealers on foreign exchange markets who began to dump the Japanese currency. It was only when White House officials cleared up the confusion that the yen's earlier losses were won back.

And who could forget how Bush tried to portray himself as the champion of education by declaring: "Rarely is the question asked, 'Is our children learning?'" He has been known to complain that people "misunderestimate" him. Frankly it is hard to see how they could.

Of course, he had a good teacher. His father, plain old George Bush, once said confusingly: "I have opinions of my own – strong opinions – but I don't always agree with them." Bush Snr wasn't very good with dates either. Addressing the American Legion in Louisville, Kentucky, on 7 September 1988, he declared: "This is Pearl Harbour Day. Forty-seven years ago to this day, we were hit and hit hard at Pearl Harbour." Sadly he was three months out – Pearl Harbour was attacked on 7 December 1941. He also showed an alarming lack of sensitivity when, on a visit to the Auschwitz death camp, he remarked: "Boy, they were big on crematoriums, weren't they?" But Bush is still best remembered for this tribute to his predecessor: "For seven-and-a-half years I've worked alongside President Reagan. We've had triumphs. Made some mistakes. We've had some sex . . . uh . . . setbacks."

Reagan's finest hour was when he accidentally announced to the world that America was about to start bombing Russia. Thinking he was doing a sound check before a radio broadcast, he jokingly announced with due solemnity: "My fellow Americans, I am pleased to tell you I have signed legislation to outlaw Russia forever. We begin bombing in five minutes." However his private joke was picked up on audio tapes by radio stations across the country and ended up on news bulletins throughout the world.

It was Reagan who introduced Princess Diana as "Princess David"; who called boxer Sugar Ray Leonard and his wife "Sugar Ray and Mrs Ray"; who once described Gerald Ford as a "Communist" instead of a "Congressman"; and who told baffled dinner guests in Brazil how pleased he was to be visiting Bolivia. Geography may not have been Reagan's strong point, but he was willing to learn, and picked up a great deal from a Latin American tour in 1982. On his return, he told newsmen: "I didn't go down there with any plan for the Americas, or anything. I went down to find out from them and their views. You'd be surprised. They're all individual countries." He also had a knack for misquoting people. Addressing the Republican National Convention in 1988, he attempted to quote the second US President, John Adams, by saying: "Facts are stupid things." In fact, Adams had written in 1770: "Facts are stubborn things." To show it was no fluke, Reagan went on to repeat the error on several occasions.

And what a comfort it must have been to the American people when he forecast: "Now we are going to get unemployment to go up, and I think we're going to succeed."

In view of her husband's tendency to say the wrong thing at the wrong time to the wrong person, sometimes in the wrong hemisphere, it is only fitting that Nancy Reagan should come out with her own classic line on capital punishment. "I believe that people would be alive today," she opined, "if there were a death penalty."

Of course the Reagans and the Bushes are mere amateurs compared to the king of the *faux-pas*, Dan Quayle. He was in his element on a visit to the Luis Muñoz Rivera School in Trenton, New Jersey, where he was asked to help out with a spelling bee. A boy was asked to spell "potato" and did so correctly, only for the Vice-President of the United States to send him back to the board with instructions to add an "e" on to the end of the word. Even more alarmingly for the American education system, everyone applauded when the erroneous "e" was added, including the school principal and the teacher who had mis-spelled the word on the card Quayle was holding.

But if Desperate Dan was only partly culpable on that occasion, the following statements were all his own work:

"We have a firm commitment to NATO; we are a part of

NATO. We have a firm commitment to Europe; we are a part of Europe."

"The Holocaust was an obscene period in our nation's history . . . this century's history . . . We all lived in this century . . . I didn't live in this century."

"What a waste it is to lose one's mind. Or not to have a mind is being very wasteful. How true that is."

"I love California. I practically grew up in Phoenix."

"Republicans understand the importance of bondage between a mother and child."

"I believe we are on an irreversible trend toward more freedom and democracy. But that could change."

"We are ready for any unforeseen event that may or may not occur."

"It isn't pollution that's harming the environment. It's the impurities in our air and water that are doing it."

"One word sums up probably the responsibility of any Vice-President, and that one word is 'to be prepared.'"

By 1989 Quayle was becoming such an object of ridicule that he felt obliged to defend himself, and announced: "I stand by all the mis-statements."

Then again, Quayle was in good company. After all, it was John F. Kennedy who rounded off a 1963 speech in Berlin with the immortal phrase: "*Ich bin ein Berliner,*" which to the German people means, "I am a donut."

Royal Disasters

Eric XIV: Love's Labours Lost

Eric XIV of Sweden was a paranoid schizophrenic with a bee fixation. So when he set his heart on England's Virgin Queen, Elizabeth I, it was a courtship which was destined to be different and probably doomed to failure.

Eric was a contradictory character. On the one hand, apart from getting a buzz out of keeping insects, he played the lute and was passionately interested in astrology; on the other hand, he was wary and suspicious, convinced that treachery lurked around every corner. From time to time this mistrust manifested itself in deeds of murderous intent. Any wife had to be chosen with care.

By the mid-sixteenth century Sweden, like England, was a Protestant country, and this persuaded Eric's father, Gustav Vasa, to try and line him up with the young English princess Elizabeth. To this end, Eric's tutor, Dionysius Beurreus, was despatched to London in 1557 to open marriage negotiations, arguing that a union between the two nations would be good for trade. However Elizabeth's fiercely Catholic sister, Queen Mary, had no time for Protestants and was furious that the envoy approached Elizabeth before her. So she rejected the idea on her sister's behalf.

The following year Elizabeth succeeded Mary as Queen of England, prompting renewed optimism from the Swedes, but she politely but firmly informed Gustav Vasa that she could not marry his son because God had inbred her mind with such a love of celibacy that she could not possibly allow herself to be diverted from that path. A despairing Eric wrote back insisting that he loved her . . . even though they had never actually met.

Eric was nothing if not persistent, forcing Elizabeth to repeat her rebuttal six months later to the Swedish ambassador. Eric then sent his brother John to reason with her, but his pleas, too, fell on deaf ears. Eric decided that the only solution was to visit Elizabeth in person. His father consented to the trip and the Swedish Parliament, the Riksdag, approved money for the journey, but, on 29 September 1560, just as Eric was about to set sail, Gustav was inconsiderate enough to die, thus making Eric the new King. Eric felt obliged to remain in his homeland for the coronation, even though his heart lay across the North Sea, but as soon as he was crowned, he left on his voyage of discovery. Alas, half-way to England a terrible storm broke, and the journey had to be abandoned. Was God trying to tell him something?

Saddened though he was by the abortive trip, Eric thought that it would at least have shown Elizabeth that he was serious about winning her hand, and vowed to try again the following spring. In this respect, he was encouraged by his envoy in London, Nils Gyllenstierna, who told him how excited Elizabeth was about his impending visit. This was not so much an exaggeration as a downright lie. Nevertheless the English public were sure that a royal wedding was in the offing, and London street traders, ever alert to a business opportunity, began selling commemorative woodcuts depicting Elizabeth and Eric sitting side by side on separate thrones. Eric played his part by sending Elizabeth tender love letters in Latin, but she remained singularly unmoved. A lot of woodcuts would remain unsold.

Now that it appeared that his finest prose had turned the Queen's stomach rather than her head, Eric started to suspect that someone must be turning her against him. His paranoia settled on the Queen's favourite, Robert Dudley, Earl of Leicester, and he became so jealous of Dudley that he considered having him assassinated or challenging him to a duel. Luckily Gyllenstierna managed to convince Eric that such behaviour was unbecoming of a monarch.

Eric was starting to get desperate. He had marriage contracts drawn up, but still received nothing remotely akin to a favourable response. He then embarked on an insane course of action designed to make Elizabeth jealous by suddenly opening negotiations for the hand of the Queen's detested cousin, Mary, Queen of Scots. Not surprisingly, this hardly endeared him to Elizabeth.

When his move for Mary failed, the luckless Eric turned to Christina, daughter of the German Prince Philip of Hesse. Meanwhile, in the hope of keeping his options open with Elizabeth, he wrote to the English Queen explaining that he had approached Mary not for himself but for his brother John, and that his attempt to woo Christina was simply to test Elizabeth's love. It is highly doubtful whether such a witless strategy would have impressed Elizabeth had she received the letter, but any speculation was rendered immaterial when the missive containing these sentiments was intercepted by Eric's enemies, the Danes, who promptly sent it to Philip of Hesse. Outraged to read that his beloved daughter was, at best, third choice in Eric's affections, Philip wasted no time in marrying her off to Adolf of Holstein. As a final insult, Philip promised to "wipe the Swedish noses in the dust." Eric had now succeeded in alienating half of the eligible princesses in Europe.

Despite not receiving one ounce of encouragement, Eric refused to take the hint and persisted with his fruitless attempts to seduce Elizabeth in writing. But by now she had tired of his flattery and sought other diversions to amuse herself.

Whether it was the sense of rejection which finally unhinged Eric is not certain, but his paranoia reached crisis proportions as he started to imagine plotters everywhere. One of his more extreme measures was to order the execution of two of his guards simply because they had placed a jug, a cloak and a halter in the royal privy "to annoy the King."

Denied Elizabeth, he married his mistress Karin Mansdolter but the alliance did nothing for his sanity and shortly afterwards in 1568 he was declared mad and forced to abdicate in favour of his brother John. Eric's schizophrenic attacks grew ever more violent – in one he murdered his ex-tutor Beurreus – until in 1577 he was fatally poisoned with arsenic.

It has to be said that given his mental state, the English throne had a narrow escape. But while he may not have been much of a King, as a hopeless suitor Eric XIV of Sweden was in a class of his own.

Prince Philip: Foot-in-Mouth Disease

It was Anne, the Princess Royal, who once said that her father suffers from "donto-pedology," the unfortunate habit of opening his mouth and putting his foot in it. Over the past half-century, anyone who is worth insulting has been on the receiving end of a tirade from Prince Philip, Duke of Edinburgh. Canadians, housewives, the Chinese: they're all the same to Philip. His intemperate comments on a wide range of subjects to a wide range of people have ensured a steady stream of highly critical newspaper headlines, hastily followed by diplomatic gestures from Buckingham Palace or Westminster to try to smooth the troubled waters. Some of his verbal blunders have been ill-advised attempts at humour; others have been just plain crass.

Even his own family have not been immune to his comments. He once said of horse-loving Princess Anne: "If it doesn't eat hay, she is not interested." She may have been amused by the remark, but with Princess Anne it's always hard to tell.

Among the jokes which backfired was an exchange with Kenyan leader Jomo Kenyatta when that country was handed over by Britain in 1963. Just before midnight, with 50,000 cheering Kenyans waiting for the chimes that would herald independence, Philip turned to Kenyatta and said: "Are you sure you want to go through with this?" The flippant remark caused a veritable stink. Philip also had to eat humble pie following a 1969 US TV programme in which he said that the Royal Family were so hard up that they were "about to go into the red," adding: "We may have to move from Buckingham Palace to smaller premises." Hundreds of viewers took him seriously and sent donations, all of which had to be returned by harassed Palace staff.

Philip has always been quick to blame the Press for his problems, claiming that they exaggerate or distort his words. It has always been an uneasy relationship. On a Caribbean tour, when the patron of a hospital spoke of the trouble they had with mosquitoes, Philip said: "I know what you mean. You have mosquitoes, I have the Press." Philip was forced to apologise to the uncharacteristically over-sensitive newshounds for his remark. He may have been hard done by on that occasion, but in other instances he has nobody to blame but himself. For example:

In 1961 he told British industry to "get your finger out" – a speech which infuriated MPs who didn't want him interfering in such matters. On another occasion he called Britain and the British "overcrowded, smelly, impolite and dishonest", and in 1966 moaned that he was "fed up with making excuses for Britain."

In the early 1960s Pope John XXIII granted the Queen an audience. When it was over, Philip, spotting that one of the Vatican guards was sporting a black eye, quipped: "What happened to you then? Did you meet a Protestant?"

In 1968 he unveiled his unique policy on birth control, suggesting that there should be a tax on babies. One MP called him a "useless reactionary parasite" and even Philip conceded: "As so often happens, I discover that it would have been better to have kept my trap shut."

On a 1969 visit to Paraguay, he told the country's dictator, General Alfredo Stroessner: "It's a pleasant change to be in a country that isn't ruled by its people."

When a Chilean representative turned up in an ordinary lounge suit for a reception the Queen was attending, Philip asked: "Why are you dressed like that?" The Chilean answered: "We are poor; I could not afford a dinner suit so my party told me to wear a lounge suit." To which Philip snapped: "I suppose if they'd have said wear a bathing suit, you would have done that too."

On a state visit to Canada, he barked at an official: "We don't come here for our health, you know."

To another Canadian who greeted their arrival in Toronto by asking what sort of flight he and the Queen had, Philip replied curtly: "Have you ever flown in a plane? Yes? Well, it was just like that."

He once upset the French by saying: "Isn't it a pity Louis XVI was sent to the guillotine?"

Chatting with British students during a state visit to the People's Republic of China in 1986, he described Peking as "ghastly" and warned them: "If you stay here much longer you'll go back with slitty eyes." The remark caused outrage, but Philip wasn't finished yet. At a function attended by a number of Chinese people, he told a joke: "If it's got four legs and it's not a chair, if it's got two wings and it's not an aeroplane, if it swims and is not a submarine, what is it? Answer: a Cantonese dinner – they'll eat anything that moves!" For this latest diplomatic disaster, one British newspaper called him "the Great Wally of China."

When a Press photographer fell from a pole while trying to obtain a better view of the royal party, Philip said sympathetically: "I hope he breaks his bloody neck."

In the course of a 1988 discussion on the paradox of hunting animals while supporting conservation, he said that it was no different to a butcher killing animals and selling the meat for money. He then took his argument a step further by claiming that it was the same as wives and prostitutes. "I don't think doing it for money makes it any more moral. I don't think a prostitute is more moral than a wife, but they are doing the same thing." Philip was inundated with mail from angry wives.

On a trip to Panama, he shouted at his police escort who had sounded a siren: "Switch that bloody thing off, you silly fucker!"

In May 1990, speaking in Washington about conservation as President of the World Wide Fund for Nature, he was asked by American reporters why he didn't do more to try and solve the Northern Ireland problem. He replied: "As long as they agree on the conservation of nature, I don't care what they do to each other." For that gaffe, Philip was branded by Northern Ireland politicians as "callous, ignorant and thoughtless."

In 1993 he told a Briton living in Hungary: "You can't have been here long. You've not got a pot belly."

In 1996, following the call for tougher gun laws in the wake of the massacre of 16 children and their teacher by a psychopath in the Scottish town of Dunblane, Philip expressed the view that a gun was no more dangerous than a cricket bat in the hands of a madman. "If a cricketer decided to go into a school," he said, "and batter a lot of people with a cricket bat, which he could do easily, are you going to ban cricket bats?" His views were greeted with a mixture of incredulity and fury.

He once asked his Italian hosts if they knew what the smallest book in the world was, and then told them that it was the Book of Italian Heroes. He followed that with a crack about Italian tanks being the only ones with one forward and four reverse gears.

In 1998 he suggested that tribes in Papua New Guinea still practised cannibalism. After hearing about a student who had trekked through the mountains there, Philips asked him: "So you managed not to get eaten then?"

Also in 1998 he caused a stir during a state visit to Brunei when he told businessmen he felt sorry for overseas students coming to study in Britain. "I don't know how they are going to integrate in places like Glasgow and Sheffield," he said. "I have to commiserate."

Attending the Festival of the Future at Cardiff Castle to mark the opening of the Welsh Assembly in 1999, he succeeded in upsetting a group of deaf youngsters by joking that it was standing too close to the loud music playing at the celebration which had made them deaf. "Deaf?" he said. "If you're near there, no wonder you are deaf!" Members of the British Deaf Association were "shocked" and "insulted" by the tactless remark.

Also in 1999, while touring a factory near Edinburgh, he remarked that a fuse box "looked as though it had been put in by an Indian." Buckingham Palace was forced to issue an apology.

In 2002, while on a tour of Australia, he surprised the founder of an Aboriginal cultural park by asking: "Do you still throw spears at each other?" The comment sparked an angry response from Aboriginal activists. One said of HRH: "The man has shown by that remark that he is just plain ignorant."

Louis XVI: A Flight of Fancy

Often it is some trivial event that shapes the world in which we live. What would we know about displacement if Archimedes had taken a shower? Would we have any notion of gravity had Newton sat in the pub instead of an orchard? And how would the course of French history have changed if Louis XVI and Marie Antoinette had not stopped off for a picnic?

Although the likes of Danton and Robespierre might dispute the fact, Louis really was his own worst enemy. The excesses of the royal family had been largely responsible for the French Revolution in the first place, but even when Louis and his equally duplicitous wife Marie Antoinette were snatched from the safety of the Palace of Versailles and held virtual prisoner at the Tuileries Palace in the capital, they failed to heed the lesson. Instead of agreeing to moderate their ways and listen to the voices of reform, they entered into secret negotiations with Marie Antoinette's brother, the Austrian emperor, with a view to that country invading France. The plan was for Louis and Marie to escape from Paris, flee to the border and then return in triumph at the head of an Austrian army. The revolution would be crushed, and Louis would be free to resume his reign of tyranny.

The success of the flight to the Austrian border depended on two things – stealth and speed. It failed miserably on both counts.

The plan had more flaws than the Empire State Building, but the King and Queen were not exactly renowned for their tactical acumen. They decided to enlist the help of a sympathiser, the Marquis de Bouillé, whose area of command began at Châlons, due east of Paris, but whose expertise proved to be only marginally better than their own. The combination was to prove a gift to the revolutionaries.

Yet it all began so promisingly. Aware that being such a recognisable figure he could not just walk out of the Tuileries, Louis arranged for an identically dressed lookalike, the Chevalier de Coigny, to sneak out by night two weeks prior to the royal escape. So a fortnight later, on the evening of 20 June 1791, Louis himself was able to leave the palace unchallenged, and was so confident of not being recognized that he even paused by the main entrance to correct an unfastened shoe. To avoid drawing attention to themselves, each member of the royal party left the palace separately. The royal children's governess, Madame de Tourzel, was disguised as a Russian lady, the Baroness de Korff, and her two charges were dressed as the Baroness' children. The last of the royal party to leave was Marie Antoinette, and it was here that the problems began. For she contrived to become lost in the maze of back streets surrounding the Tuileries and was consequently half an hour late for the rendezvous with the horse-drawn carriage that was to take them out of Paris.

Unaccountably, the coach driver, Alex von Fersen, then made a detour in the Paris suburbs, dropping the royal party a further thirty minutes behind schedule. During the drive through Paris, the King and Queen remained quiet and uneasy, but once out of the city they relaxed to the point of carelessness. On the edge of Paris, they switched to a second carriage – the berline, a vehicle which, on account of the fate which was to overtake its occupants, was later dubbed "the hearse of the monarchy." The berline was a cumbersome contraption at the best of times and, weighed down by six people and sufficient provisions for a long journey, its progress was pitifully slow. There was no chance of making up the lost time.

At Bondy the royal berline was joined by a second carriage, and Fersen was replaced with an ordinary postillion, flanked by two disguised bodyguards in case of trouble. This was only the third journey of any consequence of the King's life and he was determined to make the most of it, jotting down the names of towns as the mini-procession lumbered through. Against the advice of Bouillé, who thought their presence would arouse suspicion, Louis had insisted on cavalry detachments being placed in advance in every town along the route between Pont de Sommevel and Montmédy. In the belief that he would soon have a military escort, Louis became over-confident. "When we have passed Châlons we shall have nothing to fear," he declared. "At Pont de Sommevel we shall find the first detachment of troops and we shall be safe."

Châlons was negotiated the next day without incident. At least one person recognized Louis, but it was a loyal town and the carriage was permitted to proceed. Convinced that they were virtually home and dry, Louis and Marie ordered the coach driver to stop while they enjoyed a leisurely picnic. By the time they returned to the road, they were some two hours behind the all-important schedule. Consequently they arrived at Pont de Sommevel at six o'clock that evening to find that there were no troops to meet them. After waiting patiently, the Duc de Choiseul had withdrawn his forty hussars a quarter of an hour earlier, thinking that the escape plan must have been postponed.

Worse was to follow. At Saint-Menehoulde, two hours further along the journey, the forty dragoons under Captain d'Andoins had stirred up so much disquiet among the fiercely pro-revolutionary townspeople that the Captain was afraid to use them. Instead when the berline approached, he rode up to the royal carriage and whispered to Madame de Tourzel: "The arrangements have been badly made. I am going away in order not to arouse suspicion."

But the damage had already been done. The town postmaster, Jean Drouet, recognized Louis although by the time he had convinced the authorities that the King was not a figment of his vivid imagination, the royal party had a one-and-a-half hour start.

At 9.30 p.m., the King's carriage reached Clermont where it was expecting to be met by one hundred dragoons under Colonel Damas. But here too the policy of arranging for a military welcoming committee was shown to be a disastrous idea, the locals becoming so suspicious that an unruly mob refused to allow the troops to leave with the carriage. After changing horses at the posting-house in Clermont, the royal party set off once more – alone again, naturally. Just outside the town they turned off the main road, taking a minor road to Montmédy via Varennes, as they had been strongly advised against travelling through the revolutionary stronghold of Verdun.

Behind, but gaining all the time, was Drouet. Having ascertained which route the carriage had taken from the posting-house at Clermont, Drouet was able to cut across country and reach Varennes at approximately the same time as the King. It was now 11 p.m. and, because of the long royal meals and the slowness of the carriage, Louis was three hours late. The anticipated cavalry escort had given up long ago. There was no relay-station at Varennes for a change of horses, but Bouillé had made private arrangements. The trouble was, nobody seemed to know what they were. In a blind panic, the King and Queen were reduced to knocking on people's doors in the hope that somebody had a team of horses in the back yard. In fact, the fresh horses were stabled in the other side of town across the river, but by the time they had been located, the resourceful Drouet had assembled a few men from the National Guard. The royal carriage was stopped. At first the sole male occupant denied being the King before finally declaring: "Yes, I am your King. Here is the Queen and the Royal Family. Surrounded by daggers and bayonets in the capital, I have come to the provinces to find, in the midst of my faithful subjects, the liberty and peace you all enjoy. I could not live in Paris without perishing, my family and myself. I have come to live among you, my children, and I will not forsake you."

Lying through his teeth that he only wanted to go as far as Montmédy, Louis might have saved the day had there been any hussars to protect him. Eventually the forty absentees from Pont de Sommevel put in a belated appearance, but by then the crowd surrounding the royal coach had swollen to 10,000. To attempt an escape when so heavily outnumbered represented too great a risk. Early the next morning orders came through that the royal family were to be taken back to Paris.

The abortive flight served only to harden feelings against the King. As a punishment, he was kept in isolation for three months. In April 1792, France declared war on Austria, and when it was discovered that Marie Antoinette had been leaking French military secrets to the enemy, the pair were denounced as traitors and imprisoned. Their subsequent execution was a mere formality.

As he was led to the scaffold, Louis might have cared to reflect how different things could have turned out had he reached Austria in the summer of 1791. The consequences of that fateful, time-consuming picnic must have been hard for him to swallow . . . even before the blade of the guillotine ensured that he could no longer swallow at all.

Sexual Blunders

Anne of Cleves: A Picture of Misery

Henry VIII changed his wives more frequently than some men change their underpants. So keeping track of Henry's romantic whims required a politician with an agile mind and a sensitivity to the mood of the day. Such a person was Thomas Cromwell, the Lord Privy Seal, who earned the King's gratitude by securing his divorce from his first wife, Catherine of Aragon, and from the Catholic Church. Sadly Cromwell learned that Henry's gratitude could be fleeting when he overstepped the mark by arranging the monarch's ill-fated marriage to Anne of Cleves. Cromwell had hoped that Henry would lose his heart to Anne; instead the marriage was such a disaster that Cromwell ended up losing his head.

Henry's third wife, Jane Seymour, had died in childbirth in 1537. With the French and Habsburg powers of Europe contemplating a Catholic alliance, there was a grave danger that Protestant England would be left isolated. Therefore Cromwell suggested that Henry should form an alliance with the Protestant League of Schmalkalden by taking his new bride from the German House of Cleves. The bride he had in mind was twenty-three-year-old Anne, daughter of the Duke of Cleves.

Henry had already cast his lascivious eye over a number of European beauties but he knew nothing of Anne so he sent one of his courtiers, Christopher Mont, to Germany to obtain a portrait of his prospective spouse. Mont was unable to acquire a likeness but, on his return, he conveyed his impressions to Cromwell. Eager to promote the union, Cromwell duly relayed these thoughts to the King . . . with a little exaggeration thrown in for good measure. The second or even third-hand description that was thus given to Henry made Anne sound the answer to every man's prayers. Cromwell told him: "Every man praiseth" the beauty of the said Lady Anne, as well for her face as for her person, above all other ladies excellent. She as far excelleth the Duchess of Saxony as the golden sun excelleth the silver moon. Every man praiseth the good virtues and honesty with shamefacedness which plainly appeareth in the gravity of her countenance." In short, according to Cromwell, she was modest, virtuous and much prettier than her sister, the Duchess of Saxony. This might have been perfectly acceptable had Henry any knowledge of what the Duchess of Saxony actually looked like!

In truth, precious few people had seen much of Anne's charms since on her rare public appearances she was invariably swathed in cumbersome, unflattering clothes. She was indeed modest and virtuous to the point of shyness. But she was also poorly educated, could not play a musical instrument and could perform only the most basic dancing steps. Her sole accomplishment was needlework. Unfortunately for Henry he did not learn of her assorted shortcomings until it was too late.

The Duke of Cleves wanted Henry to come to Germany to ask for his daughter's hand in person, but Henry was not prepared to go on his knees to such a minor ruler, and declined the offer. Besides, he had heard that Anne had already been promised to the Duke of Lorraine. However Cromwell still yearned for the Protestant alliance and was convinced that Henry could be won round if only a portrait could be secured which did justice to Anne's alleged beauty. With no local painter available, Mont reopened negotiations with the Duke of Cleves and asked whether he might be permitted to inspect Anne in person. The duke was indignant. "Do you want to see her naked?" he demanded. As Henry would later lament, nobody wanted to see Anne of Cleves naked.

The Duke was anxious to preserve his daughter's modesty, possibly because she had much to be modest about. However he conceded that a portrait would not be an affront to her chastity and allowed the celebrated German artist Hans Holbein to depict her likeness. Within a few weeks, Holbein's portrait of Anne was taken to England for royal approval. Henry was suitably impressed by what he saw and, since it had now been established that Anne was free to marry after all, he announced that he wished to proceed with the union. The marriage treaty was signed on 4 October 1539.

Anne set off for England at the end of the month. Henry sent a fleet of ships to accompany her across the English Channel but, surprisingly in view of the way she had been cosseted to date, none of her family travelled with her. They claimed that they were still in mourning for her late father (who had been succeeded as Duke of Cleves by her brother), but his death had been over six months previously. The first omen of stormy waters ahead came when Anne was held up for two weeks by bad weather at Calais – a delay which resulted in Henry spending a lonely Christmas at Greenwich where he waited for his bride-to-be with mounting impatience. She finally made the crossing on 27 December and reached the Bishop's Palace at Rochester four days later.

By now, Henry was so eager to catch a first glimpse of his future wife that, rather than wait for Anne to journey to Greenwich, as originally planned, he acted on impulse and decided to surprise her by riding to Rochester on New Year's Day. Ever young at heart, he chose to arrive in disguise as a grand romantic gesture. So it was that on the morning of 1 January 1540 Anne's chamber was suddenly invaded by a group of mysteriously cloaked gentlemen who announced that they were bearing a New Year's gift from the King. Given no advanced warning, Anne had no idea how to respond. She spoke hardly any English and probably feared that she was about to be kidnapped. Henry took one look at her and his face fell. She was shabbily dressed, her solemn face gave little hint of beauty, and she displayed none of the wit he had come to expect in his wives. He swiftly withdrew, reappearing a few minutes later out of disguise. Anne finally realized what was going on and they talked a little. Henry even gave her a muted embrace. It would prove to be a rare moment of physical contact between the two.

Henry did his best to hide his disappointment from Anne but was so flustered that he completely forgot to give her the furs he had brought as a present. Before returning to Greenwich, he left Sir Anthony Browne in no doubt as to his true feelings. "I see nothing in this woman as men report of her," he hissed, "and I marvel that wise men make such report as they have done! I like her not."

The particular "wise man" whom Henry had in mind was his trusted chief minister, and on his arrival back at Greenwich, the King savaged Cromwell for arranging the marriage to "this Flanders mare." He accused Cromwell of making a fool of him and complained that he was having to put his "neck in the yoke." Henry was not finished yet. "If it were not that she had come so far into my realm," he boomed, "and the great preparations and state that my people have made for her, and for fear of making a ruffle in the world of driving her brother into the arms of the Emperor and the French King, I would not now marry her. But now it is too far gone, wherefore I am sorry." Henry would go ahead with the marriage, but under protest, and with the intention of obtaining a divorce as soon as possible. Cromwell was on the ropes.

With Henry's lawyers already instructed to look for a loophole in the marriage, Cromwell desperately searched for crumbs of comfort. His only hope was that Anne would prove a success in bed and that if she provided Henry with another heir, he might actually grow to like her. However as the wedding day approached, Henry's disgust with her physical appearance made it all too apparent that he had no intention whatsoever of consummating the marriage. He complained bitterly about her excessive body odour as well as deploring her lack of education and musical ability. The only thing that could be said in her favour – apart, of course, from her skill at needlework – was that she was pleasant. Embroidery and a generous spirit were not exactly at the top of Henry's wish list.

The wedding was to take place on 6 January at Greenwich. That morning Henry reiterated his displeasure to his nobles. "My lords," he confessed, "if it were not to satisfy the world and my realm, I would not do what I must do this day for any earthly thing." And with that, he glared ominously at Cromwell.

The wedding itself passed off without incident . . . as did the wedding night. Henry put out a few exploratory feelers but Anne was not only a virgin, but an ignorant one at that. She was unaware that she had to respond to a man, that sex was a game for two. As a result of her sheltered upbringing, she needed a tender, patient lover, but Henry was neither of these. When his initial fondling elicited no response from his new wife, he gave up, as much in relief as in despair.

The morning after, Cromwell anxiously asked Henry how he liked the Queen. The reply must have sent a shiver down the chief minister's spine. Henry was in a foul mood. "I liked her before not well, but now I like her much worse!" he snapped. "She is nothing fair, and have very evil smells about her. I can have none appetite for displeasant airs. I have left her as good a maid as I found her." Cromwell feared the worst.

Henry had been intermittently impotent for years but was at pains to point out to his physician, Dr Butts, that this was more a case of selective impotence. He confided that he had experienced two wet dreams during his wedding night and was absolutely positive that he could still have sex with women . . . just not Anne. In an unprecedented admission, Henry proceeded to tell everyone at court that he had not consummated the marriage, complaining that he had found Anne's body "disordered and indisposed to excite and provoke any lust" in him. For her part, poor, sweet, innocent Anne seemed to have thought the wedding night had gone rather well and was most indignant when it was suggested by one of the English ladies that she might take a few tips on bedroom etiquette from a more experienced hand. But then for Anne ignorance was bliss as her limited command of English left her unaware that she was the butt of so many cruel court jokes.

For a time Henry suffered in silence. Anne was out of her depth at the heart of a lively, cultured Renaissance court as she was in the bedroom, but, although keen to be freed from her as quickly as possible, he remained wary of antagonizing his new ally, the Duke of Cleves. Cromwell had already informed the Privy Council that the King was unable to make love to the Queen, and since the principal aim of a politically motivated marriage was to produce an heir which would unite the two houses, the whole thing was fairly pointless. While Anne continued to believe that there was nothing out of the ordinary in the fact that her husband was not remotely interested in having sex with her, Henry was beavering away behind the scenes looking for a get-out clause. In March, he found one. He claimed to have been stricken by his conscience – a new experience for this particular monarch – and told the Privy Council that he felt unable to consummate the marriage because he was sure that there had been a pre-contract between Anne and the Duke of Lorraine's son. Reading between the lines, the Council realized that it was being instructed to find firm grounds for dissolving the marriage. The pre-contract dated back to 1527 and had been discussed at length by both German and English negotiators during the arrangement of the marriage treaty. At the time the Germans had dismissed it as insignificant, and the English, keen to finalize the marriage, had willingly accepted their assurances. Now it suddenly became a major obstacle.

The matter of dissolution became more urgent when Henry began eyeing up one of his wife's attendants – 15-year-old Catherine Howard, niece of the Duke of Norfolk. In young Catherine, Henry saw the frisky filly to succeed the Flanders mare.

On 24 June Henry sent Anne to Richmond in Surrey on the pretext that there was a plague in London and that the country air would improve her health. Still oblivious to the fact that there was anything wrong in her marriage, she waited patiently there for the King. But, as in other areas, the King never came. With Anne conveniently out of sight and out of mind, he stepped up his pursuit of Catherine while his lawyers worked overtime to secure the divorce. His wish was granted on 9 July when the clergy announced that his marriage to Anne was null and void. There were three main grounds for dissolution – the non-consummation of the marriage; the possible pre-contract with Lorraine; and Henry's original opposition to the marriage. These may have seemed flimsy grounds for divorce, but Henry had a habit of getting what he wanted.

The news was conveyed to Anne at Richmond. Typically, she showed no emotion, seeming neither surprised nor sad. She was handsomely rewarded with a £4,000 annuity and three stately homes in England, terms with which she appeared perfectly content. She was also given the honorary status of Henry's sister, by which she was to be known thereafter. She wrote back to him in flattering tones, accepting the decision unequivocally, and concluded that she was comforted "that your Highness will take me for your sister, for the which I most humbly thank you." Henry may not have cared much for her, but he bore her no ill will.

That was reserved for Cromwell. The Anne of Cleves fiasco, coupled with religious unrest in London, presented Cromwell's enemies – the Bishop of Winchester and the Duke of Norfolk – with an opportunity to topple him. They convinced Henry that Cromwell was losing his grip, and on 10 June, even before the divorce was finalized, Cromwell was arrested on a charge of treason and thrown in the Tower of London. While Henry awaited his merciful release from the disastrous marriage which Cromwell had arranged, Cromwell awaited the executioner. He did not have to linger long and on 28 July 1540, just six months after the much-trumpeted royal wedding, Thomas Cromwell was beheaded. The matchmaker had met his match.

Coitus interruptus

When Arthur Millbank and his new bride spotted that the mattress on which they were feverishly consummating their marriage was on fire, they simply threw it out of the window into the back garden and carried on from where they had left off. A few minutes later, however, just as they were rekindling the flames of passion, coitus was rudely interruptus when three firemen burst into the bedroom. A neighbour had called the fire brigade to put out the fence fire started by the burning mattress.

Sweet surprise

Forbidden from seeing the daughter of a neighbour, Darsun Yilmaz from Damali on the Black Sea resorted to drastic measures and decided to abduct her. In the dead of night, he climbed into her room, threw a blanket over her head and drove off with her into the night. It was only some time later when he raised the blanket with the intention of kissing his loved one that he discovered that he had seized her 91-year-old grandmother by mistake.

George IV and Caroline of Brunswick: Happily Never After

Women were a source of constant misery to King George IV of England. The woman he loved, he couldn't marry; and the woman he married, he couldn't love. For even by the standards of the current British royal family, his marriage to Caroline of Brunswick was an acrimonious affair, peppered with accusations, recriminations, plot and counter-plot, and downright hostility. They were a perfect match only in the respect that they probably deserved each other since he was a selfish, philandering spendthrift, and she was common, loud and vulgar.

George was the son of "Mad King George," and one can only

speculate as to the extent that having such a wastrel of a son contributed to the monarch's insanity. Yet the young Prince of Wales was not without wit or intelligence and his noble bearing, allied to the fact that he happened to be heir to the throne, meant that he had no shortage of female admirers. Once freed from the shackles of a strict education, George wasted no time in tasting the fruits of his position. His excesses – financial and carnal – became the talk of London society. A new entry into this exclusive circle was Mrs Maria Fitzherbert, recently widowed following the death of her second husband. Mrs Fitzherbert was said to be neither witty nor outstandingly beautiful, and by no means a gifted conversationalist. But she did have "exceedingly full breasts," which in George's eyes counted for a great deal. George was smitten with the woman six years his senior, even though both knew from the outset that the relationship was doomed. For under the Royal Marriages Act of 1772 the Prince of Wales was forbidden to marry without his father's consent. Clearly this would not be forthcoming in the case of a twice-married commoner who, worse still, was also a Catholic. There was never any question that the King would countenance his son's marriage to anyone other than a Protestant. Furthermore the Act of Settlement of 1701 stipulated that only a Protestant unencumbered with a Catholic wife could inherit the throne.

But George would not be denied his true love. He drank himself into several stupors and when Mrs Fitzherbert announced that she was going abroad to get away from him, he stabbed himself with a sword in an apparent suicide bid. Mrs Fitzherbert rushed to the scene and a blood-soaked George took advantage of her state of distress to tell her that nothing would induce him to live unless she promised to become his wife. While Mrs Fitzherbert hesitated, George quickly slipped a ring on her finger.

She instantly regretted the engagement and again tried to put distance between herself and her royal suitor. But George was nothing if not persistent and eventually he wore down her resistance. On 15 December 1785, by which time he was 23, the pair married secretly at Mrs Fitzherbert's London house in an illegal ceremony conducted by a dubious Anglican clergyman in return for the promise of a bishopric when George became King. A friend kept watch on the door for intruders.

Unable to live openly with the woman he loved, George became increasingly frustrated; and the more frustrated he became, the more money he started to spend. By the summer of 1786 he was nearly £300,000 in the red. Over the next decade his love of the high life saw his debts soar to the extent that parental pressure was brought on him to sort out his financial affairs. The obvious solution was for him to marry into money and so, reluctantly, he agreed to find a suitable bride, which, in this instance, meant a German bride to appease his Hanoverian father. But, still in love with Mrs Fitzherbert, the Prince of Wales showed little enthusiasm for the task, deciding that just about any German princess would do. "One damned German Frau is as good as another," he muttered. It is said that he plucked the name of Princess Caroline of Brunswick, niece of George III, out of thin air or that he chose her in a fit of pique to get back at his father. Given the stories that began to filter back from Germany about her wayward behaviour, it would seem that the latter was a likely explanation.

Caroline Amelia Elizabeth of Brunswick-Wolfenbüttel was 26 in 1794 and was described as short and dumpy but with a pleasing face. If this was scarcely the most glowing pre-nuptial recommendation, her character appeared to leave even more to be desired. It was rumoured that she had once had an affair with "a man of low birth" and that she was indiscreet to the point of recklessness. When requested to do so, Arthur Paget, the British envoy in Berlin, deemed it unwise to describe her character on paper but expressed the opinion that the proposed marriage was far more likely "to ensure the misery of the Prince of Wales, than promote his happiness." Another English diplomat considered her to be "exceedingly loose" while no less a person than George III's wife, Queen Charlotte, put about the rumour that Caroline's governess used to follow her around during dances to prevent the Princess from "making an exhibition of herself by indecent conversations with men." Writing to her brother, Queen Charlotte concluded: "There, dear brother, is a woman I do not recommend at all."

Furthermore Lord Malmesbury, who had been despatched to Germany to make the formal marriage request to Caroline, harboured grave reservations. He was particularly concerned with Caroline's lack of personal hygiene, observing that she never washed and that her underclothes were invariably dirty and rarely changed. He also thought her to be headstrong and lacking in diplomacy but, as a sole redeeming feature, essentially good-natured. However, because he had been sent only to acquire Caroline's acquiescence and not to report back on her traits, Malmesbury kept his misgivings to himself. It wasn't his place to interfere.

The Prince himself seemed indifferent to such gossip – he didn't want to marry her anyway – but his father was strangely happy with the choice, overlooking the fact that the Prince and Princess were first cousins (he had previously been against cousins marrying) and also reports that two of her brothers were mad. In view of the King's own mental health, perhaps this was not altogether surprising. For her part, Caroline was apparently ecstatic at the prospect of marrying the Prince of Wales and carried his portrait in a locket around her neck wherever she went. The Marriage Treaty was duly signed on 3 December 1794 . . . before the couple had even met.

The opportunity for that did not arise until the spring of 1795, just a few weeks before the wedding day. Caroline sailed over from Germany, arriving at Gravesend in Kent. Her future husband could not even be bothered to travel the short distance from London to welcome her on to English soil. From Gravesend, Caroline was escorted to Greenwich where she was met by the inmates of the hospital. She was kept waiting by the Prince for over an hour, during which time she displayed her talent for ill-chosen words by remarking of the crippled patients: "What, is every Englishman without an arm or a leg?" This was not well received. When George finally deigned to put in an appearance, he embraced her briefly, then hastily retreated to a far corner of the room and demanded a glass of brandy, suddenly announcing that he didn't feel well. Caroline was equally unimpressed, declaring privately that George was fat and not as handsome as in his portrait. At dinner that evening, Caroline again showed herself up by acting in a coarse and vulgar manner. By no stretch of the imagination could she be termed "regal," and one guest, Lord Holland, later remarked that she was "utterly destitute of all female delicacy." The omens were not good.

As the great day approached, George's demeanour was more in keeping with one about to face a firing squad. But it was too late to back out. Besides, he needed Caroline's money. On the eve of his wedding, he sent a message to Mrs Fitzherbert, confessing that she was the only person he would ever love. It was the last cry of a condemned man.

The following day – 8 April – the party assembled for the

wedding in the Chapel Royal at St James's Palace in London. The bride was less than radiant and her dress was so heavy that it nearly caused her to fall over. In a bid to forget, the groom had been drinking heavily beforehand, and when he lurched into the chapel, he had to be supported by aides to prevent him collapsing in a heap. The only colour in his cheeks was caused by alcohol; otherwise he looked deathly pale. Lord Melbourne remarked that "the Prince was like a man doing a thing in desperation; it was like Macheath going to execution." Throughout the ceremony, George could barely bring himself to look at his bride until, in the middle of a prayer, he suddenly stood up, as if about to leave. The Archbishop of Canterbury, John Moore, who was conducting the service, paused for a moment, unsure of what to do, but the matter was resolved when the King stepped forward and firmly pushed the Prince down again. Then when the archbishop came to the part of the service where he asked whether or not there was any impediment to lawful matrimony, the Prince began to cry! After the ceremony, the Prince hardly spoke but Caroline seemed very happy. He continued to ignore her all evening, preferring the company of drink. When he eventually made his way to his new bride's bedroom, he collapsed into the fireplace in a drunken heap and stayed there all night. He at least sobered up sufficiently to climb into bed with her in the morning and consummate the marriage, but it was more out of duty than desire. For Caroline, that was about as good as it got.

If Caroline had not already realized that she had unwittingly entered into a marriage of convenience, this was surely brought home to her just three days after the wedding when George summoned his carriage to take him to Mrs Fitzherbert, and was only restrained from going by the physical intervention of his equerry. From Caroline's point of view, the honeymoon was a disaster. After two miserable days at Windsor, they drove off to Kempshott in Hampshire where a party of the Prince's drinking partners had assembled. It was very much an all-male preserve. An abandoned Caroline later recalled how the men passed the time drinking, gambling and carousing, lying around in their dirty boots, "sleeping and snoring in bouts on the sofas . . . the whole resembled a bad brothel much more than a palace."

George and Caroline stopped sleeping together after, at the most, three weeks of marriage, but that was long enough for him to father a daughter, Princess Charlotte, who was born in January 1796. Two days after the birth, George made his will, leaving all his personal property to "my Maria Fitzherbert, my wife, the wife of my heart and soul." To "her who is call'd the Princess of Wales" he left the princely sum of one shilling. By then, the unhappy royal marriage was common knowledge. Caroline had become infuriated by George's blatant preference for the company of just about any woman other than herself, while he in turn was angered by her outrageous behaviour. He took to spending weeks on end away from Carlton House, their home in central London, many of them in the company of another of his mistresses, Lady Jersey. In his absence, the Princess of Wales entertained assorted male friends, news of whom quickly reached the royal ear. Responding angrily to tales of these unsuitable companions, George promptly reduced her capacity to entertain by having every item of furniture removed from her dining room with the exception of two basic chairs. In addition, he forbade her from entertaining anyone without his approval. With Caroline feeling increasingly isolated, George heaped further humiliations upon her. He even took back a pair of pearl bracelets which had formed part of her wedding jewels and gave them to Lady Jersey who delighted in tormenting Caroline by wearing them in her presence.

As Lady of the Bedchamber to the Princess of Wales, Lady Jersey was an ever-present thorn in her side and was in a position to report all manner of malicious gossip to both George and his mother, Queen Charlotte, who disliked Caroline with a vengeance. To make matters worse, George arranged for Lord and Lady Jersey to move in next door to Carlton House on the pretext that Lord Jersey could better perform his duties of supervising the Prince's stables. Caroline saw through the whole charade and wrote to George, complaining bitterly about his ongoing relationship with Lady Jersey. He reacted angrily and there ensued a hostile exchange of correspondence which widened the rift between husband and wife to a gaping chasm. Eventually George declared himself "tired to death of this silly altercation" but Caroline wanted an assurance that he would make no attempt to produce another heir. George gladly agreed to this request, replying, with remarkable understatement: "Nature has not made us suitable to each other." In May 1796, he demanded a formal separation, suggesting that in future they should live as man and wife in name only.

Caroline was willing to go along with this – provided she kept her royal status and privileges – but George had reckoned without the King. For when the Prince told his father about the plan for separation, the King was far from happy and flatly refused to give his consent. He laid down the law in no uncertain terms to his errant son with regard to his treatment of Caroline, telling him that if he had "attempted to guide her, she might have avoided those errors that her uncommon want of experience and perhaps some defects of temper" had given rise to.

The problem for George was that the people of England shared his father's views. They saw Caroline as a sad, lonely figure in a foreign land who was being appallingly treated by the heir to the throne. Her plight attracted enormous sympathy, and whenever she attended the opera or other public events, she was cheered wildly by onlookers. Newspapers too heaped praise on her . . . and pilloried the Prince in print. This merely served to antagonise George further. He accused the Princess of deliberately trying to foster her own popularity at his expense and, in an attempt to halt her propaganda mission, he stopped her from travelling freely around the country. In utter despair at the disaster of his own making, he described his wife as "the vilest wretch this world ever was cursed with". Such comments were hardly likely to improve relations.

George pleaded with his mother to use her powers of persuasion on the King, referring to Caroline in letters as a "fiend." He called her "treacherous" and "mischievous," adding: "I am so overpowered with unhappiness that I feel quite light-headed." But the King remained unmoved and ordered that Lady Jersey be removed from the Princess's service in the hope that this might bring about a reconciliation. Caroline was prepared to give the marriage another try but when she learned that George was still seeing Lady Jersey, it was the last straw. Indiscreet at the best of times, Caroline now talked openly of her husband's failings, making it known how drunk and inadequate he had been on their wedding night. As their sex life – or lack of it – became public knowledge, George was relegated to the role of national laughing stock. Even his own brother, the Duke of Clarence, had little sympathy for him, commenting: "My brother has behaved very foolishly. To be sure he has married a very foolish, disagreeable person, but he should not have treated her as he has done, but have made the best of a bad bargain, as my father has done."

Communication between George and Caroline was at an all-time low. It had always been strained – not helped by the fact that Caroline spoke habitually in French because her English was almost non-existent – but now George, hurt and appalled at being the object of public ridicule, announced that he would rather see toads and vipers crawling over his food than even so much as sit at the same table as her. In February 1797 – less than two years after their wedding – Caroline, declaring that she would no longer obey her husband, moved out of Carlton House and into Montague House at Blackheath. Thereafter, there was a barrier of some half a dozen miles between them, and they never again lived under the same roof.

George's marriage of convenience was proving anything but. He had suffered private and public humiliation, his popularity had plummeted, and he was engaged in a constant war of words with his wife. To rub salt into his wounds, his financial troubles – the reason for his union with Caroline in the first place – had certainly not gone away. Indeed the man who had married for money now had worse debts than ever. And despite his attempts to keep her out of the public eye, Caroline was a problem that was not going to go away either. News filtered back from Blackheath that she was continuing to entertain young men in private. She also liked to sit on the floor and gossip with her entourage – behaviour hardly becoming of a princess – and to flirt, eat raw onions and drink ale. In Caroline's mind at least, eating raw onions and flirting were appropriate bedfellows.

One visitor to Blackheath described Caroline as having a "coarse mind without any degree of moral taste" while Lord Holland thought that "if not mad, she was a very worthless woman." George himself became convinced that she was insane and tried to ensure that she had no influence over their daughter's upbringing.

While George once more sought comfort in the ample bosom of Mrs Fitzherbert, the flow of scurrilous stories emerging from Blackheath increased dramatically in 1805 following a bizarre spat between Caroline and her erstwhile friend and neighbour, Lady Douglas. The latter accused Caroline of writing anonymous letters to her and of making obscene drawings alleging that Lady Douglas was having an affair with Rear-Admiral Sir Sydney Smith. Defending her reputation, Lady Douglas countered by claiming that it was the Princess of Wales who had enjoyed an affair with Sir Sydney and that she had also had a secret son by him three years previously. Seeing the opportunity to discredit Caroline once and for all, George encouraged a government commission to investigate the accusations. Whilst the testimony did little for her reputation, the commissioners decided that there had been no secret pregnancy, and she was largely vindicated. Her popularity with the public was undiminished, and instead it was George who was blamed for bringing the charges against her. He couldn't win.

In 1811 the King's insanity reached a level where he was declared unfit to rule, and George became Prince Regent. His daughter, Princess Charlotte, had grown up to be vain, impetuous and ill-mannered – characteristics which George naturally thought were inherited from her mother. He ordered that in future Caroline be permitted to see her daughter only on formal visits to Windsor Castle and, following rumours regarding Caroline's supposed "criminal attachments," the Privy Council decreed that intercourse between Caroline and Princess Charlotte was to be subject to "regulation and restraint."

With her colourful private life under intense scrutiny, Caroline decided to flee abroad in 1814, travelling under the name of Countess Wolfenbüttel in company with her daughter's ex-lover, Captain Hesse, and a young doctor, Henry Holland. To George, it seemed that his prayers had finally been answered, but three years later he was hit by a fresh blow when Princess Charlotte died in childbirth shortly after marrying Prince Leopold who had fought with the Russian army against Napoleon.

As his father's health deteriorated, George prepared for the moment when he would become King. He was determined that Caroline should never be able to assume the title of Queen and hatched a new plan to blacken her name. In 1818 two lawyers and an army officer were sent to Milan, where Caroline was now living, to make official inquiries into her conduct. The Milan Commission, as it was called, subsequently concluded that she had indeed probably been guilty of adultery although there were too many likely candidates for any one name in particular to be put forward. This was music to George's ears, and the government was forced to agree that she should not be crowned Queen of England. In the light of these revelations, George demanded a divorce, but Caroline held firm, unwilling to surrender her claim without a fight. George became increasingly frustrated. How would he ever be rid of her?

Upon the death of his father in 1820, the Prince Regent became King George IV of England. Appealing to her basest instincts, he and the government offered Caroline an annuity of £50,000 on condition that she relinquished her title as Queen and that she remained abroad. Instead she immediately set off for England and requested that Brandenburg House in Hammersmith be set aside as her residence. To George's horror, she signed the letter "Caroline, Queen of England."

By the summer of 1820 she was installed at Hammersmith,

haunting George's initial months as a monarch like a spectre at the feast. On 5 July of that year a Bill of Pains and Penalties was introduced into the House of Lords. It accused Caroline of adultery, and sought to deprive her of her title and to dissolve her marriage. Caroline attended her trial but, typically, nodded off at one point. George was confident of the outcome but had reckoned without the splendid defence case conducted by Lord Brougham, Caroline's chief adviser, who had managed to obtain a copy of the will the King had made in which he referred to Mrs Fitzherbert as his wife. If the King had been married to a Catholic, he had no right to the throne. As it was, the wedding to Mrs Fitzherbert was illegal, thus making the "marriage" to her invalid. But George was on dangerous ground and the bill against Caroline was dropped with unseemly haste. When the news reached the masses, bonfires were lit and church bells were rung in support of the new Queen. For George, it was just about his darkest hour.

His coronation was set for 19 July 1821 at Westminster Abbey and, somewhat unusually for such an occasion, the Queen was most definitely not invited. She had ruined the rest of his life; she was not going to spoil his big day. But Caroline was equally determined and arrived at the Abbey uninvited, only to be turned away at the door.

When the French Emperor Napoleon died that year, news was brought to George that his greatest enemy was dead. According to popular legend, he replied: "Is she?"

A month after the coronation, Caroline was dead. George never did get his divorce, but is not thought to have shed too many tears at his wife's demise. Yet even in death, she was a thorn in his side, her funeral sparking off riots among the populace who still held her in great esteem. He was hugely relieved, therefore, to learn that her will indicated a desire for her to be buried in her native Brunswick. For once, he was more than happy to accede to her wishes.

Wired

A pair of teenagers kissing in a car at traffic lights in Rio de Janeiro held up traffic for two-and-a-half hours when their dental braces became entwined.

Toothsome

A 19-year-old man was charged with manslaughter in Jefferson County, Missouri, after a 1994 crash which killed a 70-year-old woman travelling in another car. He had allegedly told police at the scene of the accident that he had lost control of his car when his girlfriend bit him during a sex act.

Keeping it in the family

When legendary eighteenth-century Italian lover Giovanni Casanova finally met a young woman whom he wanted to marry, he very nearly reaped what he had sown. For it was only when meeting the girl's mother that he realized that she was one of his former conquests and that the girl to whom he was about to propose was, in fact, his own daughter!

Rudolph Valentino: Marry in Haste . . .

To be dumped on your wedding night would be a fairly embarrassing experience for anyone. So when it happened to the man trying to carve out a career as the greatest lover on screen, the episode became one of excruciating humiliation and the focal point of sniggering gossip at social gatherings all over Hollywood.

Rodolpho Guglielmi di Valentina d'Antonguolla was born on 6 May 1895 in Castellaneta, a small town in southern Italy, to middle-class parents. In 1913 he decided to try his luck in America as an actor and, although his early movie appearances were invariably in the guise of a villain, his smouldering Latin looks earned him a reputation as something of a gigolo off the set. He was convinced that he had star quality but after six years of minor roles, he appeared little closer to realizing his ambition. Then he received news from Italy that his mother had died. The news hit di Valentina hard, especially as she had not lived to see him fulfil his potential.

In despair, he plunged himself into the interminable round of Hollywood parties, hoping to bump into studio bosses, producers, anyone who might grant him that big break. At the invitation of his friend Dagmar Godowsky, he attended a small dinner party at the Ship's Café to celebrate the fiery Russian star Alla Nazimova's latest picture, *Stronger than Death*, on the understanding that a number of studio moguls would be present. Di Valentina arrived late. Nazimova took one look at him and roared: "How dare you bring that gigolo to my table! How dare you introduce that pimp to Nazimova!" This was not exactly the greeting di Valentina had been expecting, and, as jaws dropped in unison, he burst into tears and ran sobbing from the restaurant.

Many of the guests at the table felt that Nazimova had overstepped the mark, among them a young Metro starlet by the name of Jean Acker who quickly asked to be excused from the party, her exit being the signal for a procession of departures. Soon Nazimova was left alone with her temper.

Inevitably Nazimova's outburst became the talk of the town but, even in an industry where the tantrum is deemed acceptable everyday behaviour, there was widespread sympathy for poor di Valentina. Keen to cheer him up, actress Pauline Frederick invited him to a party at her new luxury mansion on Sunset Boulevard where she introduced him to Jean Acker and revealed how upset Acker had been on his behalf following the Nazimova incident. What with the death of his mother and the insult from Nazimova, di Valentina was feeling particularly vulnerable and so, not altogether unusually for an actor, was more than a little susceptible to sympathy and flattery. He remarked subsequently: "I was unutterably lonely. I longed for a great and real friend."

Although short in stature, Jean Acker certainly stood out from the crowd, wearing her hair in a short, masculine style and dressing in a suit and tie. Di Valentina had heard rumours that Nazimova's inner circle included a selection of young lesbians for her personal amusement, but it didn't occur to him that Acker might be that way inclined. So while the other party guests barely contained their mirth at seeing a man who prided himself on his virility chatting up such an unsuitable companion, di Valentina blundered in with guns blazing. He found her easy to talk to and was touched by her words of sorrow for his plight. Little did he know that she had only recently broken up with another actress. His ego massaged, he asked her for a more private date and she arranged to meet him in the restaurant of the Hollywood Hotel where she had a room. He admitted later: "I was already falling in love with this charming and beautiful young woman. Even before I met her next day, I knew that I wanted her for my wife."

Was it really love at first sight, or did di Valentina believe that Acker's contacts might prove useful in his quest for stardom? Whatever the reason, he continued his whirlwind pursuit of the bewildered actress and, after spending what little money he had on hiring a pair of horses, he invited her for a moonlight ride above Beverly Hills.

Captivated by the beauty of the setting, Acker sighed: "Isn't this romantic?"

"Yes," he replied. "But wouldn't it be more so if we rode to Santa Ana and got married?"

The poor girl was briefly lost for words before spluttering:

"You'd better not be serious about that, or I'll take you up on it."

"I am serious," he said firmly.

They rode back down into Hollywood and by the time they had reached her hotel some 20 minutes later, they had decided to marry by special licence the very next day. He had known her for just eight days.

The following morning di Valentina obtained the necessary licence and early that evening – 5 November 1919 – they were married. Afterwards, by way of celebration, they went to a party for Metro president Richard Rowland. There, Acker told the world that in future her new husband would be known as Rudolph Valentino. It was far and away the best suggestion she made during their entire marriage.

There was no indication of any discord between the newlyweds at the party – certainly not a hint of the fireworks that were to come – and the outwardly happy couple left hand in hand shortly before midnight. It was when they arrived back at the Hollywood Hotel that things began to turn ugly. By now Valentino had only one thing on his mind, and that was to mark the wedding night in the traditional manner, so when they reached the hotel lobby he all but dragged his bride to her ground-floor room.

Acker was taken aback at being manhandled in such a way. "Slow down," she hissed. "You don't give a girl time to think." Valentino wasn't too interested in thinking – he wanted some action.

By now a small gang of actors from the party had gathered outside Acker's open bedroom window ready to treat the bride and groom to a noisy welcome by rattling cans full of pebbles. But instead of eavesdropping on a scene of passionate romance, they suddenly found they had ringside seats for the fight of the century. As Acker opened the door to her room, she was already in full cry. She wanted him to leave, she yelled. Now!

She didn't love him – pitied him, perhaps – and she definitely wasn't going to let him touch her. The very thought of it made her feel physically sick, she screamed. The whole thing had been a dreadful mistake. Like a little boy lost, Valentino tried to calm her down and begged her to give their marriage a try, but she refused to listen. Again he pleaded for a second chance – not quite sure what he had done wrong the first time – but she simply said she must have been a fool to think that she could see it through. The more he pleaded with her to reconsider, the more angry she became. After being on the receiving end of a further deafening tirade, he slunk away crying to his car, leaving behind his wife of six hours.

Valentino was inconsolable. Time and again he wrote to Acker begging for a reconciliation, but she turned him down flat. He was as mystified as he was hurt. His friend Norman Kerry suggested that the best way to overcome his grief was to go partying and chase every girl in town. "You may be married," said Kerry, "but there's no way they can accuse you of being unfaithful. You haven't had the chance to be faithful yet!"

Then out of the blue, in January 1921, Acker filed for divorce. She claimed that Valentino had refused to live with her, that he had never supported her, and had deserted her. She was demanding $300 a month maintenance, plus all her legal fees. Valentino was served the legal papers tucked under his plate with his lunch. He was so livid that he picked up the lunch trolley with one hand and hurled it against the wall of his hotel suite, causing the poor waiter to run for his life. The resultant damage cost him a week's wages, but he was unrepentant and told a reporter: "I should have acted like a real husband. In Italy, when wives are disobedient they are thrashed!"

Luckily Valentino had kept copies of his conciliatory letters to her and of her curt, dismissive replies, and so he counter-filed for divorce on the grounds of non-consummation.

The case was heard in Los Angeles the following November, by which time their respective careers had progressed along vastly different lines. For while Acker had been dropped by Metro, Valentino had finally won his first starring role, in *The Four Horsemen of the Apocalypse*, the success of which had turned him almost overnight into one of Hollywood's hottest properties. The courtroom drama saw Acker playing to what was probably her largest-ever audience as hushed galleries lapped up the tale of the movie heartthrob who couldn't hold on to a woman.

Acker went straight on to the offensive, claiming that two months after their wedding day Valentino had stormed into her apartment, marched into the bathroom where she was naked in the bath, and hit her. Asked why she had thrown her husband out on their wedding night, Acker disputed the version of events and maintained that she had merely wanted him to find work. She hadn't realized that he was broke, and had been expecting him to provide for her as a good husband should. She felt that to have had him hanging around the hotel day and night would have proved embarrassing for her. Nevertheless, she said, she had tried to help him out by supplying him with money, clothes and underwear, the inference being that Valentino was not averse to wearing *her* underwear. She also claimed that Valentino had helped himself to large amounts of her most expensive French perfume. Clearly, his masculinity was as open to debate as hers. As to why she had refused to allow him to visit while she was filming on location, she said there were only two beds in her hotel room, and that a girlfriend happened to be staying with her at the time. Not altogether surprisingly, this juicy titbit was relayed to the sound of knowing sniggers from the gallery. Acker was then forced to confess that the marriage had never been consummated.

When Valentino took the stand, the courtroom was packed and several female fans fainted with excitement, causing proceedings to be halted while they were revived. He admitted striking her in the bath, but insisted that it had been under severe provocation. He said that she had agreed to meet him to discuss a possible reconciliation but had then insulted him. That was when he lashed out. Regarding his finances at the time of his marriage, he pointed accusingly at Acker and stated: "I took her to be my lawful wedded wife, for better or for worse, for richer or for poorer. What more can I say?" He then produced a letter which he had written to Acker little more than two weeks after their wedding. It ended: "I am at a complete loss to understand your conduct to me . . . Since I cannot enforce my presence on you, I guess I better give up. I am always ready to furnish you a home and all the comfort to the best of my moderate means and ability. Please dear Jean, darling, come to your senses and give me an opportunity to prove my sincere love and eternal devotion to you. Your unhappy, loving husband. Rodolpho."

To the delight of most of the gallery, Judge Thomas Toland found in favour of Valentino, granting him a divorce on the grounds of Acker's desertion. Acker left the court in tears, accompanied, fittingly, by a close woman friend. Valentino did not emerge unscathed, however, and ultimately paid off his ex-wife to the tune of $12,100. By then he could afford it.

Following the judge's ruling, Valentino went out to celebrate. That evening he proposed to the woman who would become his second wife, Nazimova's costume designer Natacha Rambova. She too would leave him although at least they managed to get through the wedding night. All in all, the great screen Romeo really didn't have much luck with his women.

Jimmy Swaggart: And the Lord Taketh Away

Jimmy Swaggart was the man who seemed to have everything. As one of America's most prominent TV evangelists, he had a multi-million dollar TV empire, a 1,000-student bible college, a 7,500-seater church, a dedicated congregation worldwide and a loving family. Unfortunately he also had a number of enemies and a penchant for prostitutes, a combination of which brought about his spectacular fall from grace in 1988.

The 1980s brought troubled times in the lucrative careers of TV evangelists. In 1986, Marvin Gorman was defrocked from his

New Orleans ministry for "immorality and conduct unbecoming to a minister" after he admitted to having had an extra-marital affair six years previously. It was Jimmy Swaggart, Gorman's bitter rival in the quest for TV ratings and earnings, who helped orchestrate his downfall. The following year, Swaggart struck again when Assemblies of God minister Jim Bakker who, with his decorative wife Tammy Faye, had built up a money-spinning Christian theme park and a cable TV network with 13,000,000 subscribers, was exposed as having committed adultery six years earlier with a 21-year-old church secretary by the name of Jessica Hahn. Amid accusations that Swaggart had been trying to steal his church, Bakker, leader of the Praise the Lord ministry, was forced to resign, and aisle-wide views of Ms Hahn appeared in *Playboy* magazine. The ultimate fire and brimstone preacher, Swaggart revelled in kicking Bakker when he was down, denouncing him as a "cancer on the body of Christ." While making huge capital – political and financial – out of his rival's misfortunes, Swaggart left nobody in any doubt that he himself was beyond reproach, whiter than white, the true voice of the Lord. "The only woman I have ever kissed is my wife," he boasted.

So when Swaggart, too, was unseated from the moral high ground a year later, there was no shortage of rejoicing in certain quarters. The feeling among many was that he had got his comeuppance.

Jimmy Swaggart was born in 1935 in the small town of Ferriday, Louisiana, where his uncle had paid for the construction of an Assemblies of God church. This is America's Bible Belt, and the entire Swaggart family were devoutly religious, including both of his parents who were committed evangelists. His grandmother studied the Bible constantly and she was with nine-year-old Jimmy at a prayer meeting when he first felt the call to the ministry. As a child, Swaggart played the piano and sang with his lookalike cousin Jerry Lee Lewis before graduating to preaching on street corners. Soon he was leading congregations in singing, whipping them into a frenzy of hallelujahs with his virtuoso piano accompaniment. In 1958, while his cousin was called to rock 'n' roll and started raking in $20,000 a week, Swaggart became a full-time preacher, earning a modest $30 a week. With a young family to feed, he brought in a little extra cash in the 1960s by recording a succession of bestselling gospel albums, and then in 1969 raised his profile – and income – still further by starting up his own radio show, the quaintly-titled *Camp Meeting Hour*. From there, he expanded into television and began to earn big money.

Of all the Bible-thumping moral guardians who sprang up on TV around this time, Swaggart was the most zealous. He once described himself as "an old-fashioned, Holy Ghost-filled, shouting, weeping, soul-winning, Gospel-preaching preacher" and his ability to experience the whole range of emotions – often within the space of a single sentence – made his services compelling viewing. At the height of his fame, his empire, based at Baton Rouge, Louisiana, was worth $156,000,000 a year, his TV show reaching over 9,000,000 US households and being beamed to 140 countries. The trappings of success included luxury houses and his own private jet. In 1987 he was the Assemblies of God's biggest single contributor, passing on $14,000,000 to the church in that year alone. Jimmy Swaggart seemed to be good news all round.

Unless, of course, your name was Jim Bakker or Marvin Gorman. Ironically, Gorman and Swaggart had once been friends, but Gorman – very much the new kid on the block – represented a threat to Swaggart's money-making machine. Louisiana wasn't big enough for both of them. The two rivals were engaged in a bitter confrontation in which Swaggart accused Gorman of adultery. Gorman confessed to one affair, but Swaggart said that he had two signed statements from other woman who had enjoyed sexual liaisons with Gorman. In fact, he contended that Gorman had slept with over 100 women, including the wife of a fellow preacher from the Assemblies of God. Gorman was defrocked and his burgeoning TV ministry crumbled. Now he was hell-bent on revenge.

Acting on a telephone tip-off, Gorman hired a private detective to follow Swaggart to a New Orleans motel on 17 October 1987. After letting the air out of Swaggart's car tyres so that Gorman could arrive and catch him at the scene, the detective photographed Swaggart in a room with tattooed prostitute Debra Murphee. Confronted by Gorman, Swaggart sat and talked to his rival for two hours in his car, during which time, according to Gorman, Swaggart admitted liaisons with "many prostitutes." Gorman said that Swaggart told him: "I've been chasing prostitutes in every city where I have conducted revivals or crusades."

Gorman had hit the jackpot. He passed the incriminating photographs on to church officials, and on 18 February 1988 the 13-member executive of the Assemblies of God denomination summoned Swaggart to discuss "matters that could affect his credentials within the church." When the photos showing Swaggart entering the motel room with Murphee were produced, Swaggart insisted that he had not had sex with the prostitute, but had paid her to perform pornographic acts. An official at the Jimmy Swaggart World Ministries helpfully confirmed that Swaggart had confessed to having been plagued by a fascination with pornography since boyhood. Given Swaggart's holier-than-thou stance, the words "pot, kettle and black" immediately spring to mind.

Nevertheless the Louisiana District of the Assemblies of God listened sympathetically to the plight of their major financial donor, and decided that a three-month ban from preaching was sufficient punishment. A church spokesman said that Swaggart had "confessed to specific incidents of moral failure. In the opinion of the Louisiana district, he has shown true humility and repentance." So that was all right then.

But Swaggart was not about to get off that lightly. The media had a field day and Debra Murphee was able to enjoy her 15 minutes of fame by appearing on TV to give a graphic account of her meetings with him. She backed up his assertion that they had never had sex but said that Swaggart paid her up to $40 to take her clothes off. "He just liked to watch naked women," she opined. "He wanted me to get naked and maybe lay on the bed and pose for him . . . To me, I think he's kind of perverted . . . talking about some of the things that we talked about in the rooms, you know. I wouldn't want him around my children."

TV stations throughout the United States delighted in replaying tapes of Swaggart's denunciations of Jim Bakker, and soon other women began emerging from the woodwork. A New York call girl by the name of Precious claimed that Swaggart had definitely been instrumental in the downfall of Bakker, and the *Washington Post* reported that Swaggart regularly turned up in his Lincoln car at Tony's Motel near Baton Rouge and checked in with a woman called Peggy Carrier. Swaggart's carefully constructed family man image was being brutally dismantled.

Swaggart concluded that the best course of action was to bare his soul and beg forgiveness, and at Sunday morning service on 21 February – before a full-house congregation of 7,500 and an estimated worldwide TV audience of 500,000,000 – he gave his finest-ever performance. It was vintage Jimmy Swaggart. "I do not plan in any way to whitewash my sin," he began. "I do not call it a mistake, a mendacity. I call it sin." At this, members of his flock gasped and wept while many TV viewers, displaying similar voyeuristic tendencies to Swaggart himself, hoped that he would be more specific about the nature of his sin. In that respect alone, they were to be disappointed. Swaggart responded with tears of his own. Turning to his wife Frances, seated dutifully behind him, his voice broke up as he delivered a humble apology. "God never gave me a better helpmate," he sobbed, "a companion to stand beside him. I have sinned against you and I beg your forgiveness." Next he apologized to the Assemblies of God, "which helped to bring the gospel to my little beleaguered town, when my family was lost without Jesus," and also to its "godly" pastors, its evangelists and its missionaries. Finally, in what was turning out to be a reversal of a traditional Oscars speech of thanks, he said sorry to Jesus, "the one who has saved me and washed me and cleansed me", but had obviously missed a few bits. Swaggart's jaw quivered, and, as rivulets of tears flowed down his cheeks, he turned his eyes towards heaven. "I have sinned against you, my Lord," he wailed, "and I would ask that your precious blood would wash and cleanse every stain until it is in the seas of God's forgetfulness, never to be remembered against me."

Swaggart had accepted the Louisiana District's ruling and hoped that, now that he had made his peace with Jesus, the matter would be closed. But he received a nasty shock in March when the denomination extended the ban to two years, the directors of the Assemblies of God also ordering him to undergo a programme of rehabilitation. A defiant Swaggart refused to accept this increased punishment and, adhering only to the local sentence, resumed preaching on Pentecost Sunday, 22 May. He was promptly defrocked by the General Presbytery for defying the church ban.

Swaggart knew that a return to the pulpit was the only way of saving his empire since his son Donnie was not yet ready to take over, but the scandal had already seen his power hugely eroded. Two-thirds of his followers deserted him in the months following the motel revelations and students at the Jimmy Swaggart Bible College clamoured for transfers to other religious institutions. The construction of a high-rise dormitory block on the college campus was abruptly halted and, as enrolments plummeted, Swaggart was forced to sell other campus buildings as retirement homes and to lease office space to the state's Department of Environmental Quality. Business was bad.

By 1991 Swaggart's ministry was $4.5 million in the red. In July of that year Marvin Gorman returned to haunt him, filing a $90-million defamation suit against Swaggart on the grounds that Swaggart had spread lies about Gorman's infidelity to elders of the Assemblies of God ministry in Louisiana, which had led to Gorman's sacking and eventual bankruptcy. The case dragged on for two months – an unseemly verbal brawl between two supposedly God-fearing souls – and at the end Swaggart had to pay $10 million slander damages to Gorman. Then in October, Swaggart was stopped by police for a traffic violation in Indio, California, and was once again found to be in the company of a prostitute, 31-year-old Rosemary Garcia. The street of cheap motels in which they were caught was known locally as Love Street.

In the wake of these fresh revelations, which inevitably heaped further scorn upon his shoulders, Swaggart considered stepping down from his ministry, only to announce a few days later that the Lord had told him to continue.

Today, as an independent preacher, Swaggart still presides over the remnants of his once vast Baton Rouge ministry. Most of the flagpoles, each of which represents a foreign nation where Swaggart's TV show is seen, are empty. Only 30 countries now take his programme. As for the 1,000-strong Bible College, it now has nearer 50 students. Swaggart has paid a heavy price for his unspecified sin. It is one of the great ironies that a man who preached so vehemently against sex should eventually be caught out by it.

For 30 years everyone looked at Jerry Lee Lewis – the "Wild Man of Rock 'n' Roll" who married his 13-year-old cousin, drank heavily, and slept around – and at Jimmy Swaggart, preacher, and they thought they knew which of the two relatives had taken the wrong turning in life. Then in 1988 they realized that it wasn't Jerry Lee after all.

Woolly Vila

Italian student Paco Vila was so conscious about his skinny build that he took to wearing thick woolly sweaters beneath his shirt in an attempt to impress girls with his physique. The ruse worked and at a hot Palermo discotheque one night in 1977 he found himself dancing with an attractive English girl. Sadly he expended so much energy in dancing the rumba that when the girl stroked his cheek afterwards, he fainted. Doctors uncovered no fewer than 17 woolly sweaters under his shirt.

The Earth Stood Still

Cuff Love

A man broke into a young woman's empty apartment in St Paul, Minnesota, in 1992, left her a note on the kitchen table, then undressed, put duct tape over his eyes, and handcuffed himself to her bed. When the woman returned home shortly afterwards, she read the note. It ordered her to go into the bedroom immediately and have sex with him because a man with a gun had kidnapped him and was waiting to kill someone else if she refused! Instead the woman ran to the police, and the "captive," who had left the key to his handcuffs on the kitchen table, was unable to free himself before officers arrived to arrest him.

Cyberlove

A 28-year-old Yorkshireman declared that he had given up using the internet after finding that his new love was a pensioner with a corpse in the freezer. Trevor Tasker flew from England to South Carolina to meet Wynema Faye Shumate who had pretended to be in her 30s the web but was really 65! She had hooked him with sexy chat and by sending him a semi-naked photo taken 30 years earlier. His shock at the airport turned to horror when he discovered that Shumate had put her dead housemate Jim O'Neil in the freezer after first chopping off one of his legs with an axe so that the door would shut properly. She had kept O'Neil, who had died of natural causes, in the freezer for a year while she lived in his house and spent his money. Shumate pleaded guilty to fraud and the unlawful removal of a dead body and was sentenced to a year's imprisonment. Back home in Selby, Mr Tasker said: "I'll never log on again. When I saw her picture I thought 'Wow!' But when she met me at the airport I almost had a heart attack."

Ola! Señor Lover-Lover!

In preparation for a night of passion, a 23-year-old Spaniard inserted coins into a condom machine outside a Madrid pharmacy. When nothing came out, he punched the machine in frustration and then pushed his hand into the opening in an attempt to pull out the pack of condoms. In doing so, he got two fingers stuck inside the flap. For the next few hours, while his girlfriend tried unsuccessfully to free him, he was subjected to ribald comments from passers-by.

A bit of a dampener

Attending a business conference at a Los Angeles hotel, Sandra Orellana and her boss, Robert Salazar, decided to have sex on the balcony of their eighth-floor room, braced against a handrail. All went well until Ms Orellana accidentally fell to her death while changing positions.

The morning after

A Berkshire woman, who enjoyed a night of passion at a wealthy stranger's luxurious home after meeting him in a night-club, woke in the king-size bed the next morning to find her lover gone but three people staring at her. They were the estate agent and two prospective buyers for the show house.

Bonus footage

The husband and wife coaches of the University of Minnesota's women's gymnastics team were fired in 1992 after team members were given a video of a gymnastics meeting for training purposes. It wasn't the back flips or somersaults that caused the problem, more the five minutes of frenetic sex between the couple that had accidentally been spliced on to the end of the tape.

Dumb Danes

Two Danes were caught filming naked women at a tanning centre in Nakskov after accidentally recording themselves setting up the camera. Turning the camcorder on too early, they succeeded in capturing their faces at the start of the tape. The camera was secreted in a plastic bag with a small hole but the first woman to use the tanning room heard a noise coming from the bag and alerted the police.

"Sod him!"

An evening of back-seat passion in a sports car in a London park turned to acute embarrassment when the cavorting couple had to be rescued by firefighters and ambulancemen. The pair were in full flow in Regent's Park in 1976 until the man, in a state of semi-undress, suddenly slipped a disc and moaned that he was unable to move. "What do you mean?" screamed the woman from a position not at all becoming of a missionary. Realizing that he was serious about being in great pain, she jammed her foot against the horn to attract attention. This quickly arrived in the form of a doctor, a firefighter and several passers-by. While the firefighter sent for cutting machinery, local residents passed mugs of tea through the car window to soothe the frayed nerves of the luckless lovers. Eventually the back of the car was sliced away and the man was carried off in agony, leaving ambulancemen to reassure the girlfriend that he would soon make a full recovery. "Sod him," she answered. "What's worrying me is how I shall explain to my husband what's happened to his car!"

Lust in France

A London businessman felt his conscience pricked after enjoying a secret tryst with his mistress in Normandy. So the following year he arranged to take his wife away on holiday. The wife liked the idea of Normandy until, browsing through the brochures in the travel agency, she happened to turn to a photograph showing her husband leaning against a harbour wall with his arm around a mystery woman. It was his clandestine mistress. Unknown to them, they had been photographed by the French Tourist Board 12 months earlier.

Dying happy

Attila the Hun died on his wedding night after bursting an artery while making passionate love to his 12th wife.

Love's a gas

A distraught 35-year-old Berlin man decided to commit suicide after his girlfriend had left him so he turned on all the gas taps in his apartment and awaited his fate. A few minutes later, however, he realized that she wasn't worth it, changed his mind and turned the taps off again. To celebrate his escape, he lit a cigarette . . . forgetting that the room was still full of gas. The resulting explosion destroyed the roof of the apartment block along with several walls, but miraculously the jilted lover was unhurt except for his pride.

Hear me moan

A sex line caller complained to trading standards watchdogs in 1995 when he found himself listening to a woman nagging her husband instead of an erotically panting girl. But officials said they were powerless to act since the line was titled "Hear Me Moan."

Expensive

Having picked up a woman in Dayton, Ohio, in 1996, a Wells Fargo Armoured Services truck driver allegedly had such great sex with her that he failed to notice that she left afterwards clutching a bag containing $80,000.

Hot p . . . otato

Finding a pack of condoms in her wayward husband's pocket, Mrs Boris Paveharik proceeded to fill each one with ground pepper. The promiscuous Pole's next visit to his mistress ended with him being rushed to hospital suffering from severe inflammation.

Out of control

A Frenchman from Orleans who was having sex with a prostitute while driving his car found his ardour dampened when he lost control of the steering wheel and ended up in the Loire River. Apparently he became so excited that he completely forgot about driving. The local fire brigade were called to fish the car and its two occupants out of the river.

Moo!

In July 2000, a man in Pleasanton, California, tried to defend himself against charges of having sexual relations with farm animals by arguing that the sex was consensual.

Sexzzzzzz . . .

A 31-year-old Berlin man ran up a bill of $67,000 after falling asleep for 11 hours while calling a sex line in the Caribbean.

Did the train stop for you?

A young German couple accidentally brought a train screeching to a halt in 2000 when the teenage girl grabbed the emergency cord at the moment of orgasm while making love with her boyfriend in the train toilet.

Medical Mistakes

"Doc" Brinkley: Kidding America

Of all the quacks in medical history, few have quacked louder and longer and ruffled more feathers than John Romulus Brinkley who promised thousands of American men that he could renew their sexual appetite by grafting onto them the glands or testicles of a goat. Over a 13-year period he performed more than 5,000 such operations which, at $750 a time, made him a very rich man indeed. But the transplants were worthless since the human body's immune system ensures that any animal tissue grafted on will quickly be rejected. Any benefit to the patient was therefore purely psychological. Brinkley was a fraud.

He wasn't even a proper doctor. Born in the remote mountain village of Beta, North Carolina, in 1885, Brinkley worked first as a telegraph operator for the Southern Railroad and then as a snake-oil salesman. But all the while he dreamed of becoming a doctor like his father and realized that ambition – after a fashion – by acting as assistant to a charlatan who handed out dubious cures for venereal infections. After divorcing his first wife, Brinkley headed for Greenville, South Carolina, where he teamed up with James Crawford, a man who would eventually be known more for his contribution to the field of armed robbery than medicine. Together they went into business as the grandly-named Greenville Electro Medical Doctors and took out a series of newspaper ads which asked readers: "Are You a Manly Man Full of Vigor?" Clearly few of the male population of Greenville fitted that description for they flocked to the two "doctors" to have a rejuvenation jab at $25 a shot. The miracle liquid was nothing more than coloured water.

Skipping town, leaving behind a trail of unpaid bills, they alighted on Memphis where Brinkley married his second wife, Minnie Jones, the daughter of a genuine doctor. No sooner had he returned from his honeymoon than Brinkley was arrested for fraud, along with Crawford, by Greenville police. Fortunately Brinkley's new father-in-law exerted his influence and the charges were dropped. Brinkley was free to carry on masquerading as a medic.

In 1915 he acquired a medical degree, courtesy of the Eclectic Medical University of Kansas City, an infamous diploma mill which sold degrees to anyone with ready cash. This fake qualification – purchased for $800 – allowed him to practise medicine in the state of Kansas, to where he and his wife soon moved. His first post was as medic at a slaughterhouse. What the job lacked in glamour, it made up for in opportunity for it was there that Brinkley watched the captive billy goats performing their mating rituals and started to wonder whether their rampant sexuality could not somehow be transplanted into humans.

A two-month stint in the US Army – four weeks of which was spent under psychiatric observation – was followed in October 1917 by a move to the tiny Kansas hamlet of Milford (population 200) where he set up business as the local doctor. Outwardly respectable, the neat, bespectacled Brinkley was every inch the rural, small-town doctor, trusted implicitly by his small dose of patients. Among them was an ageing farmer who, complaining that he had been impotent for 16 years, suggested that his sex drive might be restored if Dr Brinkley were to insert a couple of goat glands in him. Brinkley was initially sceptical but then read about the work of Dr Serge Voronoff who was implanting elderly Frenchmen with monkey glands to give them the sexual appetite of 20-year-olds. Remembering the animals at the slaughterhouse, Brinkley decided to use a young Toggenberg goat as the donor and implanted its glands in the farmer's testicles. Two weeks later, the farmer told Brinkley that he felt like a young man again and within a year he had fathered a son. Appropriately enough, he and his wife called the boy Billy.

Word spread like wildfire that Dr Brinkley was the man to revive a flagging libido and soon most of the old-timers in the area were begging for the operation. The goat symbolized sexual prowess to the average Kansan and now everybody wanted a piece of one. Luckily for Brinkley, goats' testicles were easy to obtain in the Midwest and as demand grew, the local slaughterhouses were filled to capacity with doomed goats. Business was so brisk that Brinkley was forced to move from his one-room office at the town drugstore to a larger building which became known as the Brinkley Gland Clinic. In return for $750 (cash up front) for a standard billy or $1,500 for a very young goat, Brinkley would carry out gland or testicle transplants. There were no apparent adverse side effects to the operation. The glands of the Toggenbergs were odourless which meant that the patients did not go around town smelling of essence of goat nor were they the recipients of unwelcome attention from other breeds. In his early days of experimentation, Brinkley did use Angora goats on two occasions but noted that his patients left the operating theatre smelling like a steamy barn on a hot summer's day. So he reverted to his trusty Toggenbergs. To ensure that they were getting an active goat for their money, patients were allowed to pick the billy of their choice from a herd of Toggenbergs kept in a backyard pen at the clinic. Brinkley was nothing if not fair.

As his fame spread, Brinkley became the subject of good-natured banter. A joke of the day went: "What's the fastest thing on four legs? – A goat passing Dr Brinkley's hospital." My, how everyone laughed . . . until they discovered they were being taken for a ride.

Although Brinkley knew that his work was highly unethical – he never once submitted a formal paper detailing the operation to a medical journal – he did actually believe in it, partly because he did not possess sufficient knowledge to realise that the operation could never live up to his claims. More to the point, the rich and famous started to believe in it too. Maharajah Thakou of Morvi travelled all the way from India for a transplant; *Los Angeles Times* newspaper magnate Harry Chandler was another grateful recipient and he sang Brinkley's praises to his friends in the blossoming movie industry; and E. Haldeman-Julius, publisher of the Little Blue Books, wrote numerous articles in support of Brinkley as well as allowing the "doctor" years of free advertizing because he believed so strongly in what he was doing. When Brinkley was eventually exposed as a fraud, Haldeman-Julius felt obliged to apologize profusely for his error of judgment. But in 1923 that was still a long way off.

That was the year when Brinkley, inspired by his friend Harry Chandler's purchase of Los Angeles' first radio station, KHJ, decided to start up a similar venture in Milford. And so KFKB ("Kansas First, Kansas Best") hit the airwaves with a signal so powerful that it could be heard all over America, its programming tailored to meet Brinkley's target audience – elderly men. At regular intervals the station churned out his advertizing slogan: "Let me get your goat and you'll be Mr Ram-What-Am with every lamb!" Subtle he wasn't.

Brinkley's saturation advertizing worked a treat. In addition to promoting himself on radio, he enlisted the services of most of Milford's citizens to run his mail-order scheme. Up to 2,000 letters a day were sent out to prospective clients. He also planted friendly stories in newspapers and magazines, portraying himself as a God-fearing, devoted family man, medical pioneer and friend of the aged. These articles were invariably accompanied by photographs of Brinkley in a trim goatee beard, which not only gave him the air of a distinguished scientist but also reminded his readership of the very animal which, with his help, would restore their virility.

By 1927 "Goat Gland Brinkley," as he had become known, was performing around 50 operations every month. Decrepit men converged on his Milford clinic from far and wide, all desperate to dip their toes in the fountain of youth. Everybody wanted a slice of the action . . . or at least a slice of the goat. Not satisfied with raking in nigh on $40,000 a month from the goat scam, the good doctor came up with a new radio show, *The Medical Question Box*, in which listeners wrote in about their ailments and he prescribed suitable treatments over the air. Needless to say, the medicines he recommended were always ones which he sold by mail order. He subsequently scrapped the mail order system and, in its place, enrolled hundreds of drug store proprietors across the United States to sell his prescribed medicines at wildly inflated prices. The power of radio meant that some druggists participating in the Brinkley scheme took in $100 a day, and Brinkley himself creamed off $1 per prescription. He was a millionaire.

The devoted family man began to flaunt his wealth in the form of several houses, a private yacht, a fleet of cars and two private planes. He virtually owned Milford and acquired friends in high places. However these did not include Dr Morris Fishbein, editor of the *Journal of the American Medical Association*, who accused Brinkley of "blatant quackery." Threatening to sue for libel, Brinkley launched a massive propaganda offensive against the AMA, but for once his empty bluster did not prevail. *The Kansas City Star* newspaper dealt him a further blow by running a damning exposé on the Milford clinic and its shady managing director, pouring scorn on his claims and qualifications. Brinkley was on the ropes, and in 1930 the Kansas Board of Medical Registration charged him with, among other things, gross immorality, malpractice and unprofessional conduct.

Brinkley defended himself vigorously, calling upon his many satisfied customers to testify on his behalf. But the board were not to be hoodwinked, the judge summing up: "The defendant has perfected and organized charlatanism until it is capable of preying on human weakness, ignorance and credulity to an extent quite beyond the invention of the humble mountebank." Brinkley's licence was withdrawn.

In the same year the Federal Radio Commission took KFKB off the air after ruling that the station existed primarily to line Brinkley's pockets and that, in any case, his goat-gland operation was physiologically impossible and fraudulent.

Most people would have given up at this point, but Brinkley was determined not to go down without a fight and, reasoning that the surest way to regain his state-issued licence was if he controlled the state in person, he announced that he was running for Governor of Kansas. In both 1930 and 1932, he was only narrowly beaten but his third attempt, in 1934, resulted in a severe mauling. It was time for him to get out of Kansas.

The only states in which he was now licensed to practice his goat-gland sorcery were Arkansas and Texas, the citizens of which were subjected to new claims – that the transplant could return mental patients to sound mind. Since there was no shortage of mental instability in Arkansas or Texas, this proved another winner for Brinkley. So he moved his operation to Del Rio, Texas, and erected a huge radio transmitter across the border in Mexico for his new station, XER. The goats were finally dropped from his act, but he replaced them with a new rejuvenation technique, involving shots of Mercurochrome, which was equally worthless but even more profitable. He also marketed a cure-all composed of nothing more than blue dye and a splash of hydrochloric acid.

Just when everything seemed to be going well again, Brinkley fell foul of his old adversary, Dr Morris Fishbein, who, in a magazine article, labelled him "the greatest charlatan in medical history." Brinkley immediately sued Fishbein for $250,000. The case was heard in Del Rio, Texas, in 1939. Brinkley was confident of success and called the usual suspects to speak up for him, but the jurors were less impressed and found in favour of Fishbein. Brinkley was all but finished as a medical practitioner.

In a defiant last stand, he relocated to Little Rock, Arkansas, but was unable to prey on small-town ignorance in such a big city. The vultures were circling overhead. Former patients, realizing they had been conned, sued him for malpractice and he was forced to pay out huge sums in damages. At the same time, the US government billed him for over $200,000 in unpaid taxes. In January 1941 the millionaire quack declared himself bankrupt. Shortly afterwards he suffered a massive heart attack – possibly brought about by the fall of his empire – and the following year he died at the age of fifty-six. America's goats could breathe easily again. The master of kidology was no more.

What's Up, Doc?

Girth, Wind, and Fire

The most alarming case of flatulence on record was that of a 30-year-old Danish man who, while having surgery on his buttocks, broke wind and set his genitals on fire.

The operation to remove a mole from the man's posterior was being carried out at Kjellerups Hospital in April 2002. Surgeon Jorn Kristensen was removing the offending mole with an electric knife when the patient suddenly broke wind, lighting a spark and igniting his genitals, which had previously been washed with surgical spirit.

Announcing his intention to sue the hospital, the man complained: "When I woke up, my penis and scrotum were burning like hell. I've had to be booked off work for longer than expected and, besides the pain, I can't have sex with my wife."

Dr Kristensen said: "No one considered the possibility that the man would break wind during the operation, let alone that it would catch fire. It was an unfortunate accident."

Demented in Des Moines

Visiting an elderly aunt at a mental hospital in Des Moines, Iowa, in 1950, Mrs Nancy Gordon arrived to learn that the old lady had died. Out of respect, the kindly sister showed her to her aunt's room but while looking around it and still shocked by the sad news, Mrs Gordon started to feel drowsy and decided to lie down on the bed for a short nap. Some time later a doctor, thinking that she was a patient, woke her to tell her that he was moving her to another room. She ended up staying in hospital for the next 25 years until the mistake finally came to light. Asked about the blunder, Mrs Gordon replied that she simply believed in letting life follow its natural course.

Odd in Odstock

A man who broke into a Wiltshire hospital to get a suntan ended up being scarred for life. After evading security staff at Odstock Hospital, Salisbury, and pocketing doctors' paging devices, the intruder spotted what he thought was an ordinary sunbed. So he calmly removed his clothes for a 45-minute tanning session, unaware that the high-voltage ultraviolet machine was in fact designed for treating burns victims and had a maximum length of exposure to it of just ten seconds. He eventually emerged covered in blisters, having spent almost 300 times the recommended maximum period on the bed. As the pain from his burns became increasingly unbearable, he went to Southampton General Hospital where staff became suspicious because he was wearing a doctor's coat. They tended his wounds before calling the police.

Drill bitten

A 14-year-old Stockholm boy, who went to the dentist to have two teeth filled, left with the drill bit in his stomach. The bit came loose during drilling and was swallowed by the unfortunate teenager.

Not dead, just watching TV

Told by hospital doctors that he had died, James Corr's closest relatives immediately starting phoning the rest of the family to impart the sad news. They even got in touch with his social club to tell them they had lost their chairman of 30 years. But while they were relaying details of his demise, grandfather Mr Corr was sitting happily in a nearby day room at the hospital watching highlights of England's soccer team beating Germany in Euro 2000. The hospital's blunder only came to light when a distraught April Corr, wife of Mr Corr's grandson Darren, decided to take a walk around the hospital to clear her head. As she passed the dayroom, she spotted 78-year-old Mr Corr alive and well and watching the TV. When a nurse at South Tyneside District Hospital in South Shields checked the family's name, she found that his file had been mixed up with that of another patient. Mr Corr had been admitted to hospital on 12 June suffering from a mild stroke but eight days later the hospital called his wife Vera to say that he had "taken a turn for the worse." She arrived at the hospital, accompanied by their son James and six other relatives, to be told her husband had died. A nurse said they were free to use the phones, so they began ringing friends and family. James Corr said afterwards: "I told the entire family and all his friends that he was dead while he was sitting 15 feet away in a room down the corridor watching the telly." He added that when the relieved family went into the dayroom, his father thought they had all turned up because it was Father's Day.

Ant attack

Nurses rushed 77-year-old Marion Bernhardt out of her intensive care room at the Wellington Regional Hospital, West Palm Beach, Florida, in 1994 after she complained of a burning sensation on her legs and abdomen. At first staff reassured her that the burning feeling was merely the result of her surgery, but on closer inspection they found dozens of fire ants crawling all over her sheets and body.

Smoky

A patient at a hospital in Llanelli, South Wales, blew himself up in March 1996 when he lit a cigarette next to his oxygen mask. Unable to resist the urge, he slipped under the bedclothes for a furtive smoke while nurses' backs were turned, but in doing so, created an oxygen "tent." The moment he flicked his lighter, a fireball erupted and he had to be rushed to a nearby burns unit.

Cautious

Lorry driver Herbert Scott was taking no chances with his injured neck. Instead of wearing a neck brace for four weeks as advised, he kept it on for the next 14 years! Mr Scott was admitted to Burnley General Hospital in Lancashire in 1986 following a fall at work. He was discharged several days later and ordered to wear the brace for the next month to support his badly damaged neck. However he misunderstood the instructions and kept it on for nearly a decade and a half before the error came to light.

Whistle while you work

A 35-year-old British farmer carried part of a plastic whistle around in his bronchus for ten months because doctors thought he was drunk. The farmer inhaled the whistle while dancing at a Christmas Eve party and afterwards noticed that whenever he breathed out, a whistling sound was emitted from the right side of his chest. A hospital X-ray of the right lung revealed the presence of a metallic reed which was duly removed, but the man insisted that he had inhaled a whistle. However the doctors dismissed his story because he appeared the worse for drink. Two months later he developed a wheeze, then a cough and finally a slight chest pain. Almost a year after the party, gangrene was found in his bronchus, as a result of which he was transferred to a chest hospital where surgeons did indeed locate the mouthpiece of a plastic whistle. Its extraction may have meant the end of the farmer's musical career, but it allowed him to breathe easily – and silently – at last.

Radical surgery

Bonnie Booth was rushed to hospital in Muncie, Indiana, after shooting herself in the foot while using a shotgun to remove a callus. A police officer said: "She told investigators she drank a gallon of vodka and two or three beers and tried to shoot the callus off her foot." She had previously attempted to cut off the offending callus with a razor blade.

Self-circumcision

A Taiwanese student who tried to circumcise himself with a specially made ring was rushed to hospital when his penis turned black. The man attached the ring because he was told that it would make his foreskin wither and die, but as soon as he had an erection his penis went jet black. Doctors treating him pointed out that the ring technique was not medically approved.

Hearing hindrance

A Leeds man was puzzled as to why, even with a hearing aid, his hearing was so poor until he discovered that for the past 20 years he had been wearing the appliance in the wrong ear. It was only on a routine visit to the doctor in 1978 that he realized he could hear much better when the aid was removed. It then emerged that the original mould had been made for his left ear instead of his right. Finally able to appreciate the world about him, the man remarked: "Over the years I have been fitted with several new aids, but no one noticed that I had been wearing them in the wrong hole."

Dock-tor

The promising career of a Greek doctor working in Naples came to an abrupt halt when he was visited by a fellow countryman as a patient. The latter noticed that a certificate on the surgery wall, which the doctor's Italian patients had assumed was his medical diploma, was in fact a document issued by the Greek merchant navy.

Domestic Howlers

A Matter of Life and Death

Winning at all costs

Student Robert Meythaler fell 22 feet to his death after climbing onto a balcony at Furman University, Greenville, South Carolina, to get a better shot in a spitting contest.

Unwise washer

A man in Kitwe, Zambia, was electrocuted in November 2000 when, having run out of space on his clothes line, he unwisely decided to hang the remainder of his wet washing on a live power line which passed his house.

Cupboard love

Embarking on an innocent game of hide and seek, Liz Walsh and her 11-month-old son Harry managed to get stuck in the hall cupboard of their home in Stirling, Scotland. With her husband out at work, Mrs Walsh feared they would be trapped in the cupboard for hours, but fortunately her three-year-old daughter Elle had the presence of mind to telephone the police. Nevertheless it was an embarrassed Mrs Walsh who had to explain to the officers what had happened and to promise to find roomier hiding places in future.

Statuesque Silveira

When 30-year-old Lucio Silveira fell asleep on a heap of pitch left by road workers in São Paulo, he woke up as a statue! The warmth of his body softened the pitch, and he sank deeper and deeper until only his head and shoulders were visible. By the time he awoke from his slumbers, the pitch had solidified, and he looked like a bust mounted on a black base. The local fire brigade were forced to cut a block out of the pitch and carry him to hospital.

Cobweb overkill

In attempting to clean cobwebs from the basement of his home in Elyria, Ohio, in 1999, Martyn Eskins opted to use a propane torch rather than the more conventional broom. His actions caused a fire that gutted the entire house.

Sprung from the springs

A Sheffield pensioner was held prisoner for five days without food and water when his bed collapsed, trapping him among the tangled springs. Leonard Alcock was eventually released by ambulance men who had been alerted by worried neighbours.

Lucky clover

Salvatore Chirilino was walking with his wife along the cliff top at Vibo Marina, Italy, when he picked up a four-leafed clover. Just as he was congratulating himself on his good fortune, his foot slipped on the wet grass and he fell over the cliff edge, plunging 150 feet to his death.

The biter bit

Hong Kong gourmet Tsang Kin-Keung suffered the misfortune of being bitten by his dinner. He had purchased two live piranha fish from a market and had left them to die on the floor of his home before planning to cook them for dinner. But when he picked up one of the fish, it was still alive and bit him on the finger, necessitating a visit to hospital.

Re-research

When Lancastrian Ian Lewis decided to devote 20 years of his life to tracing his family tree back to the seventeenth century, he thought it was time well spent. Travelling the length and breadth of Britain, he spoke to more than 2,000 relatives, at the end of which he announced his intention to write a book about how his great-grandfather had left to seek his fortune in Russia and how his grandfather had been expelled following the revolution. It was compelling stuff, but just as Mr Lewis was about to start work on his tome he discovered that he had been adopted when he was a month old and that his real name was David Thorton. Bloodied but unbowed, he immediately resolved to begin his family research all over again.

Father Chrishmas

A drunken reveller who was refused entry to a disco in Enns, Austria, got stuck in a chimney for seven hours after he tried an alternative method of gaining admission.

Dog shoots man

A New Zealand hunter was recovering in hospital in December 2000 after being shot by his own dog. Kelly Russell, 30, was tracking wild pigs with his six-year-old mongrel Stinky when the accident happened near Tokoroa on North Island. Having cornered a pig, Mr Russell put down his loaded shotgun, only for Stinky to jump on it and blast a shot through his master's foot.

What a send-off!

A funeral procession in Romania degenerated into farce when a priest and his mistress were thrown naked into the street directly in front of the coffin. The 35-year-old priest was caught by his lover's husband as they enjoyed a sex romp at his home. The irate husband threw the pair out of the front door without their clothes . . . just as the funeral procession was approaching. The priest had married the young couple three weeks earlier.

Chief mourner

Dulal Chandra Das turned up to his own funeral in October 1996. He had merely left his home in Calcutta to pray for a while but had been presumed dead.

Extreme measures

Romanian Gheorghe Harlaucescu decided to kill his head lice by massaging petrol into his scalp. Unfortunately he then chose to dry his head by putting it next to a wood-burning stove. The petrol ignited, leaving him with severe skin burns.

A bad day

A South African man injured in a bad car crash was then run over and killed as he tried to flag down a passing car.

Hello . . .

Ken Barger, 47, of Newton, North Carolina, accidentally shot himself dead in 1992 while answering the phone in the middle of the night. He went to pick up the phone beside his bed, but, half asleep, grabbed his .38 Smith and Wesson special instead. The gun went off when he put it to his ear.

Revenge attack

Officials at the Ministry of Tourism in Nairobi were stunned when a Masai tribesman broke into a glass case containing a stuffed lion and began to strangle the inanimate beast. When arrested, he explained that his brother had been killed by a lion, and he wanted revenge.

Travellin' cat

A woman drove fifteen miles between the Buckinghamshire towns of Newport Pagnell and Aylesbury unaware that her petrified cat had been clinging to the roof rack for the entire journey. The cat, its legs rigid with fear, eventually had to be prised from the rack by firefighters.

Safer on Everest

Having survived six Everest expeditions, veteran French mountaineer Gerard Hommel fell off a ladder while changing a lightbulb at his home in Nantes, cracked his head on a sink and was killed.

Snake!

A pest control officer called to remove an escaped python from the garage of a Rotherham, Yorkshire, house in 1996 discovered on arrival that the "snake" was a strip of rubber mastic which had peeled away from the door surround.

You are feeling sleepy . . .

A man living outside Caracas in Venezuela bet his neighbours that he could prove his supernatural abilities by hypnotizing a jaguar. The man lost the bet and his left arm as the jaguar remained singularly unimpressed by his hypnotic powers.

Bad advice

A man knocked down by a car in New York in 1977 was unscathed but a bystander said that it would be a smart move to pretend to be injured and claim on the insurance money. So the victim lay down in front of the car again and waited for the emergency rescue services. But before they arrived, the car rolled forward and crushed him to death.

Maloney death baloney

With enough food and water to keep him alive for twelve days, Ben Maloney set out alone in March 2001 to explore the remotest regions of Tasmania. When the 27-year-old hiker failed to reappear from his journey through the treacherous terrain, parties searched for him in vain. Experienced trekkers said there was no way he could have survived the terrible weather conditions and five weeks after he was last seen, his distraught family gathered at a memorial service for him. A few days later, however, Maloney had a surprise for them when he crawled from the undergrowth and announced: "I'm a bit hungry." After becoming lost he had survived by drinking from streams and eating wild mushrooms. His sister said: "We're so ecstatic that he's alive. It seems our service was a little premature."

Udderly useless

A German woman who read that camel's milk would improve her skin was in despair after not being able to find the product in any shop. So she went to her local zoo and stole a camel. Unfortunately she chose a male.

Natural justice

Stubborn Armando Pinelli, 70, won an argument with another man over who should sit on the only chair in the shade of a palm tree in Foggia, Italy. Shortly afterwards Snr Pinelli was killed when the tree fell on him.

Unlucky?

A German paraglider miraculously escaped unhurt after a freak gust of wind sent him plunging 5,000 feet into a wood in Austria. But after freeing himself, he slipped as he walked through the forest to summon help and broke his shoulder.

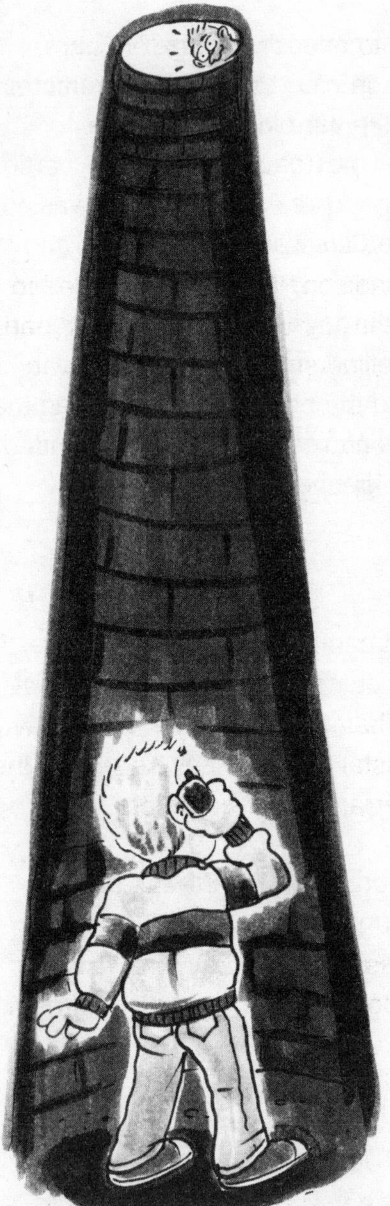

All's well

A German who climbed 50 feet down a disused well to retrieve his mobile phone then had to call for help on it after getting stuck. Rescue crews winched the emergency caller to safety from the medieval well in the grounds of Stolberg Castle.

Come on in!

Firefighters took nearly an hour to release pallbearer John Earlfield who got one of his legs jammed between the coffin and the graveside during a funeral at a church in Halifax, Yorkshire.

Throwaway couture

Having bought his wife an expensive cashmere coat for Christmas 2000, Joel Bahr of Madison, Wisconsin, decided to hide it from her until Christmas Day by storing it in a trash bag. Distracted by the chore of shovelling snow from his drive, he then made the mistake of putting the bag next to the rest of the garbage . . . on garbage collection day. The luxury coat ended up in the truck along with the neighbourhood trash.

Wrong in Warwickshire

A Warwickshire woman learned that she been tending the wrong grave for 25 years following a mix-up at the cemetery. She had been making weekly visits to lay flowers on what she thought was the grave of her father, not realizing that his grave was in the adjacent row. The mistake was discovered when the woman's mother died and she arranged for her to be buried next to her father.

Noah in France

An ultra-cautious Frenchman was so worried by forecasts of floods that he bought a rowing boat and kept it in his bedroom. One night he fell over it and broke a leg.

Lifeguards off duty

In 1985 New Orleans lifeguards threw a party to celebrate a season without any drownings. As the party came to an end, one of the guests was found dead at the bottom of the pool.

Failed suicide

The honour of making the world's least successful suicide attempt belongs to John Helms, a struggling young New York artist who decided to end it all on Christmas Eve 1977. Climbing to the 86th floor of the Empire State Building, he stepped on to the observation tower and launched himself towards the tiny dots of cars on Fifth Avenue below. Half an hour later, he woke up to discover that he had fallen no more than a few feet, and had been blown by strong winds onto a narrow ledge on the 85th floor. This not only came as a shock to Mr Helms but also to television engineer Bill Steckman on whose window the artist started knocking. "I couldn't believe it," said Steckman. "You don't get a lot of guys coming in through the window of the 85th floor. I poured myself a stiff drink . . ." Safely in the offices of the TV station, Mr Helms abandoned all thoughts of suicide and was rewarded when hundreds of families from all over America offered him a home and a meal for Christmas.

Cockroach cock-up

An explosion sparked by devices intended to exterminate cockroaches destroyed a kitchen in San Diego, California . . . but left the insects unharmed. A pilot light ignited fumes from eighteen "bug bombs," creating a blast which ripped open a ceiling and shattered windows, causing $50,000 worth of damage. The three tenants were made homeless, but amidst the rubble the offending cockroaches were still crawling around.

Sweet revenge

American poacher Marino Malerba shot a stag standing above him on an overhanging rock, and was killed instantly when the dead stag fell on him.

Defrosting disaster

A Swiss man managed to set fire to his house in 2000 while trying to defrost his refrigerator with a candle. The fridge caught fire and the blaze caused $40,000 damage.

Goldfish gulp

After hooking her pet goldfish from its bowl at her home in Rotherham, South Yorkshire, five-year-old Lesley Reed held it up for a closer look, her mouth opened in wonder. Just then a friend jogged her on the arm and the fish disappeared down Lesley's throat. Despite the exhaustive efforts of doctors, the fish could not be retrieved.

Wrong place, wrong time

A man who stopped to relieve himself next to a runway at Dundo, Angola, in January 2001 was killed when a cargo plane crashed after developing engine problems on take-off. None of the seven people on board the plane was injured.

Destroy-it-yourself

DIY enthusiast Lyn Thomas's attempts to lay a garden patio did little to impress his neighbours in Pontarddulais, near Swansea. For in doing so, he cut through a gas main, causing the whole street to be evacuated. And the intrepid Mr Thomas had one more trick up his sleeve. For no sooner had firefighters and gas engineers made the gas main safe than the local handyman returned to his task and succeeded in hitting a water pipe with his spade, flooding his own garden and those of two neighbours. "It was the day from hell," lamented Mr Thomas. "Whenever I do a bit of DIY, it turns into destroy-it-yourself." This was by no means his first brush with misfortune. Previously he had knocked himself out while building a chicken run and drilled into his finger making shelves which instantly collapsed.

Only resting

New Yorker Julia Carson was pronounced dead from heart disease and arrangements were made for her burial. Then at the funeral parlour she suddenly sat up in the coffin and asked what was going on. The shock promptly killed her daughter Julie.

Rabbit revenge

While out hunting rabbits one day, farmer Vincent Caroggio from Chartres in France paused for a rest and laid down his gun. He was immediately shot dead by a vengeful rabbit which rushed from its burrow and bumped against the trigger.

Stupid Soaita of Sibiu

Ioan Soaita of Sibiu, Romania, accepted a bet at a party celebrating the birth of his partner's baby that he couldn't slide a wheel bearing over his penis. He won the bet, but nearly lost his manhood, for having got the bearing on, it became wedged fast. To make matters worse, the chosen method of removal was a circular saw which slipped at the crucial moment, slicing off the top of his member. It took surgeons five hours to stitch it back on again.

Back from the dead, briefly

Mourners at the funeral of Anna Bochinsky were astonished to see the "dead" woman jump out of her coffin while it was being carried to the grave with the lid open – as is the custom in her native Romania. She ran straight into the road and was run over and killed by a car.

Net loss: - $2,085

A Milwaukee family literally found themselves out of pocket in 1996. A few days after his burial, relatives of Robert Senz demanded that the funeral home dig up the body because the deceased's wallet was missing. Sure enough, the wallet containing $64 was found in his pocket. Seven months later the funeral home sent the family a reburial bill for $2,149.

For Better or For Worse

Turkish disaster

Two guests at a wedding in Copenhagen were killed and nine wounded when a Turkish guest insisted on celebrating the nuptials according to Turkish custom by firing a dozen shots into the air. But he forgot that the event was being held indoors. The bullets ricocheted from the ceiling and hit the unfortunate victims.

Bridal blowback

Despite his wife's protestations, a barber in the Guangzhou Province of China agreed to offer her to a matchmaker as part of a scam in which they would sell her to a farmer, collect the fee, and then reclaim her immediately. Alas, things did not exactly go according to plan for the bartering barber. First, he was cheated out of his promised reward and then, when the police intervened, he found himself facing a life sentence in prison for selling his wife. To make matters worse, she decided that, whatever the outcome of the trial, she much preferred the farmer and had no intention of going back to her husband.

Start as you mean to carry on

In August 1994, newlyweds Tracy and John O'Donnell of Westport, Connecticut, began brawling at the reception after Tracy accused John of pushing the wedding cake too firmly into her mouth.

Kingston capers

A 1973 wedding at Kingston, Surrey, developed into a comedy of errors. First, the vicar was taken ill and had to be replaced at short notice. Then the bride, Joan Bellars, fainted at the altar as the groom, Peter Cadwell, placed the ring on her finger, and, despite attempts to revive her, remained unconscious for 20 minutes. When she eventually came round, the choir sang the anthem at the wrong point in the service. Finally the happy couple headed for their car, which contained a cement mixer – for the honeymoon hotel had burnt to the ground and bride and groom were going to spend the next two weeks building a septic tank instead.

Plain stupid

An Italian woman returned an Easter egg bought by her boyfriend to the shop without knowing a £1,300 diamond and ruby engagement ring was hidden inside. By the time the 26-year-old woman found out about the present, shop staff in Perugia had already sold the chocolate egg to another customer. She had swapped the egg in the first place because it was plain chocolate instead of milk.

Czeching out

Distraught over her husband's infidelity, Czech housewife Vera Czermak decided to throw herself out of the window of her third-floor Prague apartment, little realizing that Mr Czermak was walking along the street below at precisely the same time. His one good deed in their marriage was to break her fall, for she landed directly on top of him. He was killed outright, but she survived.

Sweet dreams

Swedish dramatist August Strindberg tried to strangle his second wife on their wedding night in his sleep. She managed to break free after a struggle and when he woke up he explained that he had dreamed that she was his first wife, and that's why he had tried to kill her . . .

Incompatible, fortunately

A real-life Romeo and Juliet ran away to the desert north of Phoenix, Arizona, vowing to kill themselves because their families disapproved of their relationship. Michael Tillery, 18, and Stefanie Townsend, 16, left a note saying next time they were seen they would be dead in each other's arms. A frantic search was launched and finally the couple were spotted – making their way home again. After two days together they had decided they weren't compatible after all.

Mrs Molefe × 2

A wedding in South Africa had to be abandoned mid-ceremony because the bride and groom were both officially women. The groom – bearded Rankoa Molefe – was mistakenly listed as female on his birth certificate. "It was terribly upsetting and embarrassing," said Mr Molefe after the ceremony had been halted just as he and his bride were about to exchange vows. He was told to see a doctor in order that he could be certified as male.

Southern beast

In search of a prospective wife, a farmer from Canneto in northern Italy asked a marriage broker to find him a good southern girl who was happy to work on the land. The broker came up with a Sicilian girl who met all the criteria except one – she was unable to send a photo of herself because there was no photographer in her village. The farmer thought this a trifling detail and set about wooing her. After exchanging numerous love letters, the couple finally met for the first time in 1976 when the girl brought her entire family to meet her future spouse. The farmer took one look at her, nearly fainted with horror and immediately tried to wriggle out of the wedding, but her family gently pointed out that he had promised in writing to marry her and that therefore, in Sicilian eyes, she was "compromised." Desperate to find some way out of the agreement, he resorted to offering 1,000,000 lire and a free honeymoon to anyone who would marry her instead. It is not known if there were any takers.

Jilted Jerzy

An hour after getting married at Kensington, London, in November 1975, Kathryn Sluckin stunned new husband Jerzy and his relatives by announcing at the reception: "It won't work." She went to live in a Finchley commune.

ER wedding

A 1958 wedding at Rochester, New York, looked more like a scene from *ER*. The bride, Miss Suzanne Archibald, wore a splint on her foot after breaking a toe in a car crash; the groom, Edward Stanton, who had been knocked unconscious in the same accident, was still suffering from concussion; the maid of honour had a black eye and a sprained ankle; and two of the bridesmaids had their arms in slings following separate skating accidents.

Honeymoon in hospital

Virginia bride Susan Merricks spent her 1982 honeymoon in hospital after a hug for one of the wedding guests left her with a punctured lung. Mrs Merrick embraced the guest, who was wearing a buttonhole fixed with a sharp pin, so vigorously that the pin penetrated her chest.

Wrong man Muldoon

Best man Albert Muldoon found himself married to the bride following a mix-up at a church at Kileter, County Tyrone, in the 1920s. Muldoon walked up to the altar with the groom but, instead of standing to the right of the groom, he stood on his left. Seeing Muldoon in that position, the priest addressed all the questions to him and Muldoon duly replied. The blunder was only discovered when the real groom demanded to sign the register too. A second ceremony was hastily arranged, this time with Muldoon on the right. Muldoon said afterwards: "The groom was so nervous that he didn't seem able to speak, so I thought I had better answer for him."

Premature celebrations

Barry and Carol Watson from Cliftonville, Kent, booked a round the world trip to celebrate their silver wedding anniversary, only to discover that they were a year too early. After spending two years planning the trip, they realized their mistake at the last minute. They decided to go ahead with the holiday and were showered with gifts wherever they went, but were too embarrassed to admit they had really only been married for 24 years.

Law suit

A Mr Robinson from Bedford was arrested after a photo of his wedding appeared in the local paper. The photo was seen by tailor James Fripp who immediately recognized Mr Robinson's suit as one which he had hired out seven years earlier for £6.50, but which had never been returned.

A short wedding

Actress Eva Bartok's third marriage (her first had been at 15) was to publicist William Wordsworth, a descendant of the poet. She left him immediately after the wedding ceremony.

Sons and lovers

A 22-year-old Los Angeles man advertised in a magazine as a lonely Romeo looking for a girl to accompany him on holiday to South America. The first reply he got turned out to be from his widowed mother.

Luckless Sorin

Few grooms are as unlucky as Sorin Archiudean. The 28-year-old Romanian saw his wife run off with their wedding day chauffeur just two weeks into their marriage and then lost his second bride to the man who made the wedding invitations. The second intended Mrs Archiudean fell in love with invitation maker Florin Cucu when she went to his shop in 2001 and promptly called off the wedding to the hapless Sorin.

Mere minutes of matrimony

Bride Marisa Carlotta left her new husband, Guiseppe Moretti, less than an hour after their wedding in Rome. At the reception she met an old flame who had emigrated to the United States but had returned just for the wedding. They quickly realized they still loved each other, sped off to the airport and caught the first flight for New York.

Religious Idiocy

The Indian Mutiny: Grease is the Word

The uprising of 1857 posed the most severe threat to British rule in India in the nineteenth century. Over a period of 14 months, hundreds of British officers and subjects were massacred as mutiny spread throughout the northern and central areas of the country. Yet this fearful bloodshed and rebellion, which nearly cost Britain its hold on India, was caused primarily because the British army, in its ignorance and arrogance, introduced a new greased cartridge without thinking of the religious consequences for the native sepoys.

The British army had decided to replace the traditional "Brown Bess" with the Enfield rifle which had a longer range, was considerably more accurate in the right hands, and had served the nation well in the Crimean War. A feature of the new rifle was a cartridge heavily greased in tallow which was thought to be a more efficient lubricant than the vegetable oil that had previously been in use. The end of the greased cartridge's paper covering had to be bitten by the rifleman before insertion into the barrel of the gun but unfortunately the tallow contained animal fat which therefore made it offensive to the sepoy troops. The Hindus, to whom the cow is sacred, objected on the grounds that the coating was cow fat; and the Muslims, to whom the pig is unclean, feared that it was pig fat. Either way, they were not at all happy about even touching – let alone biting – the new greased cartridges, saying that they would get "a bad name" if they used them. Allowing any part of the animal into one's body was considered an act of ritual defilement and such a loss of caste would automatically result in ostracism from family and friends.

The sepoys were extremely important to the British. As native soldiers of the ruling English East India Company, they made up the bulk of the 300,000-strong Indian army, allowing that relatively small force to keep a peace of sorts among a potentially hostile population of over 150 million. In contrast there were barely 30,000 British troops in India so it didn't take a genius to work out that a loss of support from the sepoy soldiers could have disastrous repercussions for British interests in Asia.

Yet the vast majority of British army officers in India chose to treat the sepoys like dirt. They had no respect for them as people, and certainly no respect for their religious beliefs. Indeed the rumour was rife in the cities, towns and villages of India that the British were attempting to convert the locals to Christianity. Undoubtedly some of the more prejudiced among the old colonial buffers seemed to consider it their duty to tame what they saw as an uncivilized rabble, but while there is no firm evidence that a conversion to Christianity was active government policy, it fitted in with the perceived image of most of the British in India at that time. Thus it was against this already simmering background of mistrust that the affair of the greased cartridges set the British on the slippery slope to military unrest.

The first batches of the new cartridges were manufactured in England and sent out to India in 1853. Nobody in authority appeared to have given a moment's thought to the fact that the inclusion of animal fats might have proved grossly offensive to the sepoy troops. The general view was that anything was acceptable provided it did not offend the British. A handful of the more enlightened British officers – who, naturally, were confined to the lower ranks – suggested that perhaps the new cartridges should be issued to European troops only. Others proposed buying inoffensive wax or coconut oil and greasing the cartridges in the presence of the sepoys to convince them that everything was above board. Inevitably those higher up the ladder saw no reason whatever to pander to the natives.

At first the British got away with it, simply because the sepoys had no idea what the coatings were made from, but by 1855 the cartridges had proved so effective in the Indian climate that production was stepped up and part of it was switched to the Dum Dum cantonment near Calcutta. From there, the rumour quickly spread that the grease contained animal fat from pigs or cows although when questioned the British blustered that it was sheep and goat fat in the hope that such an assurance would quell the rising tension. However the climate of suspicion towards the British ensured that the rumours never went away.

The new cartridges from Dum Dum were ready for issue to the sepoy troops at the start of 1857. As news of native unease reached the British high command, it became apparent that few senior officers were sure what the ingredients of the grease were either. On 29 January the Inspector-General of Ordnance and Magazines at Fort William wrote: "As soon as I heard of objections . . . I enquired at the arsenal as to the nature of the composition that had been used, and found it was precisely that which the instructions received from the Court of Directors ordered to be used – viz, a mixture of tallow and bees wax. No extraordinary precaution seems to have been taken to ensure the absence of any objectionable fat . . . it is certainly to be regretted that the ammunition was not prepared expressly without any grease at all, but the subject did not occur to me."

By nature, the sepoy troops were incredibly loyal to the British, but this insensitive handling of such a delicate matter had pushed them too far. Appalled at the thought that they had been biting into animal fat for the past few years, an increasing number of troops refused to use the new rifle. Pockets of mutiny erupted towards the end of January and soon the word of revolution was spread via the unusual means of chappaties, the local bread. These were passed from village to village accompanied by a message to the effect that the days of British rule were coming to an end.

The British treated these mutterings of mutiny with predictable contempt, none more so than Lieutenant-Colonel Mitchell, commander of the 19th Regiment of Native Infantry, who told his men in no uncertain terms that unless they handled the new cartridges, they would all be sent to Burma to die. At this stage the sepoys' attitude towards using the greased cartridges was one of polite refusal but the British intransigence served to fuel the flames of discontent. In a rare moment of compromise, Lord Canning, the newly-appointed Governor-General of India, suggested that the cartridge papers could be torn rather than bitten off if this proved more acceptable to the sepoys. Whether this conciliatory gesture would have prevented the mutiny will never be known since Lord Canning's Military Secretary, Colonel Richard Birch, chose not to circulate the offer to India's military depots, in the belief that it would be tantamount to a climbdown and would undermine British standing. Sadly Birch was by no means alone in his outmoded thinking. General George Anson, the aged Commander-in-Chief in India, could not comprehend the sepoys' objections and loftily declared that he would "never give in to their beastly prejudices." Furthermore he stated that any soldier refusing to use the new cartridges would be court-martialled immediately. A few of his underlings, tipped off by worried but loyal sepoys, tried to warn him that such a threat could backfire disastrously, but their words fell on deaf ears. The old man was not for turning.

The situation was now so fraught that it only needed one idiot to ignite the powder-keg. A suitable candidate was found in Colonel George Carmichael-Smyth, a man blessed with more names than intelligence, who had somehow risen to the rank of commander of the Third Indian Light Cavalry at Meerut military camp in the north of the country. Fresh back from leave, Carmichael-Smyth was in no mood for compromise despite being made aware of the fact that the sepoys had now taken a solemn oath not to handle the cartridges. Seemingly intent on showing them who was the boss, he ordered a parade of his men, which would require them to handle the contentious cartridges. Many pleaded with him not to proceed with the pointless parade, but he refused to reconsider on the grounds that to do so would be a sign of weakness.

On the morning of 24 April, 90 soldiers lined up on the parade ground and were instructed to take three cartridges each. Eighty-five of the 90 refused to obey the command, pointing out that using the cartridges was against their religion. With that, Carmichael-Smyth reported them to General Hewitt, no great thinker himself but someone who nevertheless despaired of the senseless confrontation. Carmichael-Smyth's obstinacy had backed the British into a corner. They could not be seen to allow such rank insubordination and so they left themselves no option but to court-martial the 85. All were found guilty and were sentenced to either five or ten years' hard labour.

On 9 May Carmichael-Smyth ordered the 85 to be shackled in leg-irons and marched down the lines of the remaining troops under the baking sun. The rest of the native troops were furious at such callous treatment. The next day, after being taunted for not helping their imprisoned fellow countrymen, the sepoys broke into open revolt. Carmichael-Smyth was informed that fires were being lit in the native quarters of Meerut, but he dismissed the reports as pure fabrication. He was obliged to take the situation more seriously when the mutinous sepoys seized the jail, freed the 85 and began murdering British officers and their families.

A superior attitude matched to an inferior intellect had seen Carmichael-Smyth and his colleagues goad the sepoys into an act of bloody rebellion which could so easily have been avoided. It was over a year before the Indian Mutiny was finally suppressed with both sides sustaining heavy losses. Britain held on to its jewel in the crown – just – although the restoration of peace saw the end of rule by the East India Company and its replacement by direct administration from the British crown. It also took considerably longer to repair relations between the Indian people and their British rulers. Some would say they were damaged beyond repair.

Heaven Help Us!

Second coming

A Christian ministry in Florida sent out 500,000 video tapes about Jesus as a special Christmas 2000 gift to residents of Orange and Seminole County . . . unaware that a handful of the tapes also contained the orgasm scene from *When Harry Met Sally*.

The Holy Goat

Among the pilgrims who joined the First Crusade in the spring of 1096 was a group from the Rhineland who dutifully marched behind a goose and a goat in the belief that the creatures had been filled with the Holy Spirit and would guide them to Jerusalem. Perhaps their zeal was understandable since one of the leading crusaders, Peter the Hermit, had an almost reverential love for his donkey.

Shoot the moon

Two people were killed and nearly 50 injured by spent bullets in 1972 when hundreds of Cambodian troops opened fire at the moon to prevent its destruction by a mythical giant frog. Ancient Cambodian legend has it that the moon is under threat of being eaten by an outsize amphibian called Reahou, so at each eclipse the soldiers fire into the sky to stop the frog in its tracks.

The consuming flames of sin

The Dean of Bletchley, the Reverend Wheeler, was conducting a service at Leighton Buzzard parish church, Bedfordshire, when the back of his surplice caught fire after brushing against a candle. At the time the congregation were singing a hymn about "the consuming flames of sin."

Yours sincerely, God

Gullible Israeli businessman Meoded Barzilai was tricked out of his savings in 1957 by a crooked rabbi who promised him King Solomon's crown in return for £2,000. Rabbi Ovadia Barati promised Barzilai that the Archangels Gabriel, Raphael and Michael would anoint him Messiah and King of Israel if he coughed up the cash. But over a period of months all Barzilai received for his money was a series of letters from God and a collection of worthless rocks. Finally losing patience, he delivered an ultimatum to the Almighty that either he be made Messiah immediately or he wanted his money back. When no refund was forthcoming, he became suspicious. Barati was eventually sentenced to eighteen months' imprisonment for obtaining money by false pretences after experts testified that 32 letters "signed" by God Almighty had all been written on the rabbi's typewriter.

Nudist nutters

Police officers stopped a car in Vinton, Louisiana, following reports that it contained naked people. The driver got out, wearing only a towel, but then suddenly jumped back in, drove off and crashed into a tree. At that point no fewer than 20 completely naked people – included a handful of children hidden in the boot – leaped out of the car and began singing religious chants. They said they were Pentecostalists from

Floydada, Texas, on their way to a religious retreat in Florida, adding that they believed the devil was after them and that he would destroy Floydada if they stayed there. They had started off in half a dozen cars, abandoning the vehicles and possessions en route. They told police that they had stripped off because they thought their clothes were possessed by the devil. "I guess it takes all sorts," commented a police spokesman.

R.I.P. H.W.P.

After eight years' searching the parish register for a name to match the initials H.W.P. on a stone slab in his church, Rev. Phillip Randall of Eye, Cambridgeshire, finally solved the mystery. The initials stood for hot water pipe.

Scientific Bungles

John Cleves Symmes: The Hollow Earth Theory

The suggestion that the Earth might be hollow had been around since the seventeenth century. Fearful of ridicule, most people preferred to keep the idea to themselves, but not former American army captain John Cleves Symmes. He wanted to tell the world.

Born in 1780, Symmes served with distinction during the war with England in 1812, after which he established a trading post at St Louis where he spent long hours reading books about the natural sciences. He was particularly fascinated by the planets and, having studied them at length, came to the conclusion that the Earth was hollow and that there was room inside for five other planets. He also firmly believed that the interior of the Earth was inhabited – a warm, green, fertile land – the sun shining through gaping holes at the north and south poles. In his estimation, the hole at the North Pole was 4,000 miles wide, and that at the South Pole was 6,000 miles wide. But he hadn't yet been able to measure them accurately.

He outlined his theories in an 1818 circular headed "To All the World" which he distributed to every member of Congress and to leading scientists, both in the United States and Europe. He despatched 500 copies in total. The pamphlet read: "I declare the Earth is hollow, habitable within; containing a number of solid concentric spheres; one within the other, and that it is open at the pole 12 or 16 degrees. I pledge my life in support of this truth, and am ready to explore the hollow if the world will support and aid me in the undertaking." Accompanying it was a doctor's note stating that Symmes was of sound mind. It was a thoughtful gesture.

To his dismay, Symmes was mocked by newspapers and scientific journals. Undeterred, he announced plans to lead an expedition which would sail from Siberia, through the hole at the North Pole and down the inside of the Earth. He appealed to every nation to fund the voyage, but did not receive one favourable reply.

With dogged determination and no little stupidity, Symmes then embarked on a nationwide speaking tour during which he spread the word to scientists and churchmen. He backed up his polar hole theory by pointing out that explorers often spoke of mysterious warm air currents melting the ice in the Arctic and Antarctic. He maintained that these currents rose from the vast cavities at the North and South Poles. He also claimed that the twilight which lit polar regions was caused by the sun's rays bouncing through the hollow Earth at the poles. Most of his audience continued to treat him with the contempt he deserved, but he did manage to pick up two influential converts in Ohio – newspaper editor Jeremiah Reynolds and millionaire James McBride.

Another convert was Kentucky Congressman Richard M. Johnson who went on to become Vice-President to James Monroe. With Johnson's help, the idea of an expedition to sail through the hole at the North Pole was revived in 1823 and received 25 votes in Congress. This, one feels, says as much about Congress as about Symmes' beliefs. It was not sufficient to gain full backing but it gave Symmes and his loyal band of followers fresh heart and a few years later Reynolds was able to persuade the Navy and Treasury Secretaries under President John Quincy Adams to prepare three vessels, reindeer, sleighs and a team of scientists for a voyage to the inside of the Earth. However sanity prevailed when Andrew Jackson took over the Presidency in 1829 and the mission was cancelled.

In that same year Symmes died, but his theories – and grandiose plans – lived on. Finally in 1838 the resourceful Reynolds persuaded Congress to approve the sum of £300,000 for a four-year voyage of discovery to the Antarctic. The expedition was unable to find the hollow earth, or even the hole, but it did find a lot of ice.

McBride and Reynolds continued to champion the hollow Earth theory with such conviction that it won new disciples in the twentieth century, among them one A. Hitler. Indeed confirmed hollow earthers are convinced that, far from committing suicide, Hitler and his cohorts evaded justice at the end of the Second World War by taking a submarine to a base below the ice-cap at the South Pole. It could be worth taking a look . . .

Piltdown Man: Bone Idol

For centuries anthropologists the world over had been looking for the so-called missing link, the key to the evolution of the human race. The second half of the nineteenth century was a particularly fertile period for significant finds, most notably the discovery near Düsseldorf in 1856 of the leg bone and skull of the creature that came to be known as Neanderthal Man. Smaller and stockier than present-day humans, with a strong jaw and prominent brow ridges on a sloping forehead, *Homo sapiens neanderthalensis* roamed the Earth some 75,000 years ago. His excavation was a major breakthrough and, followed as it was by further important finds across Germany and France, it increased the pressure on British anthropologists to come up with a contribution of their own.

Hastings solicitor and amateur fossil hunter Charles Dawson had been scouring the Kentish Weald to good effect, unearthing a succession of fossil plants, fish, and mammals. He had discovered three new species of iguanodon and the tracks of a megalosaurus, as a result of which he had been awarded fellowship of the London Geological Society at the relatively early age of 21. But, like everyone else in his field, what he really wanted to find was the missing link.

Among Dawson's closest associates was Arthur Smith Woodward, Keeper of Geology at the Natural History branch of the British Museum in South Kensington. In 1909 Dawson wrote to Woodward saying that he was "waiting for the big discovery which never seems to come."

In the hope of speeding up this "big discovery," Dawson had put most of the quarrymen in Kent and Sussex on alert. If they should come across anything remotely unusual, they were to get in touch with him. In return, he would reward them handsomely.

One day towards the end of 1911 Dawson was strolling on Piltdown Common, near Uckfield in East Sussex, when a member of a gang digging gravel for road construction handed him a piece of skull bone which they had stumbled across. Dawson was fascinated by the find and intended to search for the remaining fragments of the skull, but was prevented from doing so by the winter rains which flooded the gravel bed. Nevertheless he was sufficiently optimistic to write to his friend Woodward on 14 February 1912: "I have come across a very old Pleistocene bed overlooking the Hastings beds between Uckfield and Crowborough which I think is going to be interesting." As the weather improved, Dawson returned to Piltdown and was able to write again to Woodward a few days later, claiming that he had found part of a skull which, in terms of significance, would rival the discovery of Heidelberg Man that had been unearthed in Germany five years previously. He invited Woodward to come to Piltdown.

In May 1912 Dawson and Woodward began a systematic search of the shallow gravel bed. On the very first day of excavation Dawson dug up part of a lower jaw, along with some fossilized animal bones and a selection of stone tools. Apparently Woodward did not think there was anything out of the ordinary in the fact that Dawson had conveniently come across the jaw straight away. Or maybe he was just too eager to believe.

There was more to come. In the autumn Dawson, accompanied by Pierre Teilhard de Chardin, a young Jesuit priest and amateur paleontologist, discovered the remainder of the skull bones and half of the lower jaw. Woodward had no doubt that the bones were human and he now had enough evidence to reconstruct the head, giving it an ape-like jaw and human braincase and large, pointed teeth. The resultant ape-man look fitted in perfectly with the commonly-held theories of the time regarding human evolution.

The only note of discord came from Arthur Keith, conservator of the Hunterian Museum of the Royal College of Surgeons, who argued that the teeth should be smaller and that Piltdown Man was of the earlier Pliocene, not the Pleistocene, period. This would put his time on Earth between 5 million and 1.8 million, rather than 1.8 million and 10,000, years ago. Either way, his were the earliest remains in Europe.

On 18 December 1912 Woodward officially revealed Piltdown Man to a packed meeting of the London Geological Society. From the shape of the jaw, he felt able to announce with supreme confidence "that the creature, when alive, had not the power of speech. Therefore, in the evolution of the human species, the brain came first, and speech was a growth of a later age." This was clearly an enormous breakthrough, the most important archaeological discovery of all time, a member of a race from which both cave people and modern humans had developed. With the noble brow of *Homo sapiens* combined with a primitive jaw, it was surely the missing link in Darwin's theory of evolution.

British palaeontologists certainly thought so, but their French and American counterparts were more sceptical, pointing out that the jawbone and the skull were clearly from two different animals and that their discovery together was simply coincidence. The British attributed these doubts to a nasty case of sour grapes.

Dawson was feted for his work, and Piltdown Man was named after him, *Eoanthropus dawsoni* – Dawson's man of the dawn. But a few other dissenting voices began to be heard, the most vociferous being bank clerk and amateur archaeologist Harry Morris who claimed he had been duped by Dawson. Morris said that Dawson had swapped Morris' genuine flints for counterfeit flints stained brown with permanganate of potash and now he challenged the Natural History Museum to test the Piltdown discoveries with hydrochloric acid. Morris was convinced that the brown stain of age present on Dawson's finds would be removed by the acid, thereby proving the fossils to be fakes. The accusations were swiftly swept under the carpet. Nobody in authority was willing to jeopardize the authenticity of Piltdown Man.

In 1913 de Chardin found a tooth at Piltdown which matched Woodward's model. That seemed to satisfy most of the sceptics, except for the Americans who continued to classify Piltdown Man as a mix of human and ape fossils. The British were quietly seething. After all, even Sir Arthur Conan Doyle, who had visited the site several times, had been impressed. If the creator of the world's greatest detective was satisfied as to the validity of the finds, what right had the Americans to pooh-pooh them?

Dawson died in 1916 and Woodward went on to make further discoveries at Piltdown which seemed to put an end to any speculation that Dawson might have planted the specimens. Woodward was knighted for his work in 1924, but two years later fresh doubts were cast about Piltdown Man when a comprehensive geological survey of the gravel at the site revealed that it was nowhere near as old as had been imagined. It certainly did not correspond to the supposed age of Dawson's relics. By way of further embarrassment, a number of other ancient human finds were made during the 1920s and 1930s – and Piltdown Man simply did not fit in with them. There seemed to be no rung for him on the evolutionary ladder.

Nevertheless the British maintained a stiff upper lip and stood by their man. In 1931 Sir Arthur Keith wrote: "It is possible that Piltdown Man does represent the early Pleistocene ancestor of the modern type of man. He may well be the ancestor we have been in search of during all these past years. I am therefore inclined to make the Piltdown type spring from the main ancestral stem of modern humanity." Seven years later he unveiled a memorial to both Piltdown Man and Charles Dawson at the site. He told the gathering that Dawson had given them "the entrance to a long past world of humanity such as had never been dreamed of, and assembled evidence which carried the history of Sussex back to a period to which geologists assigned a duration from half a million to a million years."

Despite the British stance, the controversy would not go away and in 1949, fresh tests were carried out on the Piltdown remains, much more detailed than before. Four years later came the news that British anthropologists had been dreading – Piltdown Man was a fake. The results proved what American scientists had said all along – that the skull and jaw were incompatible. The skull was human all right, but only about 1,000 years old, while the jawbone turned out to be that of an orangutan, dating back some 500 years. De Chardin's solitary tooth came from a modern ape. None of these animal finds could possibly have been British in origin: they had evidently been planted there. Intensive examination of the teeth showed that they had been rubbed down artificially to make them look human.

There was more. The flint tools supposedly used by Piltdown Man showed traces of modern tool work – cuts which could only have been made by a metal blade. And the thorough chemical analysis carried out on the bones indicated that a solution containing iron had been used to stain them in order to give them an aged appearance. It was just as Harry Morris had said 40 years previously. Nobody listened then; they did now.

The leading lights of the British Museum had been the victims of an elaborate hoax – carried out by person or persons unknown – but the predicament in which they now found themselves was, in many respects, all of their own making. Right from the outset, they had been too eager to accept the finds as genuine, singularly failing to carry out sufficient detailed tests which would have exposed the hoax at once. An eminent dentist had long ago pointed out the incongruity between the heavy wear on the canine tooth found at Piltdown and its large pulp cavity, a sign of relative youth. But the dentist's suspicions were brushed aside. The teeth had never even been carefully examined under a microscope so that the erroneous wear pattern on the molars was not detected until 1953. Basically, the British Museum had always jealously guarded what it thought was its ground-breaking discovery and had refused to let experts handle the fossils. With a more open approach, the entire fiasco could have been avoided.

The finger of suspicion has since been pointed at a number of individuals, from Keith to Conan Doyle. But Dawson remains the most plausible perpetrator of the hoax, particularly in the light of an article which appeared in the *Sussex Express* newspaper shortly after the hoax was exposed in 1953. The story read: "Mrs Florence Padgham, now of Cross-in-Hand, remembers that in 1906, aged thirteen, when living at Victoria Cross, Nutley, her father gave Charles Dawson a skull, brown with age, no lower jaw bone . . . Dawson is supposed to have said: 'You'll hear more about this, Mr Burley.'"

Mariner –1

When the unmanned $10-million Mariner I space probe was launched from Cape Canaveral bound for Venus in the summer of 1962, it was intended that it would begin circling the mysterious planet in just 100 days, taking radar pictures of its surface. However just four minutes after take-off, Mariner I did an abrupt U-turn and plunged down in the Atlantic. It emerged that the accident was caused by the unfortunate omission of a minus sign from the computer programme in charge of controlling the rocket's engines.

Elisha Gray: Hanging on the Telephone

There's not much kudos in being the second person to do something. How many people can remember who was the second man to run a mile in under four minutes? Or the identity of the second person in space? Or the name of the second aviator to fly solo nonstop across the Atlantic? Elisha Gray is a case in point. He was the second person to invent the telephone, missing out by just two hours to Alexander Graham Bell who went on to earn all the acclaim and a guaranteed place in history. Poor old Gray ended up as nothing more than a footnote in Bell's triumphant tale. And what must have made it all the more galling for the American was that he had every opportunity to win the race against Bell, only for a combination of self-doubt and dithering to rob him of the prize he probably deserved.

Born in Barnesville, Ohio, on 2 August 1835, Elisha Gray was raised on a farm. He had to leave school early following the death of his father but later completed preparatory school and two years at Oberlin College while supporting himself as a carpenter. At college he became fascinated by electricity and in 1867 he received a patent for an improved telegraph relay. Sensing the importance of his discovery, he set up his own business, the Western Electric Manufacturing Company, to produce telegraphic instruments.

The spring of 1871 saw the arrival in Boston, Massachusetts, of a 24-year-old Scotsman, Alexander Graham Bell, to teach at his father's school for the deaf. As a youth in Edinburgh, Bell had conducted experiments with tuning forks and had developed an interest in the art of telegraphy, although it was little more than a hobby. Then in 1872 Western Union, the leading American telegraph company, bought a one-third stake in Gray's company. Bell read about Western Union's existing telegraph system and their hopes for expansion, and, displaying a Scotsman's intrinsic concern for money, realized that untold wealth awaited the inventor of a more efficient means of telegraphic communication. With Gray also seeking to improve the current telegraph system, the two men were thus set on collision course.

Gray held all the aces. He was the professional inventor, the one with the time and the resources, not to mention the first patent. Bell, on the other hand, was primarily a teacher. His telegraphy work was carried out on a purely amateur basis and in his spare time. Added to which, he was the new kid in town, a stranger in a foreign land.

It was Gray who set the pace. Early in 1874 he found his nephew playing with some electrical equipment in a metal bathtub. The boy was holding the live end of an electrical shock coil in one hand while running his other hand over the zinc-lined bathtub. As he did so, Gray heard a distinct sound coming from beneath the second hand. Repeating the experiment, Gray discovered that the sound emanating from the hand on the tub carried the same pitch as the vibrating apparatus that powered the shock coil. This led him to deduce that vibratory currents could be transmitted through wires. An added bonus was that the nephew apparently suffered no ill effects from playing with electricity while immersed in water although the family must have been relieved that the vulcanization of rubber would soon herald the invention of the rubber bath duck.

Armed with his major breakthrough, Gray proceeded to do . . . very little. For months he pondered over his next step before finally, towards the end of the year, an improved version of the bathtub experiment helped him reach the conclusion that different musical notes could be sent over a wire and be reproduced at the other end. Gray had come up with the prototype for the electric organ. More importantly, he realized that through musical telegraphy he could devise a method for sending speech.

Demonstrations of Gray's transmitters and receivers were subsequently given in Washington, Boston and New York, prompting the *New York Times* to quote a Western Union official as saying that soon telegraph operators "will transmit the sound of their own voices over the wire, and talk with one another instead of telegraphing." Unfortunately Gray's colleagues were not impressed and persuaded him to give up on the idea of the telephone as a money-making enterprise. His patent attorney told him that the telephone was nothing more than a scientific curiosity, which reinforced Gray's own view. To him, the telephone was just a toy and he remained convinced that businessmen would prefer to send messages rather than talk to each other. So although he had concluded that speech could be transmitted months before Bell, Gray chose not to pursue the idea . . . at least not until it was too late.

Gray devoted precious little further thought to his telephone until the autumn of 1875 when he observed two boys playing with two tin cans and a piece of string. He saw that the boy talking into one can sent vibrations in the metal that could be carried by the string to the other can, and this gave Gray the means of transmitting speech that was the missing piece in the jigsaw. At last he had cracked the mystery of the telephone. So he did what he usually did . . . nothing.

Meanwhile Bell had been busy. Using tuning forks as the basis for a new improved telegraph system, he devised the harmonic telegraph, a device which incorporated a series of electric tuning forks and a wire. Bell began playing around with the harmonic telegraph – a similar contraption to Gray's – and when his young assistant, Thomas Watson, set up an experiment in Boston involving a wire, a vibrating metallic reed (instead of a tuning fork) and a set of transmitters and receivers, Bell, too, realized that it would be possible to send speech by wire. The difference was that he actually acted upon his discovery.

Back in Chicago where Gray was based, his office was a hive of inactivity. For two long months after he had been the first person in the world to visualize how a telephone would look and work, he sat around twiddling his thumbs. It was not until 11 February 1876 that he finally put his thoughts down on paper, sketching a voice transmitter using a tin can-like voice chamber hooked to a wire. Another three days elapsed before it occurred to him that he ought to protect his idea by patenting it. The delay would prove ruinous.

As an American citizen, Gray had the advantage of being able to file a caveat with the United States Patent Office – to announce an invention which he soon expected to patent – whereas Bell, who was a British subject, had to file an application on a completed invention. Gray's caveat stated that he had "invented a new art of transmitting vocal sounds telegraphically." It went on: "It is the object of my invention to transmit the tones of the human voice through a telegraphic circuit, and reproduce them at the receiving end of the line, so that actual conversations can be carried on by persons at long distances apart." A crucial feature of the accompanying drawings was a liquid transmitter. Gray's caveat arrived at the Patent Office in New York at 2 p.m. on 14 February 1876. It was the 39th entry on Patent Office records that day. Unfortunately for Gray, Bell's entry was the fifth, filed just two hours earlier at midday. The irony was that the apparatus described in Gray's caveat would actually have worked whereas Bell's primitive design of magnets and wires would certainly not have.

Gray was not happy at being pipped at the post, but he had only himself to blame. Bell was equally unhappy with the design of his invention and on 9 March he sketched an improved liquid transmitter containing highly corrosive acid. It was almost identical to Gray's earlier drawing.

The following day – 10 March 1876 – Bell and Watson were working in a makeshift laboratory on the top floor of a boarding house at 5 Exeter Place in Boston. Watson was in an adjoining room when Bell spoke the first-ever telephone message: "Mr Watson, come here,

I want to see you." It was a defining moment in history, but it should have been Gray's.

Had he believed in his own invention Gray could have drawn and submitted a sketch to the patent office weeks before Bell made his application. But while Bell was single-minded in pursuit of his goal, Gray was decidedly half-hearted. He may have been a great scientist but he left a lot to be desired as a businessman. Gray understood perfectly the technology needed to make the telephone work but was unable to envisage any practical use for it. As far as he was concerned, a device which carried speech could never amount to anything more than a toy. Even when Bell demonstrated his new telephone at the 1876 Centennial Exhibition in Philadelphia, Gray sneered: "Its commercial value will be limited."

It is wholly in keeping with the rest of his story that Gray first showed an urgent interest in the invention of the telephone when it was too late. He sued Bell for the patent rights to the telephone, but after a protracted court case the judges ruled in favour of Bell . . . because of the two-hour time difference in submitting the applications to the US Patent Office. If only Gray had got up earlier that February morning, or if only he had invented a quicker way of getting a message from one city to another. Like the telephone.

Cowpat frenzy

An excited announcement by an expert birdwatcher over CB radio resulted in twitchers flocking to his side in a field on one of the Isles of Scilly to observe what was believed to be a nighthawk, a rare visitor from the United States. Only when scores of telescopes and binoculars were focused on the object in question was it realized that it was, in fact, a cowpat.

Blinded By Science

Merlin the rollerskating musician
A test run of his latest invention backfired spectacularly for Belgian musician Joseph Merlin. Always keen to add another string to his bow, Merlin had put together the world's first pair of roller skates and wanted to impress guests at a masked ball in London in 1760. Making a grand entrance on the skates while playing the violin, Merlin suddenly realized that he had yet to perfect how to stop or to change direction. As a result he shot across the ballroom and crashed into a full-length mirror. If Merlin's entrance was a tough act to follow, so was his exit – on a makeshift stretcher to the nearest hospital.

Frozen Bacon

In 1626 English philosopher Francis Bacon conducted one of the earliest experiments into frozen food by stuffing a chicken with snow in order to observe the effect of the cold in preserving its flesh. Alas he caught a chill from handling the snow and died shortly afterwards.

Reindeers on the moon

A staggering 90 per cent of *New York Sun* readers were said to have been taken in by an elaborate 1835 hoax which reported that reindeer, unicorns and 4-foot-high man bats had been sighted on the moon. The hoax was the work of *Sun* journalist Richard Adams Locke who capitalized on the fact that eminent scientist Sir John Herschel was in South Africa at the time to write that Herschel had built an ultra-powerful telescope capable of studying the surface of the moon in great detail. Locke filled his first article with technical jargon and complex diagrams, knowing full well that the paper's downmarket readership wouldn't understand a word of it and would therefore assume that it was all true. His second story stated that Herschel had discovered an inland sea on the surface of the moon, as well as white beaches, forests, deserts – and pyramids of amethysts. Each succeeding article reported yet more astounding finds on the moon – moose, reindeer, beavers, unicorns and finally the giant man bats, their bodies covered in hair. Herschel was quoted as saying of these man bats: "We had no opportunity to see them actually at work. So far as we could judge, they spend their happy hours in collecting fruits in the woods, eating through the skies, bathing, and loitering about on the summits of precipices." Again Locke muddied the waters by “quoting” Herschel’s detailed technical description of the creatures. “I could perceive,” he wrote, “that their wings possessed great expansion and were similar in structure to those of the bat, being a semi-transparent membrane expanded in curvilineal divisions by means of straight radii, united at the back by the dorsal integuments.” Sales of the *Sun* rocketed and rival New York papers were so impressed by the scoop that they pirated stories for their own publications, claiming that they too had access to Herschel’s data. But Locke went too far by claiming that Herschel had amassed 40 pages of calculations based on his moon studies. When the *New York Journal of Commerce* asked to see these calculations, Locke was forced to admit that the whole story had been an elaborate hoax.

Pressed flower

After years of searching for an orchid, *corybus carseii*, which only flowers for two days a year and was thought to be extinct, botanists in New Zealand found a specimen lying flattened beneath their groundsheet when they took down their tent.

Alien oven

Astronomers using a radio telescope at Parkes University in Australia believed they had discovered sensational evidence of alien life when they picked up a distinctive signal every evening around dinner time. They later realized that the signal was coming from the microwave oven downstairs.

Literary Follies

George du Pre:
The Man Who Talked Too Much

Six years after the end of the Second World War, *Reader's Digest* magazine came to hear of an epic tale of heroism which clearly deserved a wider audience. It concerned a young Canadian, George du Pre, who, recruited by British Intelligence, had apparently been trained for nine months to behave like "the village half-wit" before parachuting into German-occupied Normandy. There, he had joined the Resistance and posed as a simple French garage mechanic to help smuggle allied airmen out of France. After saving countless lives by his selfless endeavour, he had finally been captured by the Gestapo. Tortured by the Germans, he was given an enema of sulphuric acid and had boiling water poured into his clamped-open mouth, but he had stubbornly refused to talk. And in one last dramatic act of bravery, he had somehow managed to escape back to his homeland where he was feted as a national hero. The story almost seemed too good to be true. And so it proved.

Du Pre had recounted his war experiences to church and club meetings across Canada and when the story reached the ears of *Reader's Digest*, the magazine sent former war correspondent Quentin Reynolds to interview him and write an article. Reynolds was not a man to be taken in easily, but he was convinced that du Pre was genuine. His body bore all the hallmarks of Nazi torture. He had a speech impediment, no teeth, a broken nose and hideous scars on his hands and throat, all of which, he claimed, were the legacy of his ill-treatment by the Germans. Reynolds duly wrote the piece for *Reader's Digest* but also believed that du Pre's story had the makings of a compelling book, and so he approached Bennett Cerf, the head of publishers Random House. Cerf was suitably impressed, but prior to publication Reynolds submitted his manuscript to British Intelligence for verification. However they refused to look at it because of their policy of never confirming or denying that any individual had been a member of the secret service. Nevertheless the book went on to become a 1953 best-seller under the title *The Man who Wouldn't Talk*.

When Reynolds insisted on splitting the royalties from the book with du Pre, the modest Canadian at first refused but then promised all income to the Boy Scouts of Canada. It seemed a truly magnanimous gesture, but one which was perhaps born more out of guilt than philanthropy.

For shortly after the book went on sale, a Royal Canadian Air Force officer walked into the offices of the *Calgary Herald* with a photograph of himself and du Pre taken in Victoria, British Columbia, in 1942 – at a time when, according to his book, du Pre was supposed to have been in France ruffling the Germans' feathers. Intrigued, the *Herald* despatched reporter Douglas Collins, himself a former Intelligence operative, to talk to du Pre. Initially du Pre maintained the pretence but Collins soon tripped him up by getting him to say he knew Intelligence personnel and training camps that Collins had invented. Almost relieved that the truth was finally out, the "man who wouldn't talk" did. He confessed to the *Herald* that the entire story was a hoax – that he had spent the whole war in Canada and England, and had never set foot in France. What had started out as the simple, fanciful exaggerations of a country boy had now grown dangerously out of hand. Du Pre himself admitted: "The story eventually got bigger than I was."

The editor of the *Herald* phoned Cerf who was dismayed to hear that du Pre's scars were more likely to have been caused by farm machinery than the Gestapo. In turn Cerf rang DeWitt Wallace, the publisher of *Reader's Digest*, and suggested that the best way to deal with their blunder was to laugh it off. Sensing the business possibilities in a hoaxer's tale, Cerf urged the title of the book to be changed to *The Man who Talked Too Much* and suggested that booksellers move it to the fiction section where it would be more at home. As for Reynolds, he was devastated at having been taken in. "Trust George du Pre?" he said. "I'd have bet my life on that man!"

Pedro Carolino: English as she Is Spoke

In 1883 Pedro Carolino set out to write a Portuguese–English phrase book. Despite the fact that he was singularly ill-equipped for the task (not being blessed with any tangible grasp of English or even having access to a Portuguese–English dictionary), Carolino was the proud owner of both Portuguese–French and French–English dictionaries. Thus, by means of painstaking cross-referencing, the master linguist produced his inimitable tome, *The New Guide of the Conversation in Portuguese and English*, without doubt the most incompetent phrase book ever written.

Carolino's introduction gives an indication of the delights to follow: "We expect then, who the little book (for the care what we wrote him, and for her typographical correction) that may be worth the acceptation of the studious persons, and especially of the youth, at which we dedicate him particularly."

Carolino begins with some "Familiar Phrases" which might prove useful to a Portuguese visitor to Britain. These include such everyday conversation pieces as "Dress your hairs," "Take that boy and whip him to much," "That are the dishes whose you must be and to abstain," "Exculpate me by your brother's," "This meat ist not too over do," "It is a noise which to cleave the head," "She make the prude," "The rose-trees begin to button," "Do not might one's understand to speak," "He laughs at my nose, he jest by me" and, of course, "These apricots and these peaches make me and to come water in the mouth."

The genius that translates "Mind you don't get grubby" into "Take care to dirt you self" and "I feel sick" into "I have mind to vomit" then embarks on a series of "Familiar Dialogues," enabling the Portuguese traveller to have a ready saying at hand for any occasion. For example, when out fishing, one might say: "That pond it seems me many multiplied of fishes. Let us amuse to the fishing. Here, there is a wand and some hooks."

And who hasn't had this conversation with a furniture salesman: "It seems no me new?" "Pardon me, it comes workman's hands." "Which hightness want you its?" "I want almost four feet six thumbs wide's, over seven of long."

In his next section on "Anecdotes," Carolino offers a selection of stories guaranteed to liven any dinner party: "One eyed was laied against a man which had good eyes that he saw better than him. The party was accepted. I had gain, over said the one eyed: why I se you two eyes, and you not look me who one." So true, so true.

Carolino finishes with a list of "Idiotisms and Proverbs" with which all readers will be familiar. Among these are: "The stone as roll not heap up not foam," "It want to beat the iron during it is hot," "He is beggar as a church rat," "To look for a needle in a hay bundle" and the ever-popular "To craunch the marmoset."

It is reassuring to note that, in line with the policy of introducing new generations of readers to classics of English literature, Carolino's unique perspective on our language has since been republished under the title *English as she Is Spoke*.

Publish and Be Damned!

Ulf for nothing

In 1997, at the end of 13 years' hard labour writing a weighty tome about Swedish economic solutions, business consultant Ulf af Trolle finally took his 250-page manuscript to be copied. Yet it took only seconds for his life's work to be reduced to 50,000 strips of paper when a worker confused the copier with the shredder.

Cooked up

Pulitzer Prize organizers were left red-faced in 1981 after a winning entry turned out to be a fake. Janet Cooke, a reporter for the *Washington Post*, won a coveted Pulitzer for "Jimmy's World," an investigative article about an eight-year-old boy hooked on heroin by his mother's live-in boyfriend. But two days later Cooke admitted that Jimmy and the rest of her story were pure fabrications. The *Post* was forced to return the prize and Cooke resigned.

Harry who?

Nine publishers, including HarperCollins, Penguin and Transworld, turned down J.K. Rowling's first *Harry Potter* book.

Gay times

Hundreds of closet homosexuals risked being "outed" in 2000 thanks to an administrative error by Britain's bestselling gay magazine. Usually delivered in an anonymous white packet, *Gay Times* was instead dropped on 6,000 doorsteps in a partially transparent envelope following a relaunch of the magazine. Staff at the publication, which has a monthly circulation of 64,000, were alerted to the mishap after receiving complaints from readers. *Gay Times* admitted: "We could have put some readers in an embarrassing position."

Thou shalt commit adultery

In the seventeenth century London printers Robert Barker and Martin Lucas were commissioned by God-fearing King Charles I to produce a new version of the Bible. Alas, the finished article contained a number of errors, the most outstanding being the omission of the word "not" from the Seventh Commandment. Thus all readers of the good book were encouraged by the Lord to commit adultery. The angry king immediately had all 1,000 copies recalled and fined the incompetent printers the princely sum of £3,000.

Heavy weather

Production of a book on extreme weather conditions was halted in December 2000 because of storms and floods. Printers working on *The Surrey Weather Book – A Century of Storms, Floods and Freezes* had to abandon the project when rising water levels threatened to flood the Litho Techniques printing works in Whyteleafe.

Turned Doone

Lorna Doone, the novel by R.D. Blackmore, received 18 rejections before it was finally published in 1869. It has remained in print ever since.

Crawfie's howler

One of the most popular features in *Woman's Own* magazine in 1955 was a regular column by former royal nanny Marion Crawford. Due to the advent of colour printing, the magazine had to go to press six weeks in advance which meant that "Crawfie" and her staff ghost-writer struggled to be topical. Nevertheless all went well until the Crawfie Column described in glowing detail the magnificent spectacle of the Trooping of the Colour. For the article appeared on the news stands just a few days after that year's ceremony had been cancelled owing to a rail strike. The howler made Crawfie a laughing stock and her column was dropped shortly afterwards.

Intermittent service

In June 2001 the consumer service department of the UK power company Powergen sent a letter to customers promising: "If you have any questions, we're here 24 hours a day, seven days a year . . ."

The inside story

Peter Wyden's meticulously researched book *Wall: The Inside Story of Divided Berlin* was eventually published in October 1989. The following month the Berlin Wall was suddenly dismantled after 28 years and the unfortunate Wyden's book vanished from view just as quickly.

Divorce edition

Gracing the cover of a special weddings issue of *In Style* magazine for January 2001 was actress Courtney Thorne-Smith . . . just too late to take into account the fact that she and her husband had separated the previous week.

Curtilage communications

London's Lambeth Council spent over £1,000 on a series of leaflets aimed at instructing householders how to put out their wheelie bins for garbage collectors. But the guide merely talked rubbish. Among other things it told residents: "The bin must be presented within 2 metres of the curtilage on collection day." Unfortunately few people knew that "curtilage" means the edge of the front garden. The guide advised that the bins could be dispensed with "where it is impossible for the residents of the property to manoeuvre the bin from its residual stance to the presentation point without endangering themselves or anyone else involved." It then ended with the baffling warning: "Failure to comply with any of the above conditions will result in the council being obliged to restore the wheeled bins as appropriate." Resident Douglas Nel said he had no idea whether this meant the council would confiscate the bins, put them back in the right place or give them a polish. A council spokesman confessed that the leaflets' grammar left a lot to be desired and said they were being bundled into wheelie bins to be taken for a "decent burial." He added: "It's a very good example of how not to communicate with the public."

Oops!

In May 1996 New Jersey police charged 67-year-old mathematics professor Walter Petryshyn with bludgeoning his wife to death. A friend said that Petryshyn had been plunged into the depths of despair because he was afraid that his career would be ruined by an error in his latest text book, *Generalized Topological Degree and Semilinear Equations.*

Responsible journalism

Newspapers in Shimla, India, created widespread panic in December 2000 by accidentally printing a report of a mock natural disaster exercise as if it were the real thing. The fake story, which predicted that a terrible earthquake would hit the town, destroying hundreds of homes and killing thousands, caused people to flee the area in droves.

Under a foreign flag

A girl employed at a nationalized bookshop in Bratislava was arrested in 1952 for innocently arranging four books on the shelves in a manner considered anti-Communist by the local party. The books themselves were harmless enough, but it was the sequence in which they were placed that caused offence. The titles (in the order they were set out) were *We Want to Live, Far From Moscow, In the Shadow of the Skyscrapers,* and *Under a Foreign Flag.*

Lap dancing in Hakin

The world's most unfortunate misprint appeared in the *Milford and West Wales Mercury* in 2001. The newspaper was forced to apologize for the headline "Hakin Girl Wins Lap Dancing Certificate" . . . explaining that it should have read "Hakin Girl Wins Tap Dancing Certificate."

Artistic Catastrophes

Damien: An Omen?

Arguably the most significant contribution to the arts in recent years was that made by Emmanuel Asare, a humble cleaner at Mayfair's fashionable Eyesto'rm art gallery.

Arriving for work in October 2001, Mr Asare found that the room had been left in a complete mess following an exhibition party. Empty beer bottles, paint-covered newspapers and sweet wrappings were strewn all over the place. So he diligently set to work sweeping up the bits and pieces and dumping them in bin bags.

Next day he reported for duty still satisfied with a job well done, only to be told by gallery bosses: "That was no rubbish you cleared – that was a £5,000 work of art by Damien Hirst!"

After frantically rummaging through the bins, a staff member found the Hirst creation – called *Painting by Numbers* – in pieces.

Using photographs of the work, it was lovingly reassembled and a "Keep Off" sign attached to deter further do-gooders.

Mr Asare was puzzled by the fuss. "As soon as I clapped eyes on it, I sighed because there was so much mess. I didn't think for a second that it was a work of art – it didn't look much like art to me. So I cleared it all in bin bags and dumped it."

Despite what may have been considered something of an indictment of his work, the controversial Mr Hirst and the gallery were surprisingly upbeat about the incident. Eyesto'rm's Heidi Reitmaier enthused: "For Damien, it registered something very key about his work. The fact that someone interacted with it is quite a good thing from his viewpoint. And for Eyesto'rm we thought it was just a really poignant moment."

The Conqueror: A Sad Legacy?

The 1955 movie *The Conqueror*, which starred drawling all-American hero John Wayne in the unlikely role of Genghis Khan, is often described as being one of the unintentionally funniest films of all time. However behind the corny, stilted dialogue lies what in all probability is a tragic tale since there is strong evidence to suggest that filming on location contributed to the premature deaths of nearly 100 members of the cast and crew, including the Duke himself.

Although the story of the thirteenth-century Eastern warrior has its roots in Mongolia, director Dick Powell naturally chose somewhere a little closer to home to represent the arid wastelands of the Gobi Desert. He settled for Utah's Escalante Desert, in particular the Snow Canyon area close to the town of St George which was to become the crew's base for three months during the summer of 1954. It was also about 150 miles downwind from the site in Nevada where the US government had previously carried out a number of atomic bomb tests.

That summer, Powell, Wayne and co-stars Susan Hayward, Pedro Armendariz and Agnes Moorehead filmed on the sandy dunes outside St George, blissfully unaware of any possible fallout. That they never ventured far afield can be determined from scenes in the film where Wayne and Armendariz climb on their horses, ride for miles and then dismount wearily at precisely the same spot from which they had started. In fairness, this was standard procedure in many routine westerns of the 1950s and John Wayne treated this as just another western. "The way the screenplay reads," he said, "this is a cowboy picture, and that's how I am going to play Genghis Khan. I see him as a gunfighter." This did not bode well for the movie's success.

It was released to howls of derision and gales of laughter. Critics dissected the ludicrous plot and painful dialogue, sympathizing with Wayne for having to utter such lines as: "This Tartar woman is for me, and my blood says, take her!" The *New York Times* wrote scathingly: "John Wayne as Genghis Khan – history's most improbable piece of casting unless Mickey Rooney were to play Jesus in *King of Kings*."

In the face of such hostile reviews, it was scarcely surprising that *The Conqueror* failed to live up to his name at the box office. Those who did go to see it went either out of loyalty to John Wayne or sheer curiosity. Indeed it was such a disaster financially that film-makers RKO never really recovered. Producer Howard Hughes, a man not averse to the occasional eccentricity, decided that this was too bizarre even for him. He hated the movie so much that, after losing over $1,000,000 on the production, he spent another $12,000,000 trying to buy up all the existing copies so that no one could watch it! It was arguably one of his saner moves.

He was probably not amused therefore when three mountains in the Escalante Desert were renamed Mount Wayne, Mount Hughes and Mount Powell in memory of *The Conqueror*.

Sadly the movie has left a more disturbing memory. In 1960 Pedro Armendariz committed suicide while dying of cancer; in 1963 Dick Powell died of cancer; in 1974 Agnes Moorehead died of cancer; in 1975 Susan Hayward died of cancer; and in 1979 John Wayne died of cancer.

The year after Wayne's death, *People* magazine did a headcount and discovered that a minimum of 91 members of the 220 cast and crew on *The Conqueror* had contracted cancer. And over half of the cancer victims had died from the disease. St George, it was claimed, was a radioactive hot spot.

At the Pentagon one official of the Defense Nuclear Agency responded to the news by muttering: "Please, God, don't let us have killed John Wayne!"

The truth may never be known.

Celluloid Slip-ups

Lost Siam

In *Raiders of the Lost Ark* a map can be seen with Thailand marked on it. When the film was set, Thailand was still Siam.

Victorian TV

Television aerials can be seen on the roofs of Victorian London in the 1966 comedy *The Wrong Box.*

Premature sentence

Edward G. Robinson's character gets sent to Alcatraz in 1927 during the movie *The Last Gangster*. However Alcatraz didn't become a prison until 1934.

Roman jeans

A Roman extra can be seen wearing jeans beneath his tunic in the epic *Gladiator*.

Dead in Smethwick

Some of the most frightening scenes in cinema history were caused by an elderly woman who fell asleep while watching *The Sound of Music* at a Birmingham picture palace in May 1992. Waking with a start during the nuns' chorus, she created chaos and confusion because she thought she had died and was being welcomed to heaven. "It took several minutes to convince her that she was still alive," recalled the harassed cinema manager. "We don't get many out-of-body experiences in Smethwick."

Silent movie

As a gimmick the première of Howard Hughes' 1955 movie *Underwater* took place at the bottom of a Florida lake, over 100 guests being supplied with scuba-diving gear and watching the film on a special screen. It may have seemed like a good idea at the time, but unfortunately none of the audience could hear the soundtrack underwater and so they all had to swim quickly back up to the surface.

Too soon

Although *Quadrophenia* was set in 1964, a cinema is showing Warren Beatty in *Heaven Can Wait*, which was made fourteen years later. So was *Quadrophenia*.

Unsafe safety film

In 1976 the British Aircraft Corporation was forced to withdraw a safety film because the film itself was unsafe. The film, which highlighted the dangers of workers not wearing goggles, was so graphic that 13 employees at the Preston plant had to be treated for sickness and injury. One man fell off his chair in terror and needed seven stitches in a head wound while another fainted and had to be carried out. Several others complained of nausea and were led out ashen-faced to be tended in the first aid room.

Quick change artist

In the 1959 movie *Anatomy of a Murder*, Lee Remick is seen sitting in a café wearing a dress. She leaves it wearing trousers.

Hysterical, Henry

Henry Fonda rejected the role that earned Peter Finch a posthumous Oscar in the 1976 movie *Network* because he considered it to be "too hysterical."

Colour junket

Before making his 1934 epic *Cleopatra*, Cecil B. DeMille sent a team on a $100,000 trip to Egypt to study the colour of the Pyramids. The film was in black and white.

Unnatural

In the final shot of *The Green Berets*, the sun sets in the east.

Going bald

A Hollywood screen test on the young Fred Astaire famously concluded: "Can't sing, can't act, going bald. Dances a little."

Flat

Tyre tracks can be spotted on the ground in the western *Stagecoach*.

Lorry ahoy!

In *Decameron Nights*, while Louis Jourdain stands on the deck of a fourteenth-century ship, a white lorry rumbles down a hill in the background.

Prop(er) bomb

Daredevil silent movie star Harold Lloyd took to wearing gloves on screen after losing part of his hand, including thumb and forefinger, in a publicity stunt that went wrong. While shooting the 1920 comedy *Haunted Spooks*, Lloyd posed for a publicity photograph with what he assumed to be a fake prop bomb when it suddenly proved to be only too real.

Lost in translation

Scottish cinema-goers were left baffled when the cast of *Hannibal* suddenly began speaking French half-way through the film. Consequently some twenty minutes of the movie were utterly incomprehensible to most of the audience at the Belmont cinema, Aberdeen. Cinema manager Pam Green blamed the distribution company for the bilingual version.

Pre-emptive strike

In *Emma Hamilton*, Big Ben is heard to strike in 1804 . . . 50 years before it was built.

Curse of Rasputin

When MGM decided to make a movie about the life and death of Russian monk Rasputin, their screenwriters changed the names

Nearly v o'clock
Some of the chariot racers in *Ben Hur* sported wristwatches.

of anybody who was still alive for fear of incurring legal action. They replaced Prince Yusupov, who had been instrumental in Rasputin's murder, with Prince Chegodieff, a figment of their imagination. It sounded authentic enough and everyone was happy . . . until, that is, the real Prince Yusupov, who was proud of his role in Rasputin's downfall, sued MGM for denying him the credit for it. Worse was to follow. The reason that Prince Chegodieff sounded so authentic was that there was a Russian nobleman of the same name. He promptly sued MGM for libel and the filmmakers had to pay two lots of compensation.

Israel?

During a scene from *The Sound of Music*, an orange-box is clearly visible stamped with the words "Produce of Israel". Yet the film was set in 1938 – ten years before Israel was founded.

Where?

No prizes for geography for the 1968 movie *Krakatoa, East of Java*. Krakatoa was actually 200 miles west of Java.

Inspirational

The 1939 epic blockbuster *Gone with the Wind* seems to have inspired everyone it touched. Gary Cooper turned down the role of Rhett Butler because he was convinced it would be a flop. He famously remarked: "I'm just glad it'll be Clark Gable who's falling on his face and not Gary Cooper." The first studio to be offered the film rights was MGM but Louis B. Mayer was put off by one of his producers who told him categorically: "Forget it. No Civil War movie ever made a nickel." Twentieth Century–Fox and Warner Bros also turned it down before the rights finally ended up with David O. Selznick. Even then, the director, Victor Fleming, asked whether he wanted a percentage of the profits as part of his fee, replied: "Don't be a damn fool, David. This picture is going to be one of the biggest white elephants of all time!" Fans of detail may also enjoy the view of an electric street lamp that the film, set in the 1860s, affords.

Honest mistake

Less than a week after opening in the summer of 2000, *Honest*, the crime comedy starring pop group All Saints, was pulled from 160 British cinemas because of its poor box office performance. The film's chances were not helped by the fact that its content of violence, nudity, and drug abuse meant that it had to be awarded an 18 certificate, thus rendering it inaccessible to the group's legions of teenybopper fans. The £6 million movie earned just over £100,000 on its opening weekend.

Magic flowers

In *The Desk Set*, Katharine Hepburn leaves her office carrying a bunch of white flowers but by the time she reaches the pavement they are pink.

Before their time

Two Volkswagen Beetles can be seen in the 1979 production of *The Prisoner of Zenda*, a film set in the nineteenth century.

Blue-sky thinking

The first 52 days of filming the Burton–Taylor epic flop *Cleopatra* at Pinewood Studios in Buckinghamshire produced less than 11 minutes of useable material. This was because warnings were ignored about the dubious merits of building an outside set and praying for the English weather to replicate Egypt's. Finally after nearly two months of cloud and rain with only an occasional hint of blue sky, filming was switched to the balmier climes of Italy.

A long-running project

In the movie *Triple Cross*, a Second World War newspaper carries a headline about the rising cost of Concorde.

Cut!

Marilyn Monroe needed 59 "takes" for a scene from the 1959 film *Some Like it Hot*. Her only line in the scene was, "Where's that bourbon?"

Stage Frights

Safey first

The shortest theatrical run on record was Lord Lytton's play, *The Lady of Lyons*, the first and last nights of which both took place at London's Shaftesbury Theatre on 26 December 1888. After waiting for an hour, the audience were sent home because nobody was able to raise the safety curtain.

The sound of no hands clapping

In December 1983 the comedy *Bag* opened at Grantham, Lincolnshire, to an audience of nil.

Ham acting

A 1983 Edinburgh Festival Fringe production of *Ubu Roi* by the Freie Theateranstalt company from West Berlin closed after just fifteen minutes of its sole performance. The show's director and star, Hermann von Harten, had intended the cast to include a pig as well as a number of parrots and cockatoos, but had forgotten about the quarantine restrictions. The pig in particular was a key character since it played Ubu Roi's wife so an understudy porker was hastily acquired from the nearby East Lothian city farm. Alas, it was something of a "ham" actor and after a quarter of an hour, van Harten decided to abandon the rest of the show and give the audience their money back.

As Seen on TV

Bonkers Ciboncо

It was best to be prepared for all eventualities when listening to Indian weatherman Ciboncо Mala. When he forecast sun, it snowed; when he warned of frost, the country was gripped by a heatwave. TV chiefs finally pulled the plug on his New Delhi forecast when he began sobbing on screen . . . presumably at his own incompetence. The unfortunate Mr Mala was then forced into hiding after receiving death threats from irate viewers.

Fluff

On a live edition of *Top of the Pops* in 1964, disc jockey Alan "Fluff" Freeman accidentally introduced the Sounds Orchestral hit "Cast Your Fate to the Wind" as "Cast Your Wind to the Fate".

Hair today

A hairdresser's error on the detective series *Randall & Hopkirk (Deceased)* meant that Kenneth Cope, who played Marty Hopkirk, wore his wig back-to-front for two episodes before anybody spotted the mistake.

Cat lover

Filming a live TV show to promote the adoption of stray cats in 2000, Michael Daley of Massachusetts became frustrated because the cat his wife was holding refused to keep still. Shocked viewers finally heard him yelling in the background: "Choke the fucking cat!"

Wacky woods

For a 1950s BBC production of *Robin Hood*, the back-projection plate was inserted wrongly so that all of the trees in Sherwood Forest appeared on screen upside-down.

Thank God for that

In 1985 the last episode of Jackie Collins' mini-series *Hollywood Wives* was accidentally screened in Britain with 15 crucial minutes missing. None of the 10 million viewers rang in to complain.

Quiet life

On an edition of the BBC's *Antiques Roadshow*, expert Arthur Negus dropped someone's prized clock, causing it to shatter into a hundred pieces. "Never mind," said the forgiving owner. "It will give me something to do in the evenings putting it back together."

Laird of Lancashire

Channel Four paid out £5,000 for distress caused to Keith Laird in 2001 after a bungling character by the name of Keith Lard had featured on the comedy show *Phoenix Nights*. Like Mr Laird, Keith Lard was a Lancashire fire safety officer with a fringe, a moustache and a catchphrase of "It's not fire that kills – it's ignorance." At first Mr Laird laughed off the similarities but, following constant ribbing from workmates, he complained to Channel Four and received an apology plus the £5,000. The show's creator, comedian Peter Kay, who, like Mr Laird, hails from Bolton, said: "Uncanny as it may seem it was a total coincidence. The name Keith Lard was delicately chosen for its inanimate and descriptive nature. We also took time to check there were no Lards in the Bolton phone book."

Press on

In June 1978 Bob Specas prepared to break a world record by knocking down 100,000 dominoes in a row at New York's Manhattan Centre. A TV crew was on hand to record the event for posterity and filmed Specas positioning the last dominoes prior to the big moment. Specas had painstakingly reached 97,499 when a TV cameraman dropped his press badge and accidentally set off the whole wave of dominoes.

Soul darts

A misheard instruction to the *Top of the Pops* crew meant that Dexy's Midnight Runners performed their soul tribute "Jackie Wilson Said" in front of a huge blow-up of Scottish darts player Jocky Wilson.

Once more, from the bottom

At the conclusion of an interview with Duran Duran on *The Tube*, presenter Paula Yates discovered that she had been sitting on the microphone and nobody had heard a word.

Crap announcer

Introducing Sir Stafford Cripps for a 1951 political broadcast, BBC announcer McDonald Hobley declared: "And now, the moment you have been waiting for – the Chancellor of the Exchequer, Sir Stifford Crapps."

Dangerous demonstration

Mike Stewart, President of the Auto Convoy Company, Dallas, Texas, was killed instantly in 1983 when a flatbed truck attempted to pass under a low-level bridge. At the time Mr Stewart had been standing on the back of the truck presenting a piece to camera for a TV item about the dangers of low-level bridges.

Late Lahti

Thinking her category was some time away, American actress Christine Lahti left a live TV awards ceremony and nipped to the ladies' room to powder her nose. But in her absence, she was called up to receive her award. Robin Williams was forced to ad-lib for a few minutes until a sheepish Lahti emerged from the toilet to loud cheers.

Polite fob-off

When nurse Ian Payne wrote to the BBC in 2000 asking for a film season dedicated to his favourite actress, Jean Simmons, he was surprised to receive a reply branding him a "nutter." Mr Payne, an avid autograph hunter, had also requested the signature of new BBC One controller Lorraine Heggessey, but stuck to the letter of reply was a Post-It note reading: "Nutter, polite fob-off – no autograph." Mr Payne immediately returned the letter, complete with the abusive note, to BBC Director-General Greg Dyke who ordered an immediate investigation into the blunder. A grovelling apology was sent to Mr Payne, and a Corporation spokesman stressed: "At the BBC, we love hearing from viewers and listeners, particularly when people have programme proposals. They are our lifeblood."

The prank which backfired

Derbyshire's Radio Buxton played a joke on listener Catherine McGowan, telling her that she had won a new car – a Renault Clio – in a phone-in competition and that if she came in to the station she could collect it. But her joy turned to anger when she was presented with a toy model car instead. However she had the last laugh when she sued and the court ordered that she be paid £12,000 for the cost of the car. The DJ responsible for the prank that fell flat was fired.

Sound Bites

Napoleon's comeback

In September 1950 Sweden's state-owned radio station announced that the country's territory had been invaded by a Western power and that Sweden was on the point of joining Russia in a "gigantic East-West clash." Hearing the solemn declaration, thousands of listeners went on full war alert. Home Guard units turned out while several ships in the Baltic changed course and headed straight for the nearest port. In their panic, they had missed the explanation, broadcast 30 seconds later, that all this had happened in 1812 and that the invading forces were those of Napoleon. The radio station later apologized and admitted that the effects of its history lesson had been "far stronger than anticipated."

The phrase that pays

Three employees of Kiss 103.3 FM, a radio station in Boise, Idaho, had the bright idea of telling a group of teenage boy callers that they could win an undisclosed sum of money by dialling an 800 number and saying: "The phrase that pays: I'm going to kill the President." The phone number they gave the boys was that of the White House, as a result of which Secret Service officials stormed the boys' house while they were still on the line. When the Secret Service men then went to the radio station, the three employees had to listen to a phrase that definitely didn't pay: "You're fired."

Deathray drama

A few minutes after 8 p.m. on Sunday 30 October 1938, a voice interrupted an American radio broadcast to warn: "Ladies and gentlemen, I have a grave announcement to make." The voice went on to report that Martians had landed in New Jersey and were sweeping all before them. Little did the American public know that the announcement was part of a CBS radio production of H.G. Welles' *War of the Worlds*, presented by Orson Welles and his Mercury Theatre of the Air, and nothing more than a hoax designed to boost ratings. Although people were warned not to, they immediately panicked, all the more so after hearing "witnesses," many played by actor Joseph Cotten, relaying how thousands had been killed by Martian deathrays. The programme ended with an announcer shouting hysterically from the top of the CBS building that Manhattan was being overrun. His commentary tailed off in a strangulated scream. By then, the roads of New Jersey were jammed with cars heading for the hills. Many fled from their homes with wet towels on their heads in the belief that this might protect them from the nauseous space gases they had heard about. Restaurants emptied in New York, and in the Deep South women prayed on the streets. Marines were recalled to their ships in New York harbour, ready to defend the nation against the Martian invaders. When the hoax was eventually revealed, Welles was the butt of angry complaints. Dozens filed lawsuits against CBS but all were later withdrawn.

Very late night radio

Listeners to a late-night radio phone-in show in June 2001 were treated instead to 20 minutes of a radio reporter struggling with studio technology after he accidentally pressed the wrong button. Michael Buchanan, of the BBC Radio Four *Today* programme, was trying to send an election story from the Leeds studio to London when he unwittingly pressed an override button and put himself on air to thousands of people across Yorkshire who had been expecting to hear the Andy Peebles Late Show. Puzzled listeners heard Mr Buchanan becoming increasingly angry from the constantly ringing telephone as he struggled with the equipment. He was heard to swear when a colleague made successive calls to his mobile phone. The mistake was only discovered when listeners phoned the BBC switchboard. Rod Liddle, editor of the *Today* programme, said: "We are all very embarrassed, especially Michael. He's a great reporter, but let's hope he never gets a job in a nuclear power station."

"My Sweet Lord": So Fine a Line

With thousands of tracks released every year, the quest to compose a wholly original tune becomes increasingly difficult. Many "new" songs contain short sequences, or sometimes even entire verses, that are reminiscent of an earlier number, but most are allowed to pass quietly without making the legal profession wealthier than they already are. It was George Harrison's bad luck to be the exception to the rule, to be found guilty of "subconscious plagiarism" on the grounds that segments of his 1971 smash "My Sweet Lord" bore a distinct resemblance to the Chiffons' 1962 Billboard number one "He's So Fine." It was a mistake which cost the former Beatle over half a million dollars.

Harrison's first solo effort following the break-up of the Beatles was a triple album, "All Things Must Pass," and the first single to be released from that album was "My Sweet Lord" which topped the Billboard charts and spent five weeks at the top of the UK charts from January 1971. The song was born while Harrison and American gospel singer Billy Preston, who was a member of George's band, were in Copenhagen. Excusing himself from a press conference, Harrison slipped away to his room where he began "vamping" some guitar chords. He was at the peak of his Indian mystic phase and began trying to incorporate the words "Hallelujah" and "Hare Krishna" into the chords he was playing. After a while, he went back to join the rest of the band and asked them to listen to what he had come up with. Ideas were exchanged and Harrison started to develop the song from there.

The following week, the group flew back to London where they had booked studio recording time. Harrison supervised the recording but in the studio Billy Preston was the principal musician. Harrison did not actually play on the session. Somewhere in the song's gestation period, the incriminating seven notes – the first three of the verse and four ("really want to see you") in the chorus – were inserted.

The success of "My Sweet Lord" (it went on to earn over $2,000,000) alerted the Bright Tunes Music Corporation who owned the rights to "He's So Fine." Representing the song's writer, Ronnie Mack, who had died in 1963, Bright Tunes claimed that Harrison had lifted the tune for "My Sweet Lord" from the Chiffons' hit, and sued for damages on 10 February 1971. Endeavouring to underline the alleged similarities between the two songs, the Chiffons even recorded their own version of "My Sweet Lord" in 1975. To many observers, there was a certain poetic justice in the fact that it was a resounding flop.

The trial took place in New York in February 1976. Harrison had assembled a high-powered team of copyright lawyers and during the three-day trial was required to demonstrate his counsel's argument on guitar. Among the various visual aids posted around the courtroom were huge wall charts of musical staves. The case centred on the presence in both songs of two short musical phrases, sol-mi-re (motif A) and sol-la-do-la-do (motif B). In "He's So Fine" there are four repetitions of motif A, followed by four repetitions of motif B. In the second repetition of motif B, a grace note is inserted to make the phrase sol-la-do-la-re-do. "My Sweet Lord" also uses the same motif

A four times, followed by the same motif B repeated three times. In place of the fourth repetition of motif B, "My Sweet Lord" has a similar-length passage containing the same unique grace note used in "He's So Fine." It was undoubtedly the inclusion of this identical grace note in the identical place in both songs which tipped the scales against Harrison.

In the end, District Judge Richard Owen ruled that Harrison, who acknowledged on the stand that the two songs were substantially similar, was guilty of committing "subconscious plagiarism" against Bright Tunes. In his judgement, he said: "I conclude that the composer, in seeking musical materials to clothe his thoughts, was working with various possibilities. As he tried this possibility and that, there came to the surface of his mind a particular combination that pleased him as being one he felt would be appealing to a prospective listener; in other words, that this combination of sounds would work. Why? Because his subconscious knew it already had worked in a song his conscious mind did not remember. Having arrived at this pleasing combination of sounds, the recording was made, the lead sheet prepared for copyright and the song became an enormous success. Did Harrison deliberately use the music of 'He's So Fine'? I do not believe he did so deliberately. Nevertheless, it is clear that 'My Sweet Lord' is the very same song as 'He's So Fine' with different words, and Harrison had access to 'He's So Fine.' This is, under the law, infringement of copyright, and is no less so even though subconsciously accomplished."

The judge wanted Harrison and Bright Tunes to get their lawyers together and arrange an out-of-court settlement, but hopes of an amicable agreement were dashed when Allen Klein, the sharp New York accountant who had handled the Beatles' affairs for two years, suddenly bought the rights to "He's So Fine." Ironically, it was Klein who had engaged Harrison's lawyers for the case back in 1971, but, following his acrimonious split with the Beatles, Klein now appeared to have changed sides! As the saga dragged on, Harrison noted dryly: "Now Allen Klein has bought the right to 'He's So Fine' and the right to continue the law suit. It's a joke; having settled all the Beatles' law suits, he must have felt lonely not having somebody to sue." Harrison was so disenchanted with the whole business that he tried to give "My Sweet Lord" away, just to get the case settled, but the lawyers wouldn't let him.

Instead Harrison took out his frustration musically, penning "This Song," a satire on the affair, and which contained lines like: "This song ain't black or white and as far as I know, don't infringe on anyone's copyright." It became a hit in the United States, prompting a Warner Bros official to remark: "Harrison picked a mighty tough way to get a hit record."

When the question of compensation was finally brought before the court in 1981, instead of awarding $1,599,987 damages (the portion of "My Sweet Lord"'s earnings which were said to be reasonably attributable to the music of "He's So Fine"), the judge took note of the fact that Klein had recently purchased the rights and limited the damages to precisely the sum which he had paid for the song – $587,000.

So the matter was settled at last, but it still left a nasty taste in Harrison's mouth. He reflected: "I'd be willing every time I write a song if somebody will have a computer and I can just go up to the thing and sing my new song into it and the computer will say 'sorry' or 'yes, OK.' I'm willing to do that, because the last thing I want to do is keep spending the rest of my life in court. Once you get people thinking, 'Oh well, they beat Harrison on "My Sweet Lord," let's sue . . .' they can sue the world! It made me so paranoid about writing. And I thought, 'God, I don't even want to touch the guitar or the piano, in case I'm touching somebody's note.' Somebody might own that note!"

The general consensus of opinion is that Harrison was a shade unlucky to be caught out when so many others have escaped retribution. Then again, "He's So Fine" was an extremely well-known song, and one which he admitted being familiar with. John Lennon certainly thought that Harrison should have known better. In one of his last interviews, Lennon said: "George walked right into it. He must have known, you know. He's smarter than that. George could have changed a few notes and nobody could have touched him, but he let it go and paid the price."

Bum Notes

Too bad

Performing the role of Vitek in *The Makropulos Case* at New York's Metropolitan Opera House in 1995, tenor Richard Versalle suffered a fatal heart attack and fell from a ladder as he sang the line "Too bad you can only live so long." The audience heard 63-year-old Versalle's voice falter and then saw him tumble ten feet to the stage from the ladder on which he had been perched. However, because the play was receiving its New York première, they thought it was all part of the plot.

Pianissimo

Travelling with the itinerant Middle East Symphony Orchestra, pianist Eileen Joyce sat at the piano for a wartime performance of Tchaikovsky's *Piano Concerto No. 1*, opened the lid but found no keyboard. The furniture removers who had transported the piano from the previous army base had forgotten to put it in.

Breakneck Berglund

Finnish conductor Paavo Berglund broke his neck while conducting an orchestra rehearsal in 1958. Berglund always shook his head while conducting forte passages, but got

Don't worry

Chicago frontman Terry Kath died during a game of Russian roulette in 1978. His last words were: "Don't worry, it's not loaded."

particularly carried away during a piano concerto by Usko Merilainen, which contains a number of forte sections. When Berglund suddenly turned to a soloist, he felt a sharp pain in the neck.

The show must go on

Romanian folk singer Joan Melu attracted an audience of nil for her 1980 concert at the 2,200-seater Capitol Theatre in Melbourne. Undeterred by the lack of audience response, she proceeded to fulfil her contractual obligation by giving a two-hour performance, complete with interval and encores.

Lola cola

In censoring the Kinks' 1970 hit "Lola," the BBC completely overlooked the song's transsexual lyrics, concentrating instead on the line which mentioned Coca-Cola. Ever vigilant about advertizing, the Corporation forced Ray Davies to change the words to "Cherry-Cola" when performing on *Top of the Pops*.

Baton blackout

When drum-major Steve Harding proudly threw his twirling baton into the air, he succeeded in blacking out a ten-block area of Ventura, California, as well as putting a radio station off the air and starting a grass fire. His baton had hit two 4000-volt power lines.

Berlin beat

A drummer from Kagel, near Berlin, was practising so loudly in his bedroom in 2001 that he didn't hear burglars smash a window to break into his house, empty the house of valuables and drive off in his car.

Sopping violinist

About to start an 1893 concert at a Baptist church, violinist Ovide Musin decided to step behind a curtain at the back of the platform to take a furtive look at the audience. Instead he found himself in three feet of water, having stepped into the baptismal font. Fellow orchestra members dragged him out sopping wet in his immaculate evening dress.

The less grateful living

The widow of The Grateful Dead's Jerry Garcia thought it would be a nice gesture to scatter his ashes in San Francisco Bay. Sadly she failed to take into account the prevailing wind which promptly blew the ashes back into the faces of the startled mourners.

Back-to-front bagpipes

In the 1960s a Scottish record company released a bagpipe record under the Waverley label on which the music was back to front. The error arose after the master tape had been processed from a tape that was accidentally played in reverse. More alarming was the fact that hundreds of copies were sold before anybody spotted the mistake.

Architectural Clangers

The Millennium Bridge: The Wrong Kind of Walking

The appendage "Millennium" to any London project invariably proved to be a prelude to excruciating embarrassment. One by one, the attractions unveiled to celebrate the year 2000 demonstrated capital unreliability of a magnitude usually reserved for the London Underground. The Millennium Dome was a fiasco from day one; the "river of fire" firework display on the Thames turned out to be a damp squib; and the London Eye wheel had to run empty on New Year's Eve 1999 after engineering problems postponed its official opening. So it came as little surprise when the much-vaunted, £18.2-million state-of-the-art Millennium Bridge had to close down just two days after its grand opening because of a tendency to sway alarmingly from side to side.

Conceived by sculptor Sir Anthony Caro and designed by eminent architect Lord Foster to provide a pedestrian link between St Paul's Cathedral on the north bank of the Thames and the Tate Modern Gallery on the south bank, the 1,050-foot-long aluminium and stainless steel structure was seen as a breakthrough in bridge construction. Its closest living relative was across the Seine in Paris. Lord Foster promised: "While the basic concept is that of a suspension bridge, the objective was to push tried and tested techniques as far as possible to create a uniquely thin bridge profile forming a slender blade across the Thames." It was subsequently dubbed the "Blade of Light."

The long thin design was tested in three separate wind tunnels to determine how it would withstand gusts, but time constraints prevented further testing. Indeed delays in construction meant that the final sections of deck were put in place just five days before the official opening to the public on 10 June 2000.

The amount of publicity generated by the new bridge saw 100,000 people queuing up to walk across it on the day of opening. The sheer volume of pedestrians seemed to take everyone by surprise, and police and security staff decided to limit the weight on the bridge by restricting access to groups of just thirty at two-minute intervals. With the strong wind typifying a British summer's day, the police became increasingly worried as the narrow walkway began to wobble ominously, causing some pedestrians to stumble. As they stepped off, many complained of feeling seasick. Eventually safety concerns held sway and the footbridge was closed on the advice of the police. It was supposed to move a little from side to side but the effect was intended to be akin to a gentle ripple on a mill pond rather than being tossed about in a force ten gale in the North Atlantic. Officials from the Millennium Bridge Trust were mystified.

It was thought initially that the high winds were to blame but two days later when the walkway was swaying even in moderate winds, it was apparent that the problem went deeper and it was announced that the latest line in bridge-building technology would be closed to the public for the foreseeable future while repairs were carried out. The engineers remained bullish. One said reassuringly: "The bridge is never going to fall down. No bits are going to come off it."

Thus the aesthetically pleasing but physically unnerving bridge was shut down so that engineering experts could look into what was causing the instability. At the end of June they released their studied findings: it was all due to the wrong kind of walking. The technical term for the embarrassing phenomenon which caused the closure was "synchronized resonance," the result of large numbers of people walking in step. Apparently when the bridge started to sway gently in one direction, all of the pedestrians put out a foot to steady themselves, then switched to the other foot when it moved the other way. All of those feet, clomping down in unison, set up vibrations which made the sideways movements of the bridge progressively greater. The designers may have intended the bridge to sway, but they had reckoned without packed crowds moving in time with it. Quite what else people in danger of losing their balance were expected to do remains a mystery.

Consultant engineers Arup, who had built the bridge from Lord Foster's plans, explained that because the bridge was such an innovative structure, the possibility of synchronized resonance had never been considered. Asked whether he might have been better advised to have used a tried and tested design, Lord Foster insisted that the world-wide interest in his creation would not have arisen had he "retreated into the past." He added: "The bridge is safe. It is not going to kill anybody. If we are accused of being over-ambitious, I reply that I would rather be accused of that than of being lily-livered."

In November 2000 – by which time it had lain idle for five months – it was announced that the proposed cure for the Millennium Bridge's ills was the fitting of shock absorbers and heavy metal dampers, the addition of extra piers having been ruled out because they would spoil the look of the bridge. These repairs were reported to be costing £5,000,000 and the bridge would remain closed until the summer of 2001 at the earliest.

And so the showpiece bridge across the Thames – a tourist attraction which was expected to pull in four million visitors in its first year – was open for just two days during that period. Praised by the Queen at the official unveiling, it has been an unfortunate design victim, the design of the bridge being incompatible with the design of the human being. One of them would have to change, and Lord Foster – or "Lord Wobbler" as he was christened by the British Press – remained adamant that it would not be his bridge. "I am convinced my bridge will be popular and well used," he said defiantly. In the meantime he certainly acquired the "worldwide interest" he so craved as the Millennium Bridge became a laughing stock from Toronto to Tokyo.

Finally on 22 February 2002, after a 20-month closure, the Millennium Bridge reopened for business. The shock-absorbent dampers had done the trick. It no longer wobbled. Lord Foster looked on proudly but did now concede that the saga had been something of an embarrassment.

Dome Sweet Dome

Britain wanted something uniquely grand, something spectacularly successful, to mark the start of the year 2000. It wanted a tourist attraction which would encourage millions of people of all ages to flock to London from all over the world. It wanted a symbol of British ingenuity and know-how. Instead it got the Millennium Dome.

Over a 12-month period when it lurched from crisis to crisis, hand-out to hand-out, and missed an endless stream of targets, the Dome became a byword for costly failure, a monumental flop.

Heralded as a showpiece project which would be the envy of the world, it ate up £628 million in lottery funds but attracted barely half the predicted number of visitors. It was hailed as a milestone in British history, but ended up as one of the New Labour government's biggest millstones.

Far from producing a wave of back-slapping congratulation, the Dome saw an unseemly squabble between the two major political parties in Britain as to precisely who was to blame for spending so much money for so little return. Labour blamed the Conservatives, saying it was their idea in the first place; to which the Conservatives responded by blaming Labour, saying they inherited the project and wasted millions of pounds on it. The petulant recriminations didn't quite stoop to the level of "my dad's bigger than your dad" but it was a close-run thing.

The building that has subsequently been described as "the last joke of the twentieth century" opened to a wealth of expectation on New Year's Eve 1999. Its prohibitive cost was to be funded by a combination of National Lottery money and sponsorship in the belief that the Dome would attract 12,000,000 paying visitors by the end of the year, at which point it was due to close. These figures, around which all the financial spending plans were based, had supposedly been reached via market research. Whether it was Smithfield or Billingsgate Market has yet to be established.

If others had their misgivings, Prime Minister Tony Blair was not among them. "This is Britain's opportunity," he crowed, "to greet the world with a celebration so bold, so beautiful, so inspiring, that it embodies at once the spirit of confidence and adventure in Britain and the spirit of the future in the world. This is our chance to make a statement of faith in our capacity in Britain to do this bigger and better than anyone else. We will say to ourselves with pride: 'This is our Dome, Britain's Dome.' And believe me, it will be the envy of the world." Indeed Blair identified very closely with the Dome. The feeling was mutual. For the Dome was later criticized as being empty and vacuous, just like New Labour.

Meanwhile Dome Secretary, Lord Falconer, a close friend of Prime Minister Blair, predicted that it would boost the UK's economy through tourism by up to £1 billion, although wisely he later revised this figure to £500 million. All that was missing was the minus sign.

The organization of the Dome was a complex affair – too complex according to a subsequent investigation into what went wrong. The previous Conservative government had wanted a private company to run the Dome but none would take the risk. So when the Labour government took over following its election in 1997, it set up a government-owned private company, the New Millennium Experience Company, to operate the Dome. The NMEC was accountable to the Millennium Commission (the body responsible for distributing National Lottery cash to flagship projects), to Lord Falconer as the minister in charge, and to Parliament. In turn, the Millennium Commission was responsible to Culture Secretary Chris Smith who also happened to chair the commission. In one respect, Lord Falconer "controlled" the NMEC as its single shareholder and minister responsible, but so did Chris Smith via the Millennium Commission. Amid this tangled web of bureaucracy, it was perhaps hardly surprising that nobody had the faintest idea what was going on!

On a scale of success, the Dome's opening night was on a par with King Alfred's attempts at bakery. The launch party was described as the hottest ticket in town . . . if only because nobody wanted to touch it for weeks afterwards. Ten thousand guests – VIPs and mere mortals – had been invited to the newly finished Dome site in Greenwich, south-east London, to attend the grand opening, but the whole affair rapidly degenerated into a shambles. Due to an administrative error and the failure to cater for the vagaries of the Christmas mail, 3,000 of the tickets were not sent out in time. So guests were told to collect their tickets on the night at either Stratford or Charlton station from where they would be taken to the Dome at Greenwich. Unfortunately those in charge had grossly underestimated the number of people converging on these stations which were woefully ill-equipped to handle anything more than the usual trickle of passengers. The crush at Stratford was likened to a scene from *Titanic* with guests queuing for hours to pass through the security X-ray scanners and claim their tickets before catching the special trains which had been laid on to transport them the short distance to the Dome. Many couldn't be bothered and simply gave up and went home. Those who were stranded included captains of industry, who between them had secured several million pounds of sponsorship for the Dome, and a number of national newspaper editors. The resultant adverse publicity was hardly the best of starts.

Inside the Dome the party started at 11 p.m. . . . in front of rows and rows of empty seats. Comedian Stephen Fry, warming up what there was of the audience, quipped that the Queen was still queuing at Stratford for her ticket. In view of the fiasco which surrounded the distribution, it wasn't as unlikely as it sounded. Although numerous guests missed the start of the celebrations – among them a 150-strong group from the Boots pharmaceutical company which was sponsoring the Dome's chief attraction, the Body Zone – those who persevered were at least able to take their seats in time for the chimes of midnight. There they were able to witness the sight of the Queen and Tony Blair linking hands for the traditional singing of *Auld Lang Syne*. Even the most ardent monarchist might dispute that it was worth waiting six hours for.

The new millennium was less than a few hours old when the soul-searching began with police and Dome chiefs blaming each other for the first-night delays. The Dome's marketing director Sholto Douglas-Home described the debacle as "like opening a restaurant and giving every diner food poisoning."

Contrary to the title of the song with which Tony Blair and Labour swept to power, things did not get better. The opening to the public on the morning of 1 January brought fresh problems, this time in the form of huge queues at some of the 12 zones, notably the Body Zone. In a masterpiece of design, the Body Zone had been positioned near the main entrance with the result that the tailback of people waiting to get into it clogged up the entire Dome. The Dome had a capacity of 25,000 but even when 5,000 below capacity, there were still two-hour queues.

Boots, who were supposed to be paying £12 million to sponsor the Body Zone, were particularly unhappy at seeing dissatisfied customers queuing for an eternity at its showpiece. The NMEC had promised beforehand that there would never be any significant queues for attractions. Soon that promise would be kept . . . but only because there were no visitors.

The moment the school holidays were over, attendance figures slumped alarmingly. By 6 January – just five days after opening – it was announced that the Dome was to be re-launched because of poor ticket sales. On most days it was barely a third full. The British public were totally underwhelmed by the Millennium Experience.

The chorus of disapproval grew by the day. Prince Charles reportedly called the Dome a "crass waste of money" and a "monstrous blancmange" while Sir Jocelyn Stevens, chairman of English Heritage, condemned it as "completely inexplicable, unacceptable and a huge mistake." Other visitors expressed their disappointment, calling it a waste of money and a colossal white elephant. There were also complaints that parts of the Body Zone were not working and that some areas were simply boring. Two sponsors, Boots and McDonald's, were so annoyed by the bad publicity that they threatened to withhold payment. And British Airways withheld over £200,000 because the miniature "futuristic aircraft" that were supposed to fly in the Travel Zone weren't getting off the ground as often as they should.

By the end of January visitor figures had reached only half the number expected. NMEC executives continued to make optimistic noises, citing teething troubles, New Year's hangovers and so on, but it was evident to all but the most blinkered that the Dome was already in big trouble.

On 2 February the NMEC reacted to the crisis by begging an extra £60 million of lottery money to cover cashflow shortages caused by poor attendances. It accepted that the January figures of 328,821 were way below the 732,500 target but insisted that the 12,000,000 aim for the year was still attainable. Two days later, Jennie Page, the £150,000-a-year chief executive, resigned in the wake of the dismal performance. She was replaced by Pierre-Yves Gerbeau, the man credited in some quarters with having saved Disneyland Paris. One of his first jobs was to recalculate the wildly optimistic visitor figures and reduce the target to 10 million paying customers by the end of the year.

M. Gerbeau brought plenty of energy and enthusiasm to the

Dome but not too many extra visitors. Never mind, said Dome devotees, visitor levels will pick up at Easter. They didn't, and by the middle of May, with attendances still failing to hit even the revised targets, Gerbeau was going cap in hand for another £29 million of lottery money. The Millennium Commission thought long and hard about pouring more money into what had already become a sick joke but eventually agreed on condition that the Dome's most senior executive, NMEC chairman Bob Ayling, resigned. For Ayling, it represented an unwanted double. Two months earlier he had been forced to resign as head of British Airways. His successor at NMEC was David Quarmby, chairman of the British Tourist Authority.

Clutching his £29 million, Gerbeau promised that it would be the last time that the Dome would have to ask for money. He then lowered the visitor target to six million paying customers – half the original estimate.

The full entry price for the Dome was £20 but discounts – or even free tickets – were offered as an inducement to visitors. In January only ten per cent of tickets were discounted or free, but by the end of June nearly half of the Dome's tickets were being sold at a reduced price. Naturally this was matched by a similar reduction in income, particularly as the discount scheme spectacularly failed to attract additional visitors. Losses were running at over £1 million a week. It had reached the stage where you couldn't pay people to go to the Dome.

Some Dome employees were actually ashamed to admit to their involvement with the project. One designer for the Play Zone confessed that he kept quiet about the fact that he had worked on the Dome, saying: "It's a bit like saying you designed the cranes for the lifeboat on the *Titanic*!"

Even the exhibits were trying to get out, including thousands of leaf-cutter ants from Trinidad who made a break for freedom from the Mind and Body Zone by eating their way through steel cables and plastic casing. The ants' presence in the zone was intended to represent collective thinking, the very power which they then used to escape. Unfortunately after leaving their heated area, they quickly died from the cold. Perhaps they weren't such a good advert for collective thinking after all.

Whether it be a game bird or a lame duck like the Dome, one can be sure that Prince Philip would take a pot shot at it. Sure enough, in the very week that the NMEC launched a £2 million advertizing drive to try and boost visitor figures, he took a swipe at the Dome while opening a new mathematics department at Cambridge University. To accompanying ripples of laughter, the Duke told the assembled dignitaries: "This is a lot less expensive than the Dome. And I think it's going to be a great deal more useful." For once he had his finger on the nation's pulse instead of its purse.

The wonderful thing about the Dome was that there was always a fresh crisis just around the corner. And so it was that a mere six months after it opened, the state-of-the-art building – capable of housing ten St Paul's Cathedrals – developed a leaky roof. The 20-acre, Teflon-coated canopy cost £14,000,000 and was built to last 25 years but now urgent repairs were carried out to repair huge holes, some the size of dinner plates.

While Dome-mongers continued to pour scorn on the enterprise, the NMEC remained defiantly optimistic, predicting that attendances were sure to rise in the summer holidays. They didn't, and in early September, four months after Gerbeau had vowed that the Dome would not need any more hand-outs, another £47 million of lottery money was sunk into it to save it from bankruptcy. That grant brought the total of lottery funds poured into the Dome to £628 million. The original planned grant was for £399 million. Amid renewed calls for him to resign, Lord Falconer promised that this latest injection would be "enough to ensure a solvent conclusion to the project," adding, "If one looks at it in the longer term one will see a project that people went to and enjoyed." Labour backbencher Bob Marshall-Andrews was not convinced, labelling the input of cash as a "national scandal." He went on: "There is a total lack of accountability for this public money."

The Millennium Commission expressed its "deep disappointment" at the situation and spoke of "serious failings in NMEC's financial management." The commissioners had been particularly alarmed to learn that the Dome had faced immediate insolvency unless it received the £47 million and that the NMEC had massively underestimated the costs of running the Dome until the end of the year and then closing it down. The costs of shutting the Dome were found to exceed £30,000,000. Faced with that ultimatum, the commissioners reluctantly agreed to the grant – provided that the NMEC appointed a new executive chairman, accounting officer and financial director. So out went David Quarmby, to be replaced by City troubleshooter David James.

A week after the latest salvage operation Japanese bank Nomura, which had wanted to buy the Dome at the end of 2000 and keep it open as a visitor attraction, pulled out of the deal, claiming that poor record-keeping and chaotic financial management meant that nobody seemed aware of who owned what inside the giant tent. Lord Falconer said the news was "very, very regrettable."

Peter Mandelson, who had been the very first Dome Secretary three years earlier, quickly leapt to the defence of the beleaguered building and blamed the media for everything. Failing that, he blamed the Conservative administration, saying that it was Michael Heseltine's idea in the first place and that the Conservatives under John Major had taken key decisions about the project, including its general design and its location at Greenwich. When pushed, he did admit that there had been "difficulties over visitor numbers" and that "management mistakes" may have been made, but he insisted that the Dome was "something in which Britain can take pride."

His Cabinet colleague Clare Short was markedly less enthusiastic, branding the Dome a "disaster" and calling for it to be shut down as quickly as possible. While others demanded that the Dome be bulldozed to the ground, composer Sir Andrew Lloyd Webber came up with a more novel suggestion, proposing that the best way to draw crowds was to set fire to the Dome. "The public likes nothing more than a good blaze," he said.

Another casualty of the Dome's failure to attract the required number of visitors was the high-speed ferry service introduced to transport customers from Central London to Greenwich. It was forced to close in October, Whitehorse Fast Ferries announcing that the only days on which the service made a profit had been on three days back in January when the Dome still possessed curiosity value.

Although it had been in dire need of visitors for months, the Dome received an unwelcome set of callers on the morning of 7 November 2000 when a gang of robbers smashed through the walls with an earth-mover in a bid to steal £350 million worth of diamonds on display in the Money Zone. Detectives posing as cleaners were lying in wait and arrested the gang before they could make their getaway in a speedboat waiting on the nearby River Thames. That the raid was botched was somehow symptomatic of everything connected with the Dome. The incident provoked much mirth. Movie director Michael Winner remarked: "The Dome should be delighted. It's the first time they've had anyone so keen to get in."

Two days after the gang of raiders had failed to smash down the walls of the Dome, an official report published by the National Audit Office did a more efficient demolition job in writing. The report attributed much of the blame to the 12 million visitor target which it described as "ambitious and inherently risky." Outside consultants had warned as early as 1997 that eight million was a more realistic figure but the nine members of the Millennium Commission would not be swayed and nor would the directors of the NMEC. By opening night the NMEC had hoped to sell £18,900,000 worth of advance tickets, but the actual figure was a paltry £3,900,000. The report revealed that a contingency fund of £88,000,000 had been exhausted even before opening night, meaning that the Dome was effectively broke before the first visitor arrived. With much of the anticipated £175,000,000 from sponsors failing to materialize because of bad publicity and hundreds of contractors waiting to be paid, David James said he believed the NMEC had been "technically insolvent" since February.

The report highlighted a letter sent by Culture Secretary Chris Smith to Lord Falconer just five weeks after the Dome opened. In the letter Smith, who had reportedly always opposed the building of the Dome, warned Lord Falconer that the "quality of corporate governance" at NMEC "will have to improve." He went on: "The NMEC board does not appear to us to have played the role we would have expected in confronting the problems and providing leadership. Either the board did not see or chose to discount the warning signs of the cashflow crisis." It took Lord Falconer six weeks to reply.

The report was also critical of the failure of the NMEC to agree on an emergency plan in case visitor numbers were lower than expected. In essence, it concluded that the Dome was an enormous gamble with public money – a gamble which did not pay off.

In the wake of the report, former NMEC chairman Bob Ayling was suitably contrite. “Those of us responsible for the Dome,” he said, “owe everyone else an apology for not having achieved the aspiration of attracting 12,000,000 visitors.” Fresh calls came for Lord Falconer’s head, but he stood firm. However even he struggled to put a favourable spin on the findings of the report and was forced to concede that the Dome had failed. Naturally it wasn’t his fault.

Ironically, the impending closure of the Dome heralded an increase in the flow of visitors over the last three months of 2000. A total of 609,487 people (48,137 of them free) passed through the gates in October and the six millionth visitor arrived on 12 December. If she had brought six million friends with her, the Dome would have broken even.

As it was, the Dome was £229 million over budget when it closed for good on 31 December 2000, the end of a miserable year for the attraction which Tony Blair had once predicted would be “the envy of the world.” Even the Official Yearbook of the United Kingdom appeared to try and gloss over the Dome’s existence. Whereas the December 1999 issue had featured pictures of the Dome on the front and back covers along with a glowing description inside, the following year’s publication saw the Dome relegated to a derisory twenty-word sentence on page 529. No photographs. No praise. No wonder.

Back in 1997 Peter Mandelson had said: “If the Millennium Dome is a success, it will never be forgotten; if it’s a failure, we will never be forgiven.” “Failure” barely begins to describe it.

Fonthill Abbey: One Man's Folly

Writer and traveller William Beckford was one of the most eccentric individuals in Georgian England. The death of his father in 1770, leaving an estate worth one million pounds, made young William just about the wealthiest ten-year-old in the land, and he used the money to pursue his wild dreams and fantasies.

Wherever he travelled, he was accompanied by his personal physician, cook, valet and baker, plus two dogs, three footmen, 24 musicians and, for good luck, a Spanish dwarf. It is said that for one trip to Portugal Beckford even took with him a flock of sheep to improve the view from his window. Wherever he stayed, he supplied his own bed, cutlery, crockery and wallpaper, flatly refusing to occupy any bedroom until it had been redecorated to his personal taste. But probably his greates eccentricity of all was the building of a huge folly, Fonthill Abbey, in Wiltshire.

In 1786 Beckford had published *Vathek*, a Gothic novel in which the hero lived in a mighty tower, the master of all he surveyed. Beckford dreamed of his own tower, reaching high into the sky, taking him ever closer to heaven. He wrote to a friend: "I am growing rich and mean to build Towers, and sing hymns to the powers of Heaven on their summits." On top of the tower, he envisaged a tall spire so that the whole would extend to the incredible height of 450 feet, thus surpassing Salisbury Cathedral by 50 feet.

To realize his dream, Beckford engaged James Wyatt, the most eminent architect of the day and the man responsible for the restoration work at Lichfield and Salisbury Cathedrals. It was to be a chaotic association. For all his expertise and charm, Wyatt was hopelessly unreliable and was often absent from the site for months on end, much to the frustration of Beckford who was impatient to see the building completed as quickly as possible. Wyatt over-stretched himself by taking on too much work in different parts of the country, but it wasn't only other projects that kept him away from Fonthill. For he was also a lover of wine and women in equal measures, prompting Beckford to give him the nickname of Bagasse – the Whoremonger. In spite of Wyatt's shortcomings, it appears that Beckford felt a great deal of affection for him.

Not that Beckford was the easiest person to work for. His plans for the Abbey, which he wanted to be a cathedral dedicated to the arts, were on a grand scale, but he insisted on everything being rushed. His first mistake was made right at the outset when he refused to wait for proper foundations to be dug, insisting that those which had already been laid for a small summer house would suffice. When Wyatt and the builders demurred, Beckford ignored their concerns and demanded that work proceed at once.

He boasted that he would soon be living in the tallest private residence in England.

A letter which Beckford wrote to his mother in November 1796 indicated that work on the Abbey was progressing rapidly, but this was partly because it was being constructed of flimsy materials. Rather than use stone facings, Wyatt had decided to rely on a mixture of wood and a substance called compo-cement, a form of ornamental plaster. Wyatt was a big fan of compo, but it was not designed to withstand the harshness of the English climate. As Wyatt would learn to his cost, it only lasted six years before it deteriorated so badly that it had to be stripped off. And that was provided the structure hadn't fallen down already!

By February 1797, the Abbey was reported as being half-finished, but while Beckford was away on one of his jaunts to Portugal, work virtually ground to a standstill. Wyatt had lost interest in the project, preferring to attend to the needs of his other clients, among them King George III. When Beckford returned to England and saw the minimal amount of progress that had been made in his absence, he summoned Wyatt to Fonthill. At the same time, he announced even grander plans – including extra wings – and Wyatt was instructed to draw up new designs accordingly.

Beckford was truly excited about the expanded Abbey, and Wyatt was obliged to draft in extra workmen who had been doing the alterations to Windsor Castle. Quite how the King reacted to playing second fiddle to a mad writer is not recorded.

Over 500 labourers toiled day and night to create Beckford's dream. In an attempt to encourage them, he increased their ale ration, but this merely had the effect of rendering them so drunk they were incapable of knowing what they were doing.

Then, in May 1800, even the supremely enthusiastic Beckford received what can only be described as something of a setback.

One night violent storms lashed the fragile structure of the half-built tower which was still encased in its scaffolding. A huge gust of wind caught the flag flying at the top, the standard crashed down, followed by the scaffolding and the 150-foot high tower. All that remained of Beckford's tower was a pile of wood and compo cement.

Although Beckford did not witness the collapse, the tower's demise wounded him like a dagger to the heart. He saw it as a destruction of his dream – a personal insult. It was a humiliation to all concerned, not least to the architect for his blind faith in cheap products. However Beckford wasn't the type to stay down for long, and he immediately made plans to ensure that his tower possessed a similar quality. With the dust still settling after the May storm, he decreed that the tower must be rebuilt . . . and this time in stone. He was rapidly running out of patience with Wyatt, whose negligence and lack of attention had already added £30,000 to the £220,000 cost of the Abbey, and issued him with a final warning. Beckford wrote to the architect: "Determined to sink no longer from disappointment to disappointment, I give you this plain and decided warning. If you take it as it is meant I shall soon see you at Fonthill. If not – the whole shall be stopped, every workman discharged."

The threat appeared to work at first. Wyatt became more visible at Fonthill, causing Beckford to write excitedly to Sir William Hamilton in 1802: "The tower sings a fine tune, and all the little turrets, flying buttresses, pinnacles, and gothic loopholes join in the chorus." But it proved to be yet another false dawn and by 1807 the tower was still in scaffolding while the rest of the Abbey also remained unfinished. Beckford could wait no longer, and even though there were gangs of workmen on site, he decided to move in. He was determined to eat Christmas dinner there, but the kitchens were by no means ready. The beams had not been secured and the mortar was not yet dry. As Beckford dined, the kitchens caved in around him and had to be rebuilt.

The repair work was constant. Wood and compo walls had to be rebuilt in stone, the chimney flues had to be amended and "a thousand other errors" attended to between 1812 and 1814. In the middle of this, in 1813, Wyatt was killed in a carriage accident. Despite working on Fonthill Abbey for nearly 20 years, Wyatt never lived to see its completion. That was not achieved until 1817 but even then the Abbey lacked the colossal spire which was supposed to have been built to top the 276-foot tower. Nor would the spire ever be built. In view of what was to follow, it was probably just as well.

Having lavished so much time and money on his grand design, Beckford found the place virtually uninhabitable. The tower, which housed his bedroom suite, gave particular cause for concern, swaying so ominously in one storm that Beckford said the whole place made his flesh creep. Following another violent night, in November 1815, he complained: "This habitation is deathly in the stormy season. This morning I'm more yellow, rent and wretched than a dry leaf." Four years later, he went so far as to describe the tower as being in a state of collapse. Other areas suffered from damp, notably the gallery where the cabinets and cases were "all covered with lichen and stalactites like Fingal's Cave." But an outbreak of rising damp paled in comparison to the inherent problems of the tower. In 1821 the *Gentleman's Magazine* reported that "the tower is acknowledged to be a weak and dangerous structure, and so tottering are the eight surmounting pinnacles that they are held on their bases by strong iron bars, to the no less disparagement of the building than of the builder." The most committed estate agent would have struggled to make an appealing feature out of a high tower that was liable to crash down on the sleeping resident at any time.

It was the concerns for his own safety coupled with the fact that he had over-stretched himself financially with his constantly expanding plans that forced Beckford to sell the Abbey no sooner than it had been completed. In 1822 he sold Fonthill to John Farquhar, an elderly merchant who had made his fortune in India selling gunpowder. Beckford moved to Bath where he quickly set to work on a new tower – the Lansdown Tower. While this was under construction, Beckford received news of the highly dangerous state of Fonthill Tower from Wyatt's former clerk of works. In a death-bed confession, the clerk revealed that the new stone tower was resting on the same flimsy foundations as the previous structure of wood and compo-cement. The clerk added that the intention had been to build a relieving arch into the foundations to bear the weight of the stone tower, which was so much higher and heavier than its predecessor, but for some reason this essential work had never been carried out. As it stood – and it barely did – the tower could scarcely withstand an exhalation from the Big Bad Wolf.

A horrified Beckford rushed to tell the new owner but old man Farquhar took the news stoically, simply replying that he was sure that the tower would outlast him.

Farquhar's confidence was misplaced. On 21 December 1825, he was sitting on the lawn in front of the Abbey when gaping cracks were spotted in the tower walls. Still protesting that there was no danger, he was hastily carried inside the Abbey by his staff and had just reached safety when the tower collapsed in upon itself and crumbled to the ground in a huge cloud of dust. The falling masonry succeeded in damaging much of the Abbey but luckily nobody was hurt. In that splendidly under-stated way of his, Farquhar remarked:

"Now the house is not too big for me to live in."

With two towers having bitten the dust, it was the end for Fonthill. Farquhar moved out and the ruins fell into decay. The unsteady Abbey was finally demolished in 1844 – by an uncanny coincidence the same year in which its creator William Beckford, the man with the dream, died. Beckford had enjoyed better fortune in Bath with his 154-foot-high Lansdown Tower. Apart from anything else, it didn't collapse. Not even once. As an Abbey, Fonthill may not have lived up to its name; but as a folly, it certainly did.

Here today, gone tomorrow

A demolition team at Reutte in Austria accidentally blew up the wrong railway bridge. Instead of detonating the old ramshackle bridge, they destroyed the brand new £1,000,000 structure which had been opened just three days earlier to replace it.

Doing time on the Med

A new jail on the Mediterranean island of Ibiza was decidedly prisoner-friendly. For thanks to a blunder by the builder, all of the cell door locks were put on the inside.

Henry Winstanley: The First Eddystone Lighthouse

Englishman Henry Winstanley was a renowned eccentric whose house was filled with traps to ensnare the unwary visitor. So it was only fitting that he should die in eccentric circumstances . . . while trying to prove to the world that his frail lighthouse could withstand any storm.

Winstanley was born in Essex in 1644 and began his colourful life as an engraver. Under the patronage of Charles II, his fortunes prospered and he established Winstanley's Waterworks near Hyde Park as one of London's major tourist attractions. He was also a merchant of some repute who invested money in five ships. When two of these were lost on the notorious Eddystone Rock, 14 miles off the Plymouth coast, Winstanley confronted the maritime authorities and demanded to know why no action was being taken to protect shipping from the deadly rock formation. They told him that the Eddystone was impossible to mark: it was only 30 feet across, had a 30 degree slope and barely rose above the waves at high tide. Furthermore, it was nearly 15 miles out in one of the world's roughest seas. Mere facts were no deterrent to Winstanley, however, and he immediately announced his intention to build a lighthouse there – a decision which was met with derision by the sceptics.

In 1696 Winstanley set about constructing the first lighthouse on the Eddystone Rock. Just digging the foundation holes took five months since it was a twelve-hour round trip for his workmen by boat, and the hard rock had to be broken with pick axes. On many days, the weather was too rough for the men to be able to climb on to the rock. Braving strong winds and high seas, Winstanley's workforce made steady progress after that, and it soon became apparent that his vision of a 125-foot high wooden structure, topped with a candle-lit lantern, was more than just a pipe dream.

Yet there was a minor setback in 1697 when Winstanley was kidnapped. At the time England was at war with France, and the Eddystone project was deemed so important that the Admiralty provided Winstanley with a warship for protection on days when building work was taking place. One morning near the end of June, the protective vessel failed to arrive but in its place appeared a French privateer who promptly carried Winstanley off to France. However, so many ships were being lost on the rock that the French King, Louis XIV, realized that France needed a lighthouse there too, and so he ordered

Winstanley's immediate release with the words: "France is at war with England, not with humanity."

By the autumn of 1698 the lighthouse was finished, and on 14 November Winstanley climbed up to the lantern and lit a dozen tallow candles. The lighting of the Eddystone caused great excitement as fishermen returning to Plymouth relayed the news. Sightseers with telescopes flocked on to Plymouth Hoe, straining for a glimpse of the new landmark, and the city's pubs were packed with rejoicing sailors. The only people unable to join in the celebrations were Winstanley and his team, the weather being so bad that it was another five weeks before they made it back to dry land.

Although the locals hailed Winstanley as a genius, others were less impressed and predicted that the lighthouse would never make it through the winter. They were nearly right. When Winstanley and his men returned to Eddystone Rock three months after the grand opening, they found the keeper nearing insanity and the lighthouse literally falling down around him. Undaunted, Winstanley fortified the structure, and for the next four years not one shipwreck occurred at Eddystone.

Still, Winstanley's critics were not satisfied and complained that the tower was top-heavy. Irritated by the constant carping, Winstanley boasted publicly that his lighthouse could survive any storm and, somewhat recklessly as it transpired, declared that his one crowning wish in life was "to be in the lighthouse during the greatest storm that ever was." His wish was to be granted sooner than he thought.

The month of November 1703 was marked by two weeks of terrible gales which confined all ships to port. The harbours and estuaries of southern England were filled with vessels, their captains desperately hoping for a break in the weather. The lull finally came on Thursday 25 November, and on the following morning Winstanley and his maintenance crew rowed out to the lighthouse to carry out urgent repairs for the winter. Just before midnight there blew up the worst storm Britain had ever known. Men and animals were lifted off their feet and carried for yards through the air; lead roofs were ripped like tissue paper off over 100 churches; much of London was ripped apart; 15,000 sheep were drowned in floods near Bristol; 400 windmills were blown over; some 800 houses were completely destroyed; and the ships, huddled together at port, were tossed into one another and on to adjacent rocks. Not one ship remained afloat in Plymouth. A total of 8,000 sailors were drowned that night, all within yards of land.

Fourteen miles out, on the Eddystone Rock, Henry Winstanley's wish became his dying one. He was indeed present at Britain's greatest ever storm, but he did not live to tell the tale. On the evening of Friday 26 November the Eddystone Lighthouse showed a light as usual, but by daybreak on Saturday there was no sign of the lighthouse, or Henry Winstanley. The only evidence that a structure had ever existed there was a few bent pieces of rusty iron protruding from the rock.

The lightweight lighthouse may not have stood the test of time, and its architect may have paid for his over-confidence with his life, but his vision and courage paved the way for future buildings on the same site. The current Eddystone Lighthouse, built of stone in 1882, still provides an invaluable service to shipping and sits as a lasting monument to a crazy man's crazy dream.

Back to the Drawing Board

Mystery ward

While building an extension to a hospital in Maputo, Mozambique, workmen demolished a wall and were surprised to discover a state-of-the-art, unused maternity ward hidden behind it. It emerged that seven years earlier, when the hospital was built, the original contractors had mistakenly put in a wall instead of a door. Remarkably, no one seemed to have noticed the absence of the maternity ward during the hospital's lifespan.

Bad Bonanno

The famous tilt on the Leaning Tower of Pisa is not the result of some ground-breaking feat by its original architect Bonanno Pisano, but because the foundations are too shallow. For although the tower is 179 feet high, its foundations are only 10 feet deep. Consequently the top of the tower is some 17 feet out of true.

Dumb demolition

In January 2001 the city council of Texarkana, Arkansas, sent a contractor to a street in the town with instructions to demolish a house which had trees covering the front. Unfortunately there were two buildings like that in the same street and the wrong one was demolished. The householder, who was in California at the time, was not amused.

Short-lived award

In February 1979 Britain's leading architects congregated at Skegness Pier in Lincolnshire to present an award for Best Designed Pier Theatre to Mr George Sunderland. Half-way through the ceremony a ferocious storm erupted and the theatre was swept out to sea.

Transport Foul-Ups

Beryl the Peril

Beryl Millican had never learned to drive. But she could see no harm in doing her husband a favour by starting their car to gets its engine ticking over. But as soon as the 64-year-old grandmother got behind the wheel of the automatic Toyota Corolla, she left a trail of chaos and destruction which would have done Laurel and Hardy proud. Neighbours in the quiet cul-de-sac in Caister-on-Sea, Norfolk, dived for cover as the car knocked over Mr Millican and careered out of control, smashing through six garden walls, two fences, demolishing a tree, wrecking flowerbeds and lawns and missing two other cars by a matter of inches. It finally came to rest when it crashed into a newly-built porch, leaving Mrs

Millican, who had been desperately trying to locate the brake, suffering from whiplash and acute embarrassment.

The carnage of May 2001 began when Mrs Millican, a retired shop assistant, started the engine in the driveway of the family bungalow at 30 Queensway. The intention was simply to charge the car's battery because her 65-year-old husband Dick had not been able to get into the car following a knee operation four weeks previously. But as Mrs Millican held the steering wheel in horror, the Toyota somehow lurched into reverse gear and shot backwards, knocking her husband to the ground. The car then careered over the road before knocking down a garden wall and destroying a brick flower bed at number 38 – the home of Rita and Les Shearing. The couple's 16-year-old son Oliver was revising for exams in his bedroom at the front of their bungalow. When he saw the car heading straight for him, he fled from the room. Instead of stopping there, the car then went into forward gear and shot across the road for a second time, crashing through a garden wall at number 28, the home of Alan Calver and his wife Joan. Rampaging through their garden, the errant Toyota felled an 8-foot-tall conifer and smashed a mighty hole in their wooden fence. It then lurched into the garden of number 26, just missing the car of retired lecturer John Walpole which was sitting on his driveway. The Toyota ploughed through Mr Walpole's 3-foot-high wall and into widow Kathleen Jessup's front garden, narrowly missing her Rover car. It then smashed through the wall on the other side of her garden and went into number 22 – the home of Brian and Susan King. It crossed the corner of their garden and emerged through their front wall before veering across the road for a third time and crashing through the front wall at number 44 – the home of Thelma Mills who was away in Germany. The car finally stopped when it crossed her flowerbeds and demolished her smart front porch.

Mrs Millican, who had lived in the close for 39 years, was reported as being "comfortable" in hospital. Her husband, who escaped with cuts and bruises, said: "She is very embarrassed and is worried that she might have upset all the neighbours. Not learning to drive is one of the biggest regrets of her life. A policeman asked her if she had been drinking and she said: 'Yes, a cup of coffee.'"

Jokey Japanese

Setting off to school one morning, a Japanese girl sent her father a jokey e-mail: "I'll contact you if the bus I'm riding on is hijacked." But he only read the last part of the message which said "the bus I'm riding on is hijacked" and, in a panic, instigated a massive police hunt to track down the bus.

Kiwi heavies

Twenty-eight members of a New Zealand weight-watchers club suffered the indignity of having their bus sink up to its wheels in a tarred car park when they returned to the vehicle following a day out in the sun.

William Huskisson: A PR Nightmare

When a company unveils a new food processor, just about the worst possible scenario is for the managing director to slice off the top of his finger while demonstrating the product's safety features to the world's press. Similarly when the world's first passenger railway was launched in 1830 amid widespread fears for public welfare, the worst thing that could have happened was for the local MP and champion of the project to be run over and killed by the flagship steam engine at the opening ceremony. Yet sadly that is precisely the fate which befell distinguished British politician William Huskisson at the grand opening of the Liverpool to Manchester Railway on 15 September 1830. It was the ultimate PR nightmare.

At the turn of the nineteenth century goods such as coal were generally transported around Britain via the newly-constructed network of canals. The canals were considerably cheaper than shipment by road. To carry coal by road from Liverpool to Manchester, for example, cost 40 shillings a ton but the development of canals caused the price of coal in Manchester to fall by half. Nevertheless canals still charged what appeared to manufacturers to be an exorbitant amount to transport goods, and they were also pitifully slow. So quicker, more economical methods were constantly being sought, many based upon James Watt's invention of the steam engine.

Cornish engineer Richard Trevithick produced a steam engine which ran on rails in 1804, but it was left to George Stephenson, a miner's son from Newcastle, to develop the railway as a viable alternative to the canal. Stephenson built his first steam locomotive in 1814 and nine years later was asked to build the world's first railway, from Stockton to Darlington. It opened in 1825 and carried coal rather than people – the British public saw no future in hauling passengers by rail. A coach and horses could attain speeds of 15 mph on the roads; these coal-bearing locomotives could only manage between 6 and 8 mph. And who wanted to travel on something that was noisy, dirty and smelly? There was nothing noisy, dirty and smelly about a horse . . . unless, of course, you happened to be standing at the wrong end.

The Stockton to Darlington venture may not have fired the enthusiasm of prospective passengers, but it proved a resounding success for local businessmen, so much so that in the year it opened a second railway was mooted, between Liverpool and Manchester. The merchants of both cities were looking to break the monopoly of canals, and Liverpool in particular thought that a railway leading into the heartland of Lancashire would boost its sea trade enormously. A letter to the Board of Trade in favour of the line stated "that the formation of the projected railways between Liverpool and Manchester promises to afford means of conveyance for agricultural produce and manufactures to the interior of the North of England hitherto unparalleled for cheapness and despatch; and of supplying the most populous inland town in that part of the Kingdom (Manchester) with the necessaries of life, disburthened of a large proportion of the present charge of transport." In other words, it would be cheap and quick. The President of the Board of Trade was William Huskisson, Tory MP for Liverpool, and one of the most astute financial brains of his day. With Huskisson backing the project enthusiastically, the new railway was given the go-ahead in 1826. And this time George Stephenson had more ambitious plans. He wanted the line to carry passengers and was designing a locomotive which could speed them through the countryside at an unthinkable 30 mph. Appropriately, he planned to call his wonder locomotive the *Rocket*.

The opening of the Liverpool to Manchester Railway was an eagerly-awaited event. Dignitaries including the Prime Minister, the

Duke of Wellington, and the Home Secretary, Sir Robert Peel, were in attendance and crowds flocked from all over the country to line the entire length of the route. It was estimated that there were as many as 50,000 people at Crown Street Station in Liverpool to wave the trains away. There were eight trains in all with 33 carriages carrying over 1,000 passengers between them. There were bands and bunting, and much gaiety. At the head of proceedings was the locomotive *Northumbrian* which pulled a splendidly ornate VIP coach whose thirty-something passengers included the aforementioned political giants and William Huskisson. For this special occasion, both tracks were ferrying trains in the same direction. The Duke of Wellington's train was travelling towards Manchester on the southern line, and the other seven trains, of which the *Rocket* was third in the procession, rode on the northern track.

At first everything went according to plan. The trains set off amid wild scenes of jubilation and by noon had reached the Sankey Viaduct below which even the ships on the canal stopped to watch the magnificent locomotives pass by. At Parkside, some 17 miles from Liverpool and the approximate half-way point on the line, the engines were going to stop to take on water. The Duke's train was to stop first with the other seven overtaking it on the adjacent line, thereby allowing the VIPs to review all of the locomotives as they passed. The Duke's party were requested to stay on board at Parkside but a number, among them William Huskisson, decided to get out and stretch their legs. Having taken on water, the *Phoenix* and *North Star* locomotives steamed past the stationary *Northumbrian*. Next in line was the famous *Rocket*, driven by Joseph Locke. At 60, Huskisson was very much one of the elder statesmen of British politics and his health had never been the same since catching a chill at King George IV's funeral earlier in the year, an illness which had left him slightly paralysed down one side. Consequently he was not quite as nimble on his feet as some of his younger colleagues. This particular section of the railway was extremely narrow with barely enough space for the double track. There was certainly no standing room at either side so Huskisson and his friends were obliged to mill around on the other track. In their defence, it has to be said that at this early stage in railway history they were probably unaware of the potential dangers of steam locomotives. According to eye-witnesses, Huskisson was lingering outside the Duke of Wellington's carriage, the door of which was open, the Duke having obeyed the request to remain inside. Seeing others re-entering the carriage, Wellington said to Huskisson: "Well, we seem to be preparing to go on – I think you had better get in." As Wellington spoke, the *Rocket*, on its way back from watering, was seen approaching at great speed on the adjacent track, some 200 yards away. Confused and infirm, Huskisson appeared frozen to the spot. Wellington shouted out: "Huskisson! Do get to your place! For God's sake get to your place!" Huskisson reached out for the door but slipped while trying to climb into the state carriage and fell back. The passing *Rocket* knocked him down and the wheels ran over his left leg. With a badly mangled thigh, the old man wailed: "I have met my death."

Huskisson was carried into the band wagon – the musicians and their instruments making a hasty evacuation – and two doctors from Liverpool stemmed the flow of blood with a tourniquet. George Stephenson attached the *Northumbrian* to the coach and drove the patient personally to a track-side vicarage at Eccles, attaining unprecedented speeds of 36 mph on the way. There, surgeons from Manchester fought valiantly to save Huskisson's life.

Wellington and Peel were so shaken by the accident that they wanted to return to Liverpool, but were told by a local JP that the crowd awaiting the arrival of the trains at Manchester was so large that civil unrest was feared if the journey was not completed. So, with heavy hearts, they agreed that the show must go on. At a celebration dinner that evening, only 47 of the 230 invited guests turned up. They drank to Huskisson's health but it was to no avail. He died between 9 and 10 o'clock that evening. Ironically his last view from the vicarage was of the railway which he had championed and which had prematurely ended his life.

One correspondent wrote of the day's festivities with commendable understatement: "A terrible damper was thrown upon the proceedings by an accident that occurred to poor Mr Huskisson which has terminated in his death." Yes, it must have been a bit of a blow – not least to the directors of the railway who were worried in case the mishap shattered public confidence in the new form of transport. Already people thought that travelling at speeds as great as 30 mph might cause mental disorders, suffocation (since the speed might suck the air from their lungs) or, more dramatically still, their heads might blow off. This unhappy occurrence might just confirm their worst fears.

Huskisson was buried nine days later in Liverpool in front of 15,000 mourners. Shops in the city were closed for the funeral. Luckily as far as the railway was concerned, his misfortune proved to be an isolated incident and the steam locomotive went from strength to strength. There were no reports of headless passengers wandering around the Lancashire countryside, and no more MPs perished beneath engine wheels. Railways the world over would recover from their inauspicious beginnings.

Dallas motel

A woman in Dallas, Texas, investigated a noise in her hotel bedroom and found a car on her bed. The car had missed a turn in a multi-storey parking building next door, leaped a six-foot gap and crashed through the wall of the third-floor bedroom.

Spruce Goose: The Flying Lumberyard

Aviator and Hollywood producer Howard Hughes was no stranger to eccentricity. This is the man who was so obsessed with hygiene that nobody else, not even his wife, was permitted to touch his food; who was so terrified of germs that any visitors had to stand in a chalk square drawn outside the house for inspection before being allowed anywhere near the front door; who was so appalled at contact that his own doctor could only "examine" him from the other side of the room; who became a recluse, stored all of his urine in giant containers, ate nothing but ice cream for weeks on end, and had his hair and nails cut just twice in ten years. To put it mildly, Howard Hughes was barking mad.

It should therefore come as no surprise that Hughes' most famous foray into the field of aircraft design should result in a monstrous creation which cost millions of dollars, took five years to build and flew just one mile in its lifetime.

In the early 1940s Hughes was an American hero. An accomplished pilot, he was one of the first men to fly around the world single-handed. Eventually his thoughts – and those of his country – turned towards the war. The US government was becoming increasingly concerned by the number of cargo liners, used to ferry American troops and supplies across the Atlantic to the war in Europe, that were falling victim to German submarines. These ships were little more than sitting ducks so, in their place, the government proposed the construction of a fleet of flying boats which could transport men and supplies above, and therefore safe from, the Nazi U-boats.

On 20 July 1942 Hughes received a confidential tip-off from a source in the White House that a multi-million dollar contract authorizing the building of the flying boats had just been awarded to metal magnate Henry Kaiser. Hughes was particularly interested to learn that the flying boats were to be made from wood, an area in which he had already worked. So he suggested to Kaiser that they join forces. Hughes and his team worked on a design and within months he and Kaiser were given $18,000,000 by the War Production Board to construct a fleet of seaplanes. The prototype was to be the largest aircraft ever considered, let alone built, equipped with eight engines, a wing span longer than a football field, and a hull taller than a three-storey building. It would be called the HK-1 (Hughes-Kaiser 1), and Hughes promised to have the first one operational inside a year.

It quickly became apparent that Hughes' assessment was recklessly optimistic. The design, using non-essential materials, mainly birch wood, was dogged by incompetence, not the least of which was that it was too heavy to fly. This was not thought to be a useful trait for an aircraft. As one obstacle was cleared it was quickly replaced with another, and the costs escalated. The government began to lose patience with Hughes and the Spruce Goose, as the flying boat was nicknamed in honour of its timber frame. Germany and Japan were defeated, the war was over, but still the Spruce Goose was nowhere near completion.

Since there was now no need for a troop carrier, Washington

pulled the plug on it in 1946. Kaiser also withdrew and the plane was re-named the H-4 Hercules. A change of name did not bring about a change in fortune, but Hughes and his designers plodded on. To salvage what remained of his reputation, he was determined to get the Spruce Goose airborne, no matter how long it took or how much it cost.

In the meantime he was hauled before a Senate committee to explain why he had wasted so much government money on such a flawed project. One senator disparagingly referred to the plane as a "flying lumberyard." Hughes was accused of war profiteering, but was acquitted and emerged to declare: "If the Hercules won't fly, I will leave the United States for good." He was advised to start searching for his passport.

The first step towards getting the Spruce Goose airborne was to find some water, and so the huge hull and the two wing sections made the 26-mile journey from Hughes's Culver City plant to Long Beach's Terminal Island. It cost Hughes $60,000 to move the vast load and the whole exercise involved over 2,000 people and 23 separate organizations. Traffic had to be re-routed, and bridges and roads were checked for strength. It wasn't only the weight that was a problem. More than 3,000 trees had to be trimmed by parks departments and some 2,300 utility wires were temporarily taken down just so that the monster plane could pass by. It may have been a logistical headache but it provided a rare treat for local schoolchildren who were allowed to skip lessons to watch the Hercules as it lumbered through California. When it finally reached Long Beach, it was dismantled and lowered into dry dock. It may have moved, but it still hadn't flown.

Privately, Hughes had set himself a target of getting the Hercules airborne by the end of 1947. Considering that he had originally promised to deliver it by 1943, he wasn't being unduly hard on himself. On the morning of 2 November 1947 he finally unveiled his colossal creation at Long Beach. Hundreds of pleasure craft bobbed around in the harbour, and the waterfront was lined with spectators gazing in wonderment at the 320-foot wing span. Hughes had insisted that this was to be nothing more than a taxi test across the water, that the maiden flight would not take place until the following spring, but the truth of the matter was that he was having difficulty finding a pilot. He was prepared to offer $1 million to anyone brave enough to pilot it, but there had been no takers. So that morning, wearing his familiar fedora, Hughes himself took the controls on two test runs across the choppy waters. At the end of the second and supposedly final run, all of the reporters on board bar one left to file their stories. So when Hughes decided to make a third run, only radio reporter Jim McNamara was on board to describe the scene. Along with those watching from the shore, McNamara got the shock of his life when Hughes suddenly hauled the 400,000-pound craft into the air. At an altitude of just 70 feet, the Spruce Goose flew for about a mile before belly-flopping back into the water. Its first and last flight lasted less than one minute.

On his return to land, Hughes was mobbed by the crowds who were curiously impressed by what they had witnessed. He beamed triumphantly: "Well, the airplane seems to be fairly successful."

Hughes may have seen it that way, but the US government certainly didn't. Unwieldy, impractical and obsolete before its time, the Spruce Goose never flew again. Instead it became a major tourist attraction, first at Long Beach and latterly in Oregon. And it still divides the nation. Many see it as a brave engineering feat – at worst, a heroic failure; but to others it was just a white elephant . . . except that an elephant would have had a better chance of flying than the Spruce Goose.

Wrong-Way Corrigan: Blunder or Blarney?

Pilot Douglas Corrigan took off from a Brooklyn airfield on 17 July 1938 and touched down safely 28 hours later at Baldonnel Airport, Dublin. The trouble was, he was aiming for Los Angeles. But was his unscheduled transatlantic flight, which he attributed to compass failure, the biggest aviation blunder of all time, or was it really part of a cunning plan?

Born in Texas in 1907, Corrigan first went up in a plane at the age of 20. It cost him $2.50 for the privilege and lasted just ten minutes, but it was enough to get him hooked on flying. He gained employment working on planes in San Diego and that led to a job as a welder on the *Spirit of St Louis*, the plane in which Charles Lindbergh would become the first person to fly solo nonstop across the Atlantic in 1927. Lindbergh's achievement inspired Corrigan to emulate the feat, and in 1932 he bought a battered single-engine 1929 Curtis-Robin off a scrapheap for $310. He told anyone who would listen that he intended to fly the Atlantic, just like Lindbergh, but few took him seriously.

Day and night Corrigan worked on the plane, modifying it for long-distance flight, but it still looked like a heap of junk.

In July 1938, the intrepid Corrigan flew nonstop from California to Floyd Bennett Airfield in New York. He then boldly announced that his next port of call would be Ireland, but the aviation authorities refused to give him permission to fly the Atlantic in something they considered to be an old rust bucket. They had a point, for his plane had no radio, no beacon finder or anything remotely resembling a safety device. It was an accident waiting to happen. Corrigan appeared to take the rejection of his plan stoically and simply said that he would fly back to California instead.

At dawn on 17 July before a handful of onlookers, Corrigan prepared to take off, supposedly bound for California. The little plane was laden down with so many cans of fuel that he could hardly see out of the cockpit window and had quite a struggle to get airborne at all. Those on the ground were puzzled when, shortly after take-off, he appeared to do a 180-degree turn, moments before vanishing into dense fog. Had he lost his bearings? If so, with no radio on board, there was no way he could be contacted.

The rickety old plane rattled through another 24 hours of thick fog above the Atlantic, defying most of the laws of aeronautics. At one point Corrigan pushed a broom handle out of the window to remove ice that had formed on the wings. And when gasoline from the leaky tank began to slosh around on the floor, he allowed it to drain away by poking a hole through the plane's wooden body with a screwdriver! Needless to say, he had no fuel gauge, so he had no idea how much fuel he had left.

He was not heard of again until the morning of 18 July when he stepped out of his plane in Dublin. "Just got in from New York," he announced, bewildered. "Where am I?" When the Irish authorities told him that he was in Dublin, Corrigan exclaimed: "Oh my God! In the darkness I must have followed the wrong end of the compass needle!"

Even by Irish standards, an accidental crossing of the Atlantic was an unusual event and they made a tremendous fuss of their unexpected visitor, treating him like one of their own. Corrigan repeated that he had meant to fly to California, but must somehow have got turned around at the start of the flight and that, in the thick fog, his compass had either malfunctioned or he had simply misread it. To the Irish, both explanations seemed entirely plausible.

The American authorities were less convinced and suspended Corrigan's licence for five days – the precise length of time it took him to return to New York by ship. He arrived home to a hero's welcome, and a ticker tape parade through the streets of New York which was more spectacular than the one the city had given Lindbergh eleven years earlier. The American nation took the bemused pilot to their hearts and christened him "Wrong-Way Corrigan." What it may have lacked in invention, the sobriquet made up for in accuracy.

Corrigan became a test pilot during the Second World War and played himself in the film of his story, *The Flying Irishman*. To all inquirers, he insisted that his flight to Dublin had been an accident, even when sceptics made him an honorary member of the Liars' Club of America.

After the excitement had died down, he retired to lead a quiet life as an orange grower in California. Then in 1988, when he was 81, his old Curtis-Robin was dusted off and taken out of storage to be displayed at an airshow. The hitherto reclusive Corrigan suddenly became so enthusiastic that aviation authorities put a special guard on the plane, just in case he tried to take to the skies again.

Douglas Corrigan died in 1995, and in doing so took the real story of his transatlantic flight with him to the grave. Had it been a deliberate act in protest at the ban imposed on him, or was he simply a bungling pilot who flew east instead of west? Whatever the truth, the legend of Wrong-Way Corrigan still has plenty of mileage left in it.

Home rescue

A French pilot sparked a full-scale rescue operation after accidentally setting off a distress beacon which he had taken home. After the emergency signal had been detected by satellite, two helicopter crews spent six hours searching for the "aircraft" in distress and were joined in their quest by a gaggle of radio hams. The signal was finally traced to the pilot's home between Valence and Romans.

Sailor, Beware!

A self-taught sailor with poor eyesight and even poorer navigational skills had to be rescued by coastguards on a dozen occasions in just over a year after creating the sort of terror at sea not witnessed since *Jaws*. His uncanny ability to get lost, miss harbour entrances or run into inanimate objects made Eric Abbott, a 57-year-old former house-painter, the scourge of rescue services from Liverpool to Belfast.

During that period the myopic mariner's incompetence cost the Royal National Lifeboat Institution and coastguards an estimated £35,000. One experienced lifeboatman complained: "We've never seen anyone as bad as this. If he had been on the road, he would have been disqualified by now."

Mr Abbott, who built his 24-foot yacht, *Plus VAT*, at his home in Northwich, Cheshire, said he went to sea in order "to find himself." Unfortunately, more often than not, he tended to lose himself.

His first adventure occurred on 23 July 1999 when Liverpool Coastguard logged his departure from the city as "not without mishap." Within two days of setting out he twice had to be towed to safety by Rhyl lifeboatmen after getting into difficulties. Then on 23 April 2000 he told Holyhead Coastguard that he couldn't read his chart and was lost. An inshore rescue boat towed him to Amlwch on Anglesey. Later that same day he managed to run aground outside the harbour.

On 5 June 2000, he contrived to lose the Isle of Man. To help him find it, Manx Coastguard switched on bright lights and a lifeboat towed him in. The following day, after hearing that Mr Abbott had been at sea for 17 hours bound for Strangford Lough, Northern Ireland, the same coastguards sent a lifeboat to take him from his yacht. On 18 June he told Belfast Coastguard that he didn't know where he was, as a result of which they towed him to Portaferry at the southern end of the lough. One of the coastguards there remembered that "he said he did not know how to use his compass."

Continuing to wreak havoc in Ireland, Mr Abbott sent a mayday call to coastguards on 8 July to say that he was taking in water in the lough. He was towed to a nearby yacht club. The lifeboat coxswain wrote in his log: "The owner appeared to lack any ability whatsoever."

On 18 July, Mr Abbott informed Liverpool Coastguard that he was lost. He was towed to Portaferry again. Two days later, he reported to Dublin Coastguard that he was unsure of his position, and was towed by lifeboat to Balbriggan.

Returning to North Wales from Howth, near Dublin, on 8 August, he was nearing the end of a trouble-free,15-hour voyage when he started to feel confused and lost. He told Holyhead Coastguard that he couldn't find Amlwch harbour and was towed in by the same lifeboatmen who had rescued him just four months previously. They were not amused.

At 2 a.m. on 10 August, Mr Abbott set off on the relatively simple 35-mile voyage along the coast to Rhyl – his final voyage of the season before resting up for the winter. This time he was just 100 yards from the safety of Rhyl harbour when he ran aground on a sandbank after going round the wrong side of a marker post. A coastguard at Rhyl, who saw the *Plus VAT* heading for trouble, urged Mr Abbott by radio to make a left turn, but he failed to do so and missed the harbour entrance channel by 30 yards. Rhyl lifeboat coxswain Pete Robinson said: "We were getting ready for our flag day when he came into view. We had been warned he was on his way. Getting into harbour is fairly elementary, but you have to research it first. You can't just feel your way in. Once he grounded, we had to go out because he could have turned broadside-on to a breaking sea, which could have swamped the boat and washed him out of it. We towed him to a safe mooring and advised him to get some basic instruction in navigation and boat handling before putting to sea again. We gave him the same advice when we towed him in last year."

But Mr Abbott's run of bad luck didn't end there. That night he was moving his boat in Rhyl Yacht Club when he fouled the mooring chain of another vessel. It meant yet another trip for the lifeboat crew – to help him move to a different berth.

Mr Abbott, whose wife wisely refuses to join him on the boat, insists: "I know my limits and err on the side of caution. I'm a self-taught sailor with no formal training but I was in the Scouts for several years. I have a very keen interest in boating but I am just not sure about the sea. There is such a vastness out there."

Travel Chaos

Pilot prang

An airplane rolled down the runway, crashed into a fence and ploughed into an outbuilding, causing an estimated £10,000 worth of damage, after the pilot had jumped out of the cockpit to talk to a friend. Pilot Eddie Cannon-Jones had put on the Cessna 210's parking brake at Auckland's Ardmore Airport, leaving the engine and propeller ticking over, before hopping out to chat to a colleague. But to his horror, the plane began rumbling away along the tarmac. As Mr Cannon-Jones turned to stop the plane, he pulled a hamstring and fell to the ground, and was thus powerless to prevent the destruction which unfolded before his eyes.

Lost driver

A rail driver who abandoned his locomotive to go and buy cigarettes became lost on the way back and had to ask for directions to his train. The driver was in charge of a 36-wagon coal train travelling from Liverpool to Ironbridge Power Station near Telford, Shropshire, in March 2001. Five miles from his destination, he was told to wait at signals in a queue of trains. Thinking the delay would be a long one, he decided to walk the one-and-a-half miles into the centre of Telford to buy some cigarettes. But on the return journey, he became lost in a maze of shopping arcades and had to phone a friend to find the way back to his train. In the meantime, signallers had been trying to contact him to tell him that it was safe for his train to proceed. Instead they found his cab empty with the engine door wide open. A rail spokesman promised: "We are taking the matter very seriously."

Mr Bean the bus driver

On his second day as a Glasgow bus driver in November 2000, Barry Bean succeeded in getting hopelessly lost and wedging his bus under a low bridge. As he tried to release the vehicle, he crashed into a parked car, knocked down garden fences and hit a lamp-post. A passer-by remarked: “It was chaos, but we couldn’t keep our faces straight when the driver said his name was Mr Bean!”

Wilson’s Wey

Mrs Margaret Wilson was forced to abandon her driving test after finishing up in the middle of the River Wey at Guildford in Surrey. She had just turned sharply into the ominously-named Riverside Road when things started to take a turn for the worse. Mrs Wilson, who was driving her husband’s Hillman Hunter, said afterwards: “This was my fifth test and it had been going much better than the previous four. I’d just gone round the corner in first gear on full lock. I said to myself, ‘I’m too close to the edge,’ and then I must have put my foot on the accelerator instead of the brake because I went straight through the railings into the river. The car started to sink. I had my window open and got on to the seat and half out. The examiner opened his door and the water rushed in. Then he got out of the window.” Mrs Wilson and the examiner were sitting on top of the car when they were rescued by a passing motor-cruiser. The examiner was subsequently sent home “in a state of shock,” but, in accordance with procedure, he managed to hang on to his briefcase and clip-board during his climb to safety. A Ministry of Transport official commented: “We cannot say whether the lady passed or failed until the examiner makes his report.”

Rowboat Romeo

After a few drinks in the pubs of Felixstowe, Suffolk, jobless Graeme Bethell decided to pay his girlfriend a visit. The trouble was that he was on one side of the River Deben and she lived in Alderton, on the other side in the village. Going by road was clearly too far, but a rowing boat moored on the river bank proved a tempting proposition. Ignoring the fact that the 14-foot-long vessel had no oars, engine or sail and that he himself could not swim, the 28-year-old Romeo set off across the river in the hope that he would drift over to the opposite bank. Instead the boat drifted out to sea and he spent a terrifying night in the busy North Sea shipping lanes, praying that he wouldn't be crushed by a passing ferry en route for Scandinavia. He was finally towed back to Felixstowe the following morning by a fishing boat. "It was meant to be a bit of a romantic surprise to turn up and see her in a boat," said Mr Bethell, "but it all went wrong. On the way out of the river I clipped the edge of a jetty and thought I had holed the boat because I heard this hissing noise which sounded like water gushing in. It was only later that I discovered it was a bottle of Coke which had started hissing after its top was loosened. While I was at sea I saw a couple of ferries, a tanker and something that looked like a battleship. I did get quite close to them." Mr Bethell insisted on keeping his girlfriend's identity a secret. "We're still together but she is quite embarrassed about the whole episode."

Spectacular failure

A Canadian pensioner was aggrieved to fail his driving exam in 2001 after reversing through a window at the test centre. Under British Columbia law, motorists are required to re-take their test every two years once they reach 80, but the unnamed 83-year-old man spoilt his chances somewhat by pressing the accelerator instead of the brake. His wife, who was waiting inside the building, was taken to hospital with chest pains brought on by shock. And a woman motorist escaped with minor injuries when the man's car ripped her driver's-side door off as it careered backwards into the test centre. A police spokeswoman ventured that the pensioner had become confused at the wheel. Almost unnecessarily she added that he would not be getting his licence back.

Blown away

A helicopter blew over benches and put a student in hospital during a practice landing at Central Connecticut University for a forthcoming visit from President George W. Bush. Students were watching a nearby softball game when their bench was blown ten feet by gusts from the Marine Corps chopper. One suffered a cut head and was taken to hospital while three others suffered minor injuries. President Bush was visiting the university to promote education.

Road trip

In 1996, former traffic policeman William Alexander set out to drive the 15 miles from Hereford to Ross-on-Wye. He and his wife were found confused 36 hours later, after a 1,000-mile drive, going the wrong way down the M1 near Barnsley.

Bypass detour

An ambulance crew transferring a heart bypass patient to another hospital in June 2001 became hopelessly lost and took nearly five hours to complete what should have been a 90-minute journey. Allan Lowden, 59, who days earlier had undergone a quadruple bypass, was alarmed when he realized the ambulance taking him from Glasgow to Dumfries was travelling in completely the wrong direction. After a 150-mile detour, Mr Lowden alerted the crew and helped show them the right way as he lay in the back of the ambulance. His son Michael said: "My father heard the crew laughing and joking and saying they were lost. Naturally he wondered what was going on since it's a direct route from Glasgow to Dumfries."

Lost in . . . Spain

A stag night reveller ended up 1,500 miles from home when he fell asleep on a "booze cruise" and found himself in Spain. To celebrate Ray Cole's forthcoming wedding, his friends decided to book a round ferry trip from Portsmouth to France, but as the party returned to Portsmouth, one guest, Lee Wearn, nodded off in the ship's toilet. He failed to wake up when the ship docked and was still on board when it sailed again . . . for Bilbao.

Gunshot mechanic

Repairing a car can be a costly business, as 20-year-old Joseph Aaron of Wesley Chapel, Florida, found in 1995. Aaron needed to bore a hole in the exhaust pipe, but was unable to find a drill. In a flash of inspiration he decided to shoot a hole instead and ended up being taken to hospital with fragments of bullet lodged in his leg.

The greatest queen

The British liner the *Queen Mary*, launched in 1934, would been called the *Queen Victoria* but for a bizarre misunderstanding. Prior to the launch, Sir Thomas Royden, a director of shipbuilders Cunard, met King George V to obtain permission to call the new liner *Queen Victoria*. Unfortunately Royden made his request in rather flowery language, asking whether the vessel could be named "after the greatest Queen this country has ever known." The King misunderstood and, visibly moved, answered: "That is the greatest compliment ever paid to my wife. I shall ask her." The King's wife, Queen Mary, readily assented, leaving Cunard with little option but to revise its plans.

Ferrari fiasco

A parking valet at a plush California hotel couldn't resist taking a guest's gleaming $175,000 Ferrari for a spin round the block. Ten yards from the hotel he crashed into a palm tree and wrecked the car.

From Claggan to Laggan

The Automobile Association sent one of its mechanics on a 300-mile round trip requiring an overnight hotel stay because of a mix-up over place names. An AA member called for assistance just outside Laggan, near the Scottish town of Fort William, but a control centre operator misheard it as Claggan, near the Isle of Mull, and sent a mechanic from there. When the mistake came to light, the mechanic had to catch a ferry from Mull to Oban, drive on to Fort William and then tow the stranded driver 110 miles to his home in Clackmannanshire. Due to the long journey, he had to stay overnight in a hotel. The car's fault was subsequently repaired at a Stirling garage for £12.

Clearly unacceptable

A high-speed, 130-mile train journey from London to Nottingham, which is scheduled to take under two hours, lasted an agonizing nine hours for 30 irate passengers on 27 November 2000 – longer than it takes to fly from London to Moscow and back. The 10 p.m. Midland Mainline service from London St Pancras set off 18 minutes late following problems with one of the power cars, but that was nothing to the delay which awaited the passengers south of Bedford where a power failure left them stranded for over four hours. When that little difficulty was eventually rectified, the train could only crawl towards Kettering because of speed restrictions on the line. The bleary-eyed travellers pulled in at Kettering shortly after 3.30 a.m., but by then the line ahead had been closed for engineering work so they were told that they would have to get off and board a bus for Nottingham. The unheated bus finally made it to Nottingham at 7 a.m. where the hardy souls had a further 30-minute wait for taxis to take them home despite being promised by Midland Mainline that taxis would be ready and waiting. A company spokesman admitted that the standard of journey offered on this occasion had been "clearly unacceptable."

When in Wales . . .

Motorists in Bristol were puzzled and confused to see roadwork diversion signs in Welsh. The contractors who had installed them had thought they were in Wales.

The long U-turn

Driving along a French motorway while on holiday, Vivienne Vanderwalt-Hudson from Sheerness in Kent missed her turning and panicked when she was unable to find another. She ended up driving 5,000 miles across the Pyrenees, through Spain to Gibraltar before finally finding a turning place. She said afterwards: "I kept hoping there would be a gap in the road but there wasn't, so I decided to keep going."

Rescuers rescued

A party of lifeboat men from Harwich in Essex, who hired a boat to take their families on a river trip, ran aground on mud flats. They had to be rescued by their own lifeboat manned by a reserve crew.

Turnpike interruption

Fire trucks speeding down the Massachusetts Turnpike, with sirens blaring and lights flashing, to put out a brush fire around the town of Westfield were delayed for several minutes when a toll collector insisted on charging each driver. A turnpike spokesman later said that the collector had been disciplined.

What you don't know can't hurt you

When petrol rationing swept through Britain in the autumn of 2000, Derby taxi driver Saqib Bashir thought he had the perfect solution. Desperate to keep his business going, he bought 80 litres of fuel and stored it in his terraced house. Unfortunately, in what magistrates later described as a "gross act of stupidity", he chose to keep some of it in a plastic dustbin. The petrol melted the plastic, leaked into the house and caused most of the street to be evacuated. The operation and resulting clean-up cost over £100,000 and the house was only declared safe five months later. Bashir told a trading standards officer: "I didn't know petrol was highly flammable."

Caronia carry-on

A shipmate who decided to honour the vessel by painting her name on a Norwegian mountain completely missed the boat and was only re-united with his fellow crew members after a frantic chase by aircraft, bus, and steamer. Assistant steward McNulty from Southampton was working on the liner *Caronia*, and when the ship stopped in a Norwegian fjord, he hopped ashore, climbed the 1,500-foot-high Merok mountain and painted the *Caronia*'s name in large white letters. But in his haste to rejoin the liner, he slipped on the way down and fell 20 feet. In desperation, he waved his shirt at the ship to try and attract attention. An officer on the bridge spotted the flapping garment and alerted a rescue team, but not before the ship had set sail. The red-faced McNulty was put on a seaplane but the *Caronia* was travelling too fast for him to land nearby, so he was flown to the nearest town. From there he caught a bus and then a steamer to Bergen where he finally met up with his ship . . . and an angry captain.

An easy mistake to make

A Florida teenager demolished the front window of Euclid's post office when she crashed her car on the morning of her driving test. Indira Bachoo from St Petersburg made the mistake of confusing the brake with the accelerator. Charged with careless driving, Ms Bachoo announced that her test had been postponed.

Sixteen-minute shop

Due to a highly imaginative bus timetable for 2001, villagers from Wilsford in Lincolnshire were left with just 16 minutes to do their Saturday shopping in the town of Grantham. The Lincolnshire Road Car bus, the only service of the day on the eight-mile route, dropped them off in Grantham at 1.49 p.m. and started out on the return journey at 2.05 p.m. prompt. The penalty for missing the bus was an £11 taxi fare. Wilsford Parish Council chairman Robert Lewis complained: "I'm 68 and I can't go running round the shops in a quarter of an hour at my age." The bus company said that the service was not designed to allow people to go shopping.

Red bus, red face

Taking delivery of the first £50,000 bus in a brand new fleet of vehicles, a London Transport engineer went out on a test run and promptly tried to drive the 20-foot-high double-decker under a 13-foot bridge. He succeeded in slicing off most of the upper deck, leaving him with a face as red as his bus.

Listen up, Bret!
Mrs Christine Lauritzen of Tacoma, Washington, filed a lawsuit against her husband Bret for failing to heed her map-reading. She claimed that because he had ignored her directions on a visit to Miami, they had found themselves in a rough neighbourhood where they were subjected to a robbery, in the course of which she sustained an arm injury. So she sued her husband for the negligence that subjected her to injury.

Lucky coincidence
A banned driver with no insurance crashed his car into a £50,000 Jaguar carrying Metropolitan Police chief Sir John Stevens in London in 2001.

Train hits boat

The only known collision between a boat and a train took place in February 1913 on the Memphis branch of the Louisville and Nashville Railroad. The area was severely flooded at the time and in the dark a freight train collided with the boat *Lochie S* which was sailing above the tracks at Cumberland, Texas. Nobody was injured and liability for the damage was never settled.

Tight fit

Drivers in Marlborough, Wiltshire, were put in a tight spot in May 2001 after workmen repainting 27 parking bays in the town's High Street made the spaces too narrow. Contractors had been ordered to mark the spaces to a width of 2.26 metres, but instead they made each one over half a metre too small. One motorist complained: "It was ridiculous. I tried to get in three times. Each time I thought it was me getting it wrong. But every time I got in I couldn't open my doors to get out. Shoppers in the street were laughing at me."

Back to school for Schling

Czech transport minister Jaromir Schling, a former driving instructor, failed the written part of the national driving test that he himself had introduced to the country. He was unsure of the meaning of several road signs and got a number of insurance questions wrong. Afterwards he admitted: "I'm not too happy about the result."

Whisky wind-up

To combat the theft of miniature bottles of whisky from one of their aircraft in 1978, Pan-Am security staff set a trap by wiring up a cuckoo clock inside the drinks cabinet. Unfortunately they neglected to tell the plane's crew with the result that a stewardess, on hearing the ticking, thought it was a bomb. She quickly alerted the pilot, and the Boeing 727 was forced to make an emergency landing at Berlin. The cost of the emergency landing came to £6,500; the miniature bottles of whisky cost 17p each.

Shelter but no bus

A top-of-the-range, Victorian-effect bus shelter, costing £7,500, was erected at Swanley in Kent . . . despite the fact that buses had stopped using the route five years earlier. Swanley Town Council, who approved the building of the new shelter to replace one which had been demolished, admitted: "There seems to have been a lack of communication. I'm afraid if anybody actually tries to use the shelter, they will have a very long wait for a bus."

Way to go

A Toronto woman talking on her mobile phone drove into the back of a police car . . . minutes after getting a speeding ticket from its driver.

Lost train

Commuters on an InterCity 125 train from Bristol to Swansea in 1997 faced a 90-minute detour after the driver got lost. Owing to a signalling mix-up, he accidentally turned off the main London to South Wales line east of Neath and on to a quiet country track. After half an hour of driving through unfamiliar scenery, he announced to passengers that he hadn't a clue where he was. He pulled into a siding and then waited for a relief driver to arrive and get the train back on track. One passenger sighed: "I've never known anything like it. How on earth can a train driver get lost?"

Relax!

While on a flight from Zurich to Gatwick in 1991, passengers listened in horror as a stewardess was heard to declare over the tannoy in measured tones that the plane was about to ditch in the sea. A number of passengers had already donned their inflatable life jackets and were hunched in the brace position preparing for the moment of impact when a few moments later the captain came on to apologize. The plane was not in trouble at all. "We meant to tell you we were about to serve the duty frees," he said jauntily. "Someone pressed the wrong pre-recorded tape button."

Minimum voyage

An Essex man postponed his dinghy voyage around the coast of Britain after crashing a few minutes into his journey. Stuart Hill, 58, from Manningtree, was planning to travel 2,000 miles in 20 days in a 14-foot craft called *Maximum Exposure*, but as he set sail on the River Stour, part of the boat's mechanism jammed and he hit another boat moored on the riverside. It was not the first setback Mr Hill had encountered on the challenge. He was poisoned by resin fumes as he worked on his boat which capsized on its maiden voyage.

Dangerous cargo

On the night of 25 November 1875, the *Royal Adelaide*, an iron sailing ship bound from London to Sydney, was driven ashore on Chesil Beach, Dorset. The impact caused her to break up and hundreds of cases of spirits were washed from her holds on to the shore. Six of the 67 passengers drowned in the wreck but there were greater casualties among the thousands of onlookers, 20 of whom were dead by the morning after drinking too much of the washed-up cargo.

Curiosity killed the cat

Husband and wife Paul and Bonnie Stiller from Andover Township, New Jersey, were taken to hospital after being injured by a quarter-stick of dynamite which exploded in their car. The bored couple were driving around at 2 a.m. in the morning when they decided to light the dynamite and throw it out of the car window to see what would happen. Unfortunately they forgot that the window was closed . . .

Dedicated mechanic

A woman told Southend police that she had seen a car being driven at Leigh-on-Sea with what appeared to be a body protruding from the open boot. Police found the car – with two legs sticking out of the back. They belonged to a garage mechanic trying to trace a noise which was irritating the driver.

Martinez . . . and keep them coming!

In the summer of 1953, 64-year-old Juan Martinez, who spoke only Spanish, was planning to travel from New York to his home in Puerto Rico. At the airport it was found that his boarding ticket bore no flight number so he was mistakenly shuffled on to a flight for Frankfurt in Germany. Asked by a stewardess, who spoke only English, whether he would like a drink, he answered with his name, Martinez, and was rewarded with a succession of Martinis. It was not until the plane stopped at Gander,

Newfoundland, and Martinez thought it was rather cool for the Caribbean in July that he realized he was on the wrong flight. Admitting its blunder, the airline paid for an overnight stay in Gander before sending him back to New York on another flight and then on to San Juan.

Watered down

Drivers who filled up at an Irish petrol station were alarmed to find that their cars spluttered to a halt a little way down the road. Motoring organizations investigating the spate of break-downs in Lurgan, County Armagh, quickly discovered the cause – the drivers had been filling their tanks with four-star water. The garage had just taken delivery from a tanker which had recently been cleaned out with water. Unfortunately before the tanker set off on its rounds, nobody had remembered to empty it and fill it with petrol instead.

Cycle path to nowhere

The world's shortest cycle path was unveiled in Dudley, West Midlands, in 2001. Immaculately marked, the two-way path, laid out at a cost of £2,000, ran for just 15 yards between two solid wooden fences. "It's a bit mystifying really," said an Automobile Association spokesman. "What on earth do you do once you have cycled the 15 yards and come to the end? Dismount and climb over the fence?" Dudley Metropolitan Council explained that the path was a prototype which could lead to greater things although there were no plans to extend it in the near future.

Hapless handler

An airport luggage handler made an unscheduled flight from Dallas to Mexico in 2001 after accidentally locking himself in the plane's cargo hold. The hapless handler banged on the walls of the plane as it prepared for take-off but he wasn't found until it landed in Puerto Vallenta. Crew members reported hearing a knocking sound in Dallas, but had been unable to trace the source.

One for the road

A Romanian man was so nervous before taking his driving test in November 2000 that he drank half a bottle of vodka to calm his nerves, as a result of which he failed the test before even starting the engine. A centre spokesman said: "We couldn't report him for drunken driving because he didn't go anywhere."

Ditched again

An unlucky retired police officer managed to crash and end up in the same ditch twice in one day. Carolann Henderson, 44, was driving her Ford Escort on the morning of 15 June 2000 when it skidded on the slippery road at Hoton in Leicestershire and finished up in a 20-foot ditch. She was taken to Nottingham's Queen's Medical Centre with minor bruising before being collected by her brother Colin that afternoon. He was driving her home when a car travelling in the opposite direction lost control at Hoton, skidded into them and pushed them into the very ditch from which she had been rescued a few hours earlier. She remarked ruefully: "Who says lightning doesn't strike twice?"

First for Belgian motorways

A Belgian motorway was brought to a standstill when a hot air balloon carrying ten passengers landed on the carriageway near Ghent. It had been intended to land the balloon in a nearby park but the plans were changed after that became flooded. "We are used to seeing strange things on Belgian motorways," said one driver, "but a hot air balloon is a first."

Margate mystery

In 1971 Mr and Mrs William Farmer of Margate, Kent, took a summer holiday trip to Wales. At the start of the week they signed up for a mystery tour organized by British Rail . . . which promptly took them straight back to Margate. Declining the proposed guided tour, they nipped home for a cup of tea instead.

Auburn mishap

Mrs Helen Ireland of Auburn, California, is a strong contender for the fastest failure of a driving test. She got into the car, bade the examiner "good morning," and started the engine. Unfortunately she mistook the accelerator for the clutch and drove straight into the wall of the test centre.

Mole misery

A Lincolnshire man who tried to stop moles digging up his lawn caused £6,000 worth of damage to his car and house instead. Oscar Ejiamike used the headlights of his Jaguar to illuminate the furry miscreants but after a while had to re-charge the battery by starting the engine. Suddenly the automatic car shot backwards and ploughed through the wall of his house and into the lounge where it dislodged a wall heater. Sparks from the heater then ignited fuel leaking from the car's now damaged petrol tank, and the Jaguar burst into flames. As his wife fled the inferno wearing only her nightdress, Mr Ejiamike was left feeling as gutted as his car.

Missing Murphy

When a boy of 13 was found to be missing from his school party on a cross-Channel ferry, a £100,000 air and sea search was launched amidst fears that he must have fallen overboard. It was only after the five-hour operation had revealed no trace of him that teachers realized that they had left him at a bus stop in France. Michael Murphy was a member of a school party returning from Barcelona to Birmingham until the coach pulled in for a midnight rest stop at Lyon. For some reason he just missed the coach's departure, but his absence went unnoticed by teachers and pupils alike. It was only when the party docked at Dover and teachers carried out a head-count that they discovered he was missing. Some pupils thought they had seen Michael's distinctive shaven head in the ferry's amusement arcade, on the strength of which police called in the coastguard and the RAF to search the English Channel in case he had gone overboard. The hunt involved four helicopters, an aircraft, and several boats, and an emergency call was transmitted to all shipping to keep a lookout for the missing boy. French authorities were also alerted, and it was they who eventually called to say that Michael was alive and well 350 miles away, having spent the night with the gendarmerie. The school hinted that it may review its procedures.

Test too short

A 22-year-old man from The Hague had to retake his driving test after it was sandwiched between two trains on a Dutch level crossing. The learner driver was in the middle of his test when he had to stop for the barriers of a railway crossing at Rijswijck. When the lights changed, he attempted to drive off but the car stalled on the crossing and both the driver and the examiner were obliged to jump out just before the car was hit by two trains travelling in opposite directions. The examiner said afterwards that he could not award a pass or a fail because the test had been cut short.

Legless (and armless)

A drunken driver in Japan drove for over a mile unaware that his right arm had been sliced off by a passing lorry. A passer-by found the severed limb on the road and informed the police, but the owner was only traced when a man called in to report that his right arm was missing.

Connex cancellation

On 3 November 2000, representatives of all of Britain's rail companies met in Nottingham to listen to passengers' grievances – all except Connex, that is. Their representative couldn't make it. His train was cancelled.

Mallard mayhem

A motorist ended up in a duck pond after swerving to avoid a mallard which had left its habitat and wandered on to the A448 between Kidderminster and Bromsgrove in the West Midlands. Three other vehicles were also involved in the smash as they, too, tried to take evasive action. The duck crossed the road safely.

Business Cock-Ups

Martin Frobisher: Fool's Gold

Elizabethan England witnessed a golden age of seafaring exploration. Intrepied adventurers such as Walter Raleigh and Francis Drake set off in search of distant, undiscovered lands in the hope of bringing back untold riches for their grateful Queen who would promptly reward them with a knighthood. Bearing in mind that Raleigh returned with little more than the potato, it is clear that, at least where her explorers were concerned, Her Majesty was easily pleased.

One of the most sought-after routes was the so-called "North-West Passage" around the north of Canada which, it was thought, would open up trade to China (Cathay). The man entrusted with finding this elusive shipping lane was Martin Frobisher, a no-nonsense Yorkshireman who had risen from humble cabin boy in 1544 to the rank of captain 21 years later. In 1576 Frobisher was placed in command of an expedition to the New World, the first attempt by an Englishman to search for the North-West Passage. He set sail from England on 7 June with three small ships: the *Gabriel,* the *Michael*, and a pinnace which went down in a storm. The *Michael* deserted soon afterwards, leaving the *Gabriel* to soldier on alone and sight the mouth of what is now known as Frobisher Bay on Baffin Island. Frobisher immediately mistook this for the entrance to the North-West Passage.

Yet that was by no means his most costly blunder on that expedition. For he sent a party ashore on a small island near the entrance to the bay and told them to bring back anything they could find so that England could stake a claim to the new land. Some returned with flowers and others with grass, but one brought back a piece of black stone. It was similar in colour to sea coal, but the weight suggested that it was some kind of metal or mineral. At first Frobisher dismissed it as a worthless lump of "black earth" but the crew kept it as a novelty and took it back to England. If only Frobisher had obeyed his initial instincts, he would have saved himself a lot of time and his Queen a lot of money.

By the time Frobisher had arrived back in England, he seemed convinced that he had struck gold. The "black earth" was taken to a London assayer, Jonas Schutz, for analysis and he confirmed that the glittering stone was indeed high grade gold ore. Another assayer, Burchard Kranich, was brought in for a second opinion and he too concluded that the sample contained gold. Furthermore, he predicted that a serious mining expedition to the Arctic would bring back more than enough rich ore to cover the costs of the venture. On the strength of these optimistic forecasts, investors teamed up to form the Company of Cathay to fund a second expedition in 1577. One of the major subscribers was Queen Elizabeth who parted with the regal sum of £1,000.

The Queen also lent Frobisher the 200-ton Royal Navy vessel *Aid* to act as flagship, supported by the smaller survivors of the first expedition – *Gabriel* (25 tons) and *Michael* (20 tons). With a crew of more than 100, *Aid* led the mini fleet from England on 31 May, eventually reaching the island, where they had picked up the black stone the previous summer, on 17 July. Frobisher christened the land the Countess of Warwick's Island and instructed his team of miners to start searching for the black rock which was believed to be gold ore. The trouble was that Frobisher and his men were ignorant and had no real idea as to what they were supposed to be looking for. As for the expert miners, they were just a collection of tailors and other assorted tradesmen who had gone along for the ride and who would have been hard pressed to distinguish gold ore from a block of wood. In the course of just 20 days, they loaded a colossal 160 tons of supposed gold ore on to the three ships before heading back for England.

After being deposited for safekeeping at a castle near Bristol, the new samples were taken to London for testing. Both Schutz and Kranich claimed that they had found gold in the rock, but this prompted an unholy row between the two men who were fierce rivals and who both hoped to be appointed assayer-in-chief in the event of a third expedition. Each calculated that the more gold he identified, the more competent it made him appear, thus increasing his chances of landing the prestigious post. Schutz suspected skulduggery and accused Kranich of conducting the assaying process by using chemicals salted with gold. The inference was clear: Kranich had doctored the results in the hope of winning the contract. Kranich vigorously denied the charge and when a third expert, alchemist Baptista Agnello, also claimed to have extracted gold from the ore, it seemed that there was genuine cause for optimism.

However the waters were muddied by other assayers who declared that the amount of gold present was minimal – certainly not enough to warrant a third expedition. Schutz insisted that the reason these people had failed was because their equipment was inaccurate and, in fairness, some of the metallurgists themselves were less than enamoured with their modest furnaces. It was quite conceivable, given such inadequate facilities, that the presence of gold could be overlooked. Assaying was far from being an exact science at that time. It was not uncommon for the chemicals used in the process to become accidentally contaminated with small amounts of gold or silver, thus causing misleading results. It was all pretty much a hit and miss affair.

Frobisher had no doubts that there were huge quantities of gold to be found in the Arctic, but then again he had a vested interest since he was eager to lead a third expedition to the region. The wealthy Elizabethan courtiers also wanted to believe that vast riches lay across the ocean. They had heard stories of precious metals being retrieved from the Americas by the Spanish and were desperate to get in on the act. Consequently those reputable assayers who had suggested that the ore was worthless were dismissed as incompetents, their findings over-ridden in favour of those of Schutz and Kranich. As their advocates pointed out, these two men had been trained in Germany, the leading centre of metallurgy. Who better to trust? Well, the tooth fairy for a start.

And so, with the Queen anxious to advance her imperialistic ambitions and her courtiers keen to recoup their investment, Frobisher was allowed to go off on a third jaunt in the summer of 1578. This was the biggest Arctic expedition ever mounted, a fleet of 15 ships carrying over 400 men and the most advanced mining equipment. The fleet sailed from England on 31 May and sighted Resolution Island on 1 July, but bad weather hampered its progress and the ships spent a month drifting aimlessly around Hudson Strait. One ship was sunk by ice and another deserted to England before the remainder were finally able to assemble at the Countess of Warwick's Island.

Frobisher's objectives were two-fold. In addition to mining the gold, he was to establish the first colony in the New World. He had been instructed to settle 100 men on the Countess of Warwick's Island and, for that purpose, had been issued with prefabricated barracks and sufficient provisions to last for 18 months. The plan was that the men would mine and stockpile ore over the winter and establish commercial trade with the Inuit. By doing so, they would support the English claim to ownership of the area. However, half of the prefabricated barracks had been on the ship that had sunk in the ice and many of their supplies had been lost or ruined, including much of the beer which formed a staple food. As a result it was reluctantly decided to delay colonization for at least another year.

Frobisher fared little better with his principal objective – the ongoing quest for gold. A series of mines were opened on the island and by August the crews had quarried and loaded over 1,100 tons of rock. On the way back to England one of the ships, the *Emanuel of Bridgwater*, was damaged by storms and washed up on the Irish coast. The crew managed to salvage part of the 100 tons of ore which she was carrying, but a considerable amount was left on the wreck. As it turned out, that was probably the best place for it.

Mystified by some of the results from the previous expedition and accepting Schutz's word that poor facilities were to blame, the commission appointed by the Queen to oversee the 1578 voyage decided to build a new ore-processing works at Dartford, a few miles east of London. It was designed by Schutz who had been appointed assayer-in-chief, much to the annoyance of Kranich. The Dartford complex comprised two large workhouses, two water mills, five large furnaces, a coal house and several smaller workhouses and was completed a few weeks before the return of the expedition. Its cost was prohibitive, but the commission had little option than to trust Schutz that the expense was necessary to ensure results.

The new furnaces proved no more successful in extracting gold than their predecessors. Schutz's design was held responsible amidst criticism of the construction of the furnaces and the placement of the bellows. Schutz in turn blamed everybody else. But the truth of the matter was that the ore itself was utterly worthless. The gold content in over half of the samples was actually less than might be expected to be found in an average piece of rock, and was thousands of times less than the amount claimed by Schutz and Kranich. Most of it was just pyrites . . . or fool's gold.

While the disgraced Schutz fled abroad, the investors looked for a way of salvaging their reputations and money, but the building of the Dartford complex had placed a huge financial burden on them and the whole venture quickly collapsed. The ore supposed to have contained riches beyond their wildest dreams was thrown out and used by locals for building walls. The Company of Cathay went bankrupt and the Dartford furnaces were sold as the Queen tried to recoup her losses.

For Frobisher, the news that the ore had absolutely no value whatsoever came as a bitter blow. He was at his wits' end. It wasn't one of his longer journeys. His attempt at colonization had failed, his gold mines had been abandoned and his ill-advised pursuit of Arctic treasures had hurt the Queen financially. She was not a merry monarch. Not only did she refuse to speak to him but she even demanded the return of a gold chain which she had given him at the outset of the third voyage. Accused by other ruined investors of being a fool, at best, and a cheat, at worst, Frobisher drifted back to privateering, attacking gold-laden Spanish ships at random. At least there, he knew that the gold would be genuine. He remained an outcast until 1588 when he played a valiant role in the defeat of the Spanish Armada, for which he was knighted. Six years later, he was mortally wounded while defending the port of Brest against the Spanish.

If it was any consolation to Frobisher, he wasn't the last navigator to be made a fool of while searching for the North-West Passage. In 1818 John Ross reached Lancaster Sound but mistook a bank of cloud for a range of mountains and turned back. As Frobisher could have told him, appearances can be deceptive in that part of the world.

Bad Days at the Office

Out of the frying pan . . .

Firefighters in Baton Rouge, Louisiana, managed to burn down their own fire station after leaving fish frying on the stove when they were called out to attend to a blaze.

Suicidal sheep

Police, mountain experts and coastguards struggled for three hours in 1996 to save a pregnant sheep trapped 150 feet down a cliff on Scotland's Isle of Skye. Finally the ewe was hauled to the top where it was greeted by the grateful crofter, Neilie MacLure. When he turned to check the animal, it dived straight back over the cliff to its death.

Try-it-on Trion

In November 2000, France's social services department finally realized that one of their civil servants in Cannes had not been into work for five years. Jacques Trion, 42, used to ring in to head office every day, claiming that he was on his way to one of the many other offices on his patch. But he never showed up. He was eventually caught when his bosses decided to post someone at the door of every office to see whether he put in an appearance.

Single holiday

A man who paid £600 for a singles holiday to Tuscany found he was the only person there. Patrick Rosenvinge, whose only companions at the hotel were a handful of German couples, was so disenchanted that he flew back to Britain the same day. He had booked his trip with Small World who revealed that the others had cancelled at the last minute after learning that the holiday was under-subscribed.

"You wouldn't think that a holiday company would arrange a singles holiday for one person," complained 46-year-old Mr Rosenvinge. The company's website had promised that the holiday would be spent "in the company of other like-minded people with similar interests."

Bananas

A second-hand car dealer in Connecticut learned that it doesn't pay to use slang in advertising. He advertised a 1962 Pontiac for "1,395 bananas" (slang for dollars), but when a housewife offered him 25 bananas as a deposit, he refused to accept them. The housewife sued, alleging false advertising, and won her case. She then presented the dealer with the balance of bananas and drove off in the car.

Dumped in Detroit

A school in Detroit emptied pupils' lockers early, leaving them with no notes or books for their final exams. Trenton High School staff dumped personal belongings, papers, art projects and clothes belonging to 25 pupils. They thought the lockers belonged to senior students who had left the school.

Hope springs eternal

A Lloyds TSB cashpoint in Southsea, Hampshire, attracted a queue of jubilant customers when it started paying out £20 instead of £10 notes. As news of the double payouts spread to nearby pubs and clubs, the line of customers swelled to over 50 before police officers moved them away. A bank spokesman said customers' accounts would be debited with the amount they asked for despite their having received twice as much. "We are relying on customers' honesty," she admitted, "and hope they will pay back any extra cash they received."

Headache

California's J. Paul Getty Museum admitted in 1992 that the alleged fourth-century sculpture the Head of Achilles, which it had bought for over $1,000,000, was in fact made in the twentieth century.

Home improvement

A truck which careered into a house in Kladen, Germany, in July 2001 and demolished the front room turned out to be from a home improvement company.

The Wizard of Oz

A civic-minded Edinburgh pub landlord was left seriously out of pocket after offering "free pints all round" to a group of visiting sailors from HMS *Edinburgh*. For no sooner had Tom Ponton, landlord of the Oz Bar, made the gesture than the sailors bussed in over one hundred more crew members. Mr Ponton calculated that his generosity cost him at least £500.

Dead babies

In the late 1970s the Ideal Toy Corporation introduced a new line called Angel Babies – cute harp-playing babies with halos and wings. The new doll was introduced at the New York Toy Fair but received a negative response when toy industry buyers pointed out that no parent would want to buy a dead baby who had gone to heaven. Angel Babies never took off.

Millionaire for a day

Withdrawing $10 from an automatic teller machine to buy his girlfriend lunch, 31-year-old Tampa roofing company employee

Howard Jenkins was puzzled to discover that his bank account suddenly held a staggering $889,437. Things got better. For when he went home and telephoned the bank's computer system to recheck the statement, he was told that he had over $88 million. Trying, but failing, to resist temptation, he returned to the bank and filled out a withdrawal slip for $4 million. The teller asked him whether he had just received an inheritance and then gave him $3,000 in cash and seven cheques – one for $997,000 and the rest for $500,000 each. True to his word, Mr Jenkins took his girlfriend for lunch and showed her the money. After much discussion, they agreed that honesty was the best policy and that he should return it. So later that day he took his unexpected windfall back to the bank. A bemused bank spokesman said: "Something obviously went wrong, but we don't know what. We don't make a habit of transferring $88 million to customers' accounts for no reason."

You can leave your hat in

A woman mourner was horrified when her best hat was buried with the coffin at a South African funeral. She had planned to wear the hat to a cocktail party later in the day, but the undertaker mistook it for a floral tribute.

Best chemistry lesson ever

A chemistry teacher succeeded in blowing up the school laboratory in Weilburg, Austria, in 2001. He was about to conduct an experiment when his chemicals caught fire and exploded in a spectacular display of pyrotechnics. His class of 32 pupils were taken to hospital with minor injuries. "It was the best chemistry lesson we've ever had," said one. "It certainly taught us how certain chemicals react to a naked flame."

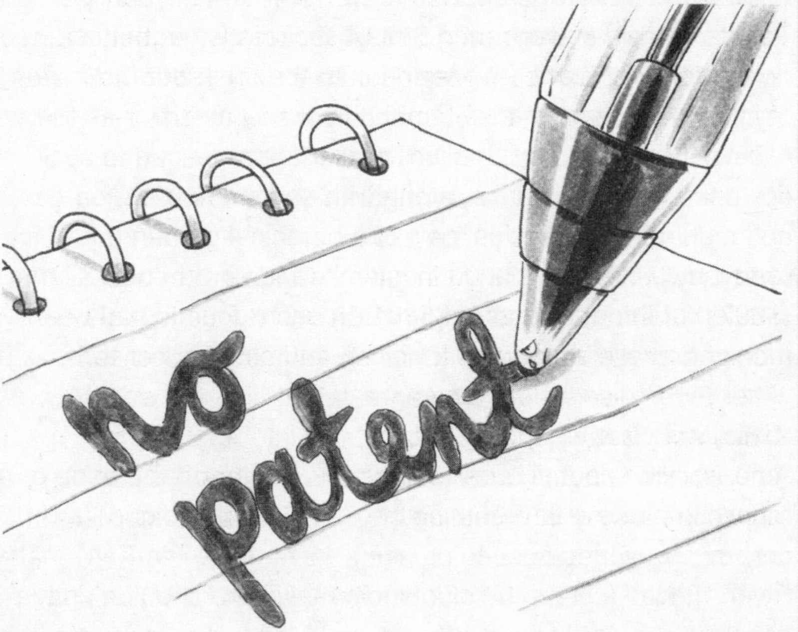

Biro balls-up

Having invented the revolutionary ball-point pen in 1943, Hungarian hypnotist/sculptor/journalist Laszlo Biro proceeded to blunder away the potential profits. First he sold the UK rights for a pittance to businessman Henry Martin, and then he forgot to patent his invention in the United States. It was a costly lapse since, hailing it as the "first pen that writes underwater," one New York department store sold no fewer than 10,000 at $12.50 apiece on the first day of sale. It was small consolation for Biro that his name entered the vocabulary.

Lost Louisiana lake

Texaco workmen were confident of success when they started drilling for oil at Lake Peigneur, Louisiana, in 1980. But instead of striking black gold, they could only watch in horror as their excavation created a huge whirlpool that proceeded to suck down the 1,300-acre lake, along with several houses, barges and tugboats, two oil rigs, part of a botanical garden and a tenth of nearby Jefferson Island. A half-mile wide crater was all that was left of the drilling attempt, which unfortunately had been made on a lake with an abandoned salt mine underneath.

Paramatta plunge

An Australian council worker drove his tractor off the edge of a cliff while mowing lawns in Sydney. The worker escaped with only minor injuries despite plunging 18 feet into the Parramatta River. "It was a steep bit of lawn so maybe he shouldn't have been mowing there," confided an ambulance spokesman.

Come back, Skippy!

Finding a kangaroo caught in a wire fence on his farm in the 1940s, farmer William Thompson from Grafton, New South Wales, kindly wrapped an old waistcoat around the animal to comfort it while he tried to set it free. It was only when the grateful kangaroo bounded off into the distance, still wearing the waistcoat, that Mr Thompson remembered that there was a £5 note in one of the pockets. The farmer and his friends immediately started searching the surrounding hillside, but to no avail.

£1-million fine

An Italian was informed he would have to pay a £1,000,000 fine for underpaying 30p in taxes. He received the fine from the tax office in Catania, Sicily, who later admitted that it had been issued "by mistake".

Best and brightest

Canadian lawyer Garry Hoy was every inch a company man. Above all, he was proud of his workplace – Toronto's Dominion Bank Tower – and when the opportunity arose to show visiting law students around the high-rise building in 1996, he extolled its virtues like a seasoned estate agent. He was particularly fond of the specially toughened windows and told his captivated audience how safe they were to lean against – even 24 storeys up. So confident was he of their resilience that he fearlessly demonstrated their qualities by barging into a pane with his shoulder. Alas the window gave way and Hoy ended up in the courtyard below. He was described by the head of his legal firm as "one of the best and brightest" members.

Cash hole crisis

A West Midlands security guard had to be dragged out of his van's cash hole after he accidentally pressed an ambush button and locked himself inside. Hearing his screams, colleagues rushed to the rescue and found him covered in red dye which had been squirted out as a security precaution.

More scents than sense

Mexican perfume manufacturer Javier Palafox decided to use the excitement surrounding the final day of the 2000 Mexican presidential campaign to promote his range of fragrances. With a new party expected to seize power for the first time in 71 years, he thought he would let the Mexican public "smell change in the air." Displaying more scents than sense, he arranged for six trucks to dump eight tons of milky perfume onto Mexico City's Periferico

Highway, and even made sure a camera crew was present to ensure extra publicity. The cameras were still rolling when dozens of cars started to skid on the slippery perfume and crash into each other, causing the highway to be closed and creating rush-hour traffic congestion right across the city. It eventually took five hours to clean up the highway, but much longer for Palafox to live down his publicity stunt.

Colfax calamity

Firefighters called out to tackle a blaze at a US fire station in December 2000 were powerless to stem the flames because all their equipment was locked inside. Crews arrived at the station in Colfax, Washington, to discover that all the hoses, tankers and protective gear were inside the burning building. "All my safety gear was in the fire engine," said Captain Ken McNaughton. "There was nothing we could do. We felt completely helpless." Damage was estimated at over $1 million.

Unless we receive a cheque for £0.00 . . .

Rugby club treasurer Ronald Lane received an account for electricity used during the close season, but since it was for £0.00, he ignored it. Later a final demand was sent to the ground at Kidderminster with the warning that the supply would be cut off unless the account was settled within seven days. Mr Lane duly sent the electricity board a cheque for £0.00. It was accepted.

Conceptual cleaner

New York City's Gramercy Hotel staged an art fair in 1995 where conceptual artists mounted exhibitions in the hotel rooms. Sadly one exhibit was ruined when a cleaning lady made the artist's bed by mistake.

Very helpful

After asking for an additional £150 on his existing overdraft, Bristol student Nick Roveta was surprised when Barclays Bank awarded him a £30-million overdraft. The letter from the bank said: "I am pleased to confirm an overdraft limit of £30,651,575 has been arranged on your account. I hope you will find this helpful." Barclays later admitted that an administrative error had been made, adding curtly: "Obviously he won't be able to draw on that amount."

Dead wrong

When he phoned Scottish Widows insurance company to ask about an overdue windfall payment, fifty-one-year-old Maurice Weitzman from Boreham Wood in Hertfordshire was twice told that he was on record as being dead. Mr Weitzman said: "I was very upset to hear I was deceased. They wrote a letter of apology, but the next time I rang, they still thought I was dead."

New surroundings

The German post office sent a card wishing a man good luck in his new home, only to find that his change of address was due to the fact that he was now in prison. Cards are automatically sent out by the post office as a customer relations exercise to welcome Germans to their new addresses, but the man from Lueneburg, whose new home was the local detention centre, was less than amused. The card read: "You've made it – and now you have earned a rest so you can get used to your new surroundings."

Baby Joey's johnson

To capitalize on the wave of publicity surrounding the Christmas 1975 birth of Mike and Gloria Stivic's baby in the hit American sit-com *All in the Family*, a US toy manufacturer decided to market a Baby Joey doll, but made the mistake of giving it a penis. Outraged moral guardians took to breaking open the doll's packaging in stores and yanking off the offending penises with the result that Baby Joey soon had to practice the withdrawal method from the nation's shelves.

Telekom trouble

Thousands of Germans were late for work on 26 March 2001 because their speaking clock forgot to change for summer time. Deutsche Telekom's morning call service failed to adjust to the new time following a computer error.

The Robinson Empire

An object displayed proudly in a Tyneside museum as a valuable Roman coin turned out instead to be a plastic token given away by a soft drinks firm. The "coin," claimed to have been minted around AD 135, was exhibited at the Roman Fort Museum, South Shields, for several days in 1971 until the error was spotted by a nine-year-old girl. A museum spokesman said: "The token was designed as a Roman replica. The trouble was that we construed the letter 'R' on the coin to mean 'Roma.' In fact it stood for 'Robinsons,' the soft drink manufacturers."

Where's the boss?

Jeweller William Joyce accidentally trapped himself in the high security walk-in safe at his shop on the Isle of Wight for four days in 2001. The 70-year-old survived on a packet of biscuits until staff began to wonder what had happened to him.

Montpellier mix-up

A worker in Montpellier, France, was sacked after sending an e-mail attachment with naked photos to the wrong person. He meant to send it to a friend, but inadvertently posted it to a female company boss in the United States who had an almost identical e-mail address.

Spendthrift Javiers

In 1977, a clerical error resulted in the Mellon Bank of Pittsburgh, Pennsylvania, paying $1,000,000 instead of $1,000 into the account of Filipino Melahor Javier and his wife Victoria. The bank quickly spotted the error and demanded the return of the outstanding amount, but the Javiers claimed that most of it had already been spent.

Pancevo post

The new owner of a house at Pancevo, near Belgrade, opened the lower shutters in front of a walled-in window . . . and discovered unopened letters, telegrams and newspapers dating back 90 years. All that time, bungling postmen had been dropping mail through an open upper shutter thinking there was a glass pane behind it. Mrs Vera Aremovic said that her grand-father and father, merchants with extensive connections throughout the Austro-Hungarian empire, had both lived in the house. Their businesses had failed because trading partners complained that they never answered letters.

Death by defecation

An overzealous zookeeper at Paderborn, Germany, suffocated to death beneath a mound of elephant excrement in June 2000 after trying extreme measures to relieve the creature's constipation. Friedrich Riesfeldt, 46, had fed Stefan the elephant 22 doses of animal laxative and more than a bushel of berries, figs, and prunes. When these administrations failed to produce the desired effect, he then attempted to give the elephant an olive-oil enema. It was at this point that the plugged-up pachyderm suddenly unloaded a colossal 150 kilograms of dung. A police detective reported: “The sheer force of the elephant’s unexpected defecation knocked Mr Riesfeldt to the ground where he struck his head on a rock and lay unconscious as the elephant continued to evacuate his bowels on top of him. With no one to help him, he lay under all that dung for at least an hour before a watchman came along.”

Sporting Dunces

Roy Riegels: Wrong Turn to Fame

The captain and centre of the University of California American football team which met Georgia Tech in the annual Rose Bowl game on New Year's Day, 1929, was a young man by the name of Roy Riegels. It is fair to say that until then his achievements had attracted little attention beyond the confines of his own team and its supporters. But that day everything changed. In one match Roy Riegels suddenly became one of the best-known sportsmen in the United States, a name that was on every fan's lips. And it was all because he committed the most appalling blunder by running 69 yards . . . the wrong way.

The game started cautiously with tension high on both sides. The first quarter was scoreless and that was still the situation in the second quarter when the Bears drove to Tech's 25-yard line before losing the ball on downs. Then Georgia's Stumpy Thompson was hit by California halfback Benny Lom and fumbled the ball at the Tech 30. Roy Riegels quickly scooped up the loose ball, but, after a heavy tackle, became confused and started running the wrong way . . . towards his own goal. Unable to believe their eyes, team-mates and Tech players headed off in pursuit of the runaway Riegels. Benny Lom led the chase and yelled to Riegels that he was going the wrong way, but Riegels couldn't hear the remonstrations above the clamour of the 71,000-strong crowd who were also screaming at him to stop. As fortune would have it, Riegels slowed down as he approached the end zone, allowing Lom to tackle him at the 1-yard line – a split second before he would have scored for the opposing team. Lom spun him around and Riegels was immediately swamped by Tech players. But although Lom had temporarily saved the day, Riegels' brainstorm still cost his side the game. For, unable to advance the ball from the 1-yard line, California had to punt, and Lom's kick was blocked out of the end zone for a safety. Those two points were to prove decisive.

During half-time a distraught Riegels sat alone in the corner of the dressing-room, a blanket draped around his shoulders, put his face in his hands and cried his heart out. Coach Clarence "Nibs" Price then announced that the second-half starters would be the same as for the first. Riegels was staying on! Everyone except Riegels headed out towards the field. "Coach, I can't do it," he sobbed. "I've ruined you. I've ruined my school. I've ruined myself. I couldn't face the crowd in that stadium to save my life." But Price was adamant and, to his credit, Riegels had a fine second half. However he couldn't stop his team losing 8–7.

Afterwards the hapless Riegels attempted to explain what had gone wrong. "I was running toward the sidelines," he told reporters, "and when I picked up the ball I started to turn to my left toward Tech's goal. Somebody shoved me and I bounded right off into a tough tackler. In pivoting to get away from him, I completely lost my bearings. As for the noise from the crowd, I thought it was the fans yelling encouragement."

Yet far from being pilloried in the press, Riegels became an unlikely national hero. He received a stack of fan mail including a proposal of marriage in which he and his bride would walk up the aisle instead of down!

Goran Ivanisevic: One Smash Too Many

Fiery Croatian tennis ace Goran Ivanisevic had to retire from the Samsung Open in Brighton in November 2000 after smashing up all of his rackets. Ivanisevic broke his third and final racket at 15–40 down in the fourth game of the final set of his second-round clash with Hjung-Taik Lee, and was forced to quit due to "a lack of appropriate equipment." Lee, who was awarded the match, was leading 7–5, 6–7, 3–1 at the time.

Ivanisevic binned his first racket in a temper after his serve was broken for 6–5 in the first set. Then he hurled his new one towards umpire Kim Craven's chair and, following a code violation, smashed the racket after missing two break points in the second game of the second set. At 15–40 down and 2–1 behind in the third and deciding set, he trashed his third racket, an outburst which was punished by a point penalty and the award of the game to Lee.

Referee Alan Mills came on to the court and when Ivanisevic told him he had run out of rackets, umpire Craven had no choice but to announce the Croat's withdrawal. Afterwards Ivanisevic moaned: "I have never won Wimbledon despite being in the finals three times. Perhaps this will be something to remember me by."

The Slowest Marathon Runner

Amid the records of outstanding athletic achievement, the name of Wallace Williams is curiously absent. Yet his unparalleled feat at the 1979 Pan American Games in San Juan is the stuff of which sporting legends are made.

Representing the Virgin Islands, Williams was considered something of a plodder whose medal hopes were, at best, negligible. True to form, he struggled from the start and soon the race leaders were but a distant memory. However he was determined to complete the course and, as a gallant loser having trudged over 26 miles in scorching heat, he felt sure of a warm reception from the crowd in the stadium.

As he wearily approached the stadium in last place, by now almost 39 minutes behind the previous finisher, it occurred to him that the crowd were strangely silent. Perhaps, he reasoned, they were saving themselves to greet his heroic entrance.

Then he realized why all was quiet. The stadium door was locked. Everyone had gone home.

Food for Thought

The French may love their food, but ironically it was the search for the ultimate gastronomic experience which was to prove the downfall of rugby player Gaston Vareilles who chose a decidedly unfortunate moment to stop for a snack.

Over *la lune* at winning his first cap for France against Scotland in 1911, M. Vareilles enthusiastically accepted the opportunity to travel to the match by train with his new team-mates. However the excitement of the occasion had left him feeling a little empty in the stomach so when the train pulled into Lyon, he decided to jump off and buy a sandwich.

Precisely how long the stop at Lyon was supposed to be remains something of a mystery, but suffice to say that by the time Vareilles had queued patiently for his French bread, paid for it and returned to the platform, there was no sign of the train. With the sharp eye of an international sportsman, he was able to see it and his team-mates disappearing into the distance.

Having no alternative means of transport, the hapless Vareilles missed the match. It possibly comes as no surprise to learn that he was never again picked to play for his country.

Freestyle federation

The four Turkish freestyle wrestlers who had won gold at the 1948 London Olympics were unable to defend their titles in 1952 because their federation forgot to post their entry forms.

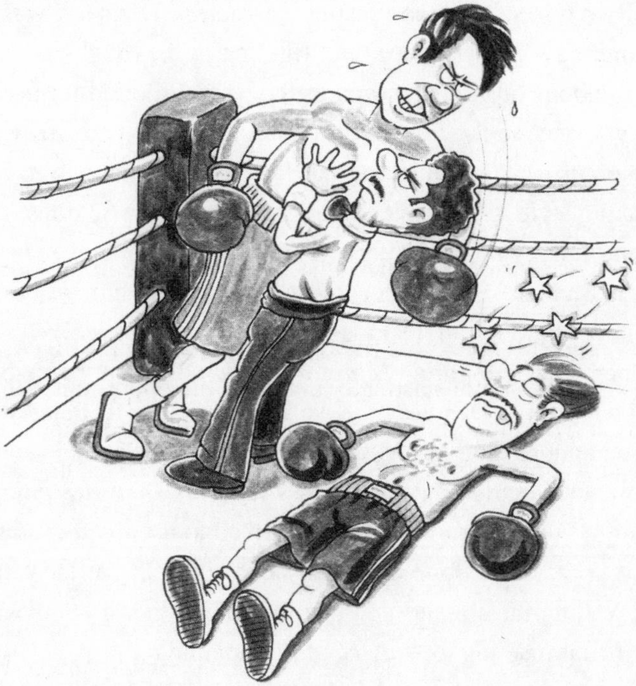

Dempsey vs Tunney: The Long Count

When world heavyweight champion Gene Tunney was allowed to spend 14 seconds on the canvas after being floored by Jack Dempsey in their infamous 1927 rematch, the fight became known as "The Battle of the Long Count." Controversy rages to this day as to whether Dempsey was robbed of victory, but who was really to blame for the fiasco – referee Dave Barry or Dempsey himself?

The two boxers were contrasting characters. Dempsey was a bar-room brawler who started out fighting in the rough-and-tumble saloons of mining towns of the west. Pilloried for avoiding military service in the First World War, Dempsey became world champion in 1919 by knocking out Jess Willard in the third round. His boxing style was a typically aggressive crouch, and his uncompromizing approach earned him the nickname of "The Manassa Mauler." Fans either loved him or hated him – but they could never ignore him. Dempsey was good box office.

Tunney – "The Fighting Marine" – was a different kettle of fish altogether. Unlike Dempsey, he was a superb ring tactician who favoured a more upright style of boxing and preferred to steer clear of close-quarter confrontations. Whereas Dempsey enjoyed slugging it out head-to-head, Tunney liked to use his feet and brain to keep out of trouble. He was also unusually refined for a boxer, reading the classics and comfortable in literary circles.

Their first meeting took place at Philadelphia's Sesquicentennial Stadium on 26 September 1926. A record crowd of over 120,000 paid $1.8 million to see Dempsey defend his title for the first time in three years. Dempsey received $711,000 for the fight, Tunney $200,000, but it was the challenger who won through, out-boxing Dempsey at every turn and winning nearly every one of the ten rounds. Dempsey showed surprising dignity in defeat and won new friends by heaping lavish praise upon his conqueror. He also provided one of boxing's most memorable quotations when he explained to his wife the reasons for his defeat: "Honey, I forgot to duck."

Following the fight, Dempsey briefly retired but boxing was in his blood and he returned to the ring to knock out Jack Sharkey and set up the contest for which the American public was clamouring – a rematch with Tunney.

More than 104,000 people crammed into Chicago's Soldier Field on 22 September 1927, paying gate receipts of $2,650,000 – a record which stood for 50 years. This time, Tunney, as champion, got $990,000 and Dempsey $450,000.

Dempsey had trained hard for the fight, and went straight on to the attack from the opening bell, but at 32 he was a shadow of his former self. Tunney was hardly troubled by these frenzied assaults, mastering Dempsey, in the words of one commentator, "like a skilled matador taming an angry bull." The *Washington Post* wrote: "The technical story of the battle can be briefly told. Dempsey, pawing, sniffing, advanced on Tunney from the outset, beckoning him to close quarters, and Tunney danced away, hitting as he danced, and sapping the strength of his foe from the start. Dempsey would come in close, lean with a pawing left, and when Tunney elected to return a blow, a slight flurry would follow, with Dempsey's head and face invariably the target."

Then, 50 seconds into round seven, Tunney was knocked from his confident stride when Dempsey connected with a long right, followed by a left hook to the chin. A further straight right drove the champion back and as he careered off the ropes, Dempsey landed another hook to the jaw. Tunney was reeling and a flurry of blows to his head sent him crashing to the canvas. With the crowd on their feet, screaming, Dempsey stood over the prone Tunney. However Illinois State Athletic Commission rules insisted that, in the event of a knockdown, the opponent must go to the farthest neutral corner before the referee begins his count. Referee Dave Barry duly motioned Dempsey towards the neutral corner, but Dempsey replied: "I'll stay here." Barry then walked over to Dempsey and half pushed him in the proper direction. All the while Tunney sat on the canvas. Five seconds had elapsed but, instead of picking up the timekeeper's count at six, the referee shouted "one." At the count of three, Tunney lifted his head and looked at Barry, but didn't get to his feet until the referee reached nine. He had therefore spent a total of fourteen seconds on the floor before resuming the fight.

Dempsey tried to carry on where he had left off, but the momentum had been lost. For the remainder of the round Tunney cleverly back-pedalled, his reluctance to do battle prompting Dempsey at one point to drop his gloves in frustration and gesture to the champion to stand and fight. Tunney was having none of it.

Able to clear his head between rounds, Tunney quickly regained control and boxed his way to a unanimous points victory at the end of the tenth. Tunney maintained that, although shaken by the seventh-round knockdown, he could easily have beaten the count even if referee Barry had resumed at "six." Dempsey was not convinced, and complained: "I was robbed of the championship." Asked why he had failed to retreat to a neutral corner, he replied: "I couldn't move. I just couldn't. I wanted Tunney to get up. I wanted to kill the son-of-a-bitch."

Although a great deal of criticism was levelled at him in the furore which followed the fight, referee Barry had merely adhered to the local regulations, no matter how unfair they may have seemed. As soon as Dempsey obeyed the referee's order to retreat to a neutral corner, Barry began the count. That Dempsey was ignorant of, or chose to disregard, these rules was his problem. In the end, he had only himself to blame.

Dempsey never fought again. He lost a fortune in the stock market crash of 1929 but redeemed himself with the American public by removing the "shirker" tag when enlisting in the Coast

Guard for the Second World War. A few weeks before his 50th birthday, he was part of the invasion force at the Battle of Okinawa, one of the bloodiest encounters of the Pacific campaign. After the war he opened a popular restaurant on Broadway and by the time he died in 1983 he was widely acclaimed as one of the great sporting heroes of the twentieth century. But in the 56th intervening years nobody would ever let him forget the "Battle of the Long Count."

Mark Thatcher: Lost in the Desert

Former UK Prime Minister Margaret Thatcher's son Mark had a passion for fast cars. He had already driven – and crashed – quite a few in competition before he decided to tackle the gruelling Paris–Dakar Rally. Although it was his first experience of desert conditions, he was not one for doubting his own ability, and was confident of completing the 6,200-mile route. Instead he became hopelessly lost in the southern Sahara and went missing for six days, necessitating a vast air and land search, the bill for which came to £300,000.

Organized by the Paris-based Automobile Sporting Association, the event was generally regarded as one of the toughest in the rallying calendar, the competitors driving day and night across hundreds of miles of inhospitable terrain on their way to the port of Dakar in Senegal on the west coast of Africa. To an experienced driver, it was a fearsome challenge; to a relative novice such as Mark Thatcher, it was simply too much.

At the age of 28, it was seven years since Mark Thatcher had made his debut in top-flight sport. On that occasion he had been disqualified from the British Open Racquets Championship for being late. So the omens weren't exactly good.

It was on 8 January 1982 that his Peugeot 504 was first reported missing, having broken down on the sixth leg of the rally somewhere in the southern Sahara Desert. Besides Mark Thatcher in the car were his French co-driver Charlotte Verney and a mechanic whom he knew only as Jackie. Agency reports on 12 January said that the three had been found unharmed and had been rescued by helicopter, but this proved to be a false dawn. As the search was stepped up, the French government sent three military planes into the desert and these were soon joined by ten Algerian planes, 20 cross-country vehicles and local units of the Algerian army. Seven other competitors were also listed as missing, but one by one they all turned up.

By 13 January there was still no sign of Mark Thatcher or his car. Unconfirmed reports of sightings came and went, and the tension became so great that his mother – the formidable "Iron Lady" and scourge of politicians throughout the world – gave a hitherto unseen display of public emotion by breaking down in tears on her way to an engagement. Husband Denis flew out to Algeria to monitor the rescue operation, and the Queen sent Mrs Thatcher a private message of concern.

Then at 11.30 a.m. on the 14th, six days after he vanished, an Algerian C130 Hercules aircraft spotted Mark Thatcher and his two colleagues standing beside their car, waving frantically to try to attract attention. They were some 35 miles off the rally route, at a remote spot known as Taoumdert, 250 miles south of Tamanrasset.

Asked to grant a rare audience to the media, Mark Thatcher related how he had been travelling in convoy with two other Peugeots near the Algerian border with Mali when a front steering arm broke on his car. The repairs took only 13 minutes, but in that time the car became separated from its team-mates and Thatcher had to continue by means of compass bearings and map references. It didn't take him long to become lost and, to make matters worse, at dusk that evening the casing on the rear axle shattered, leaving him high and very dry. With water supplies dwindling by 11 January, they managed to carry out makeshift repairs on the axle, but these gave way again after just 600 yards, and they were once again forced to wait and hope for rescue. Despite the seemingly precarious nature of their existence, Mark Thatcher insisted that he had never been remotely concerned. Indeed he expressed surprise that his disappearance had created so much interest, and said that he was amazed by all the fuss. His apparent lack of gratitude towards those who had searched long and hard for him did nothing to endear him to the British press or public.

Perhaps aware that the British taxpayer would be happier to pay for Mark Thatcher to remain in the desert than to have him rescued, the Algerian government generously agreed to settle the bill for the search. Mark Thatcher's self-confidence might not have been dented by his Saharan experience, but rally organiser Thierry Sabine doubted whether he would be allowed to enter the following year's event, adding caustically: "At a pinch, we might accept him at the finish at Dakar, as a guest."

In November 1982, Mark Thatcher went missing again during a rally in Mexico. This time it was only for eight hours.

Potted pentathlon

The modern pentathlon at the 1984 Olympics was a close-fought affair, but when Sweden's Svante Rasmuson pulled clear in the final event, the 4,000 metres cross country, he seemed assured of victory. But just 20 yards from the finish, he stumbled over a potted plant, placed there by the Los Angeles organizers to brighten up the course. Before he could get to his feet, he had been passed by Italy's Daniele Masala who went on to snatch the gold.

366

The Strange Case of Ali Dia

Most soccer players who get to play in the English Premier League do so thanks to either exceptional natural talent or sheer hard work. Ali Dia had neither, but that didn't stop him enjoying his forty-three minutes of fame one afternoon in 1996.

Ali Dia's fairytale rise from obscurity to Premiership player began when Southampton manager Graeme Souness received a phone call from someone purporting to be George Weah, a Liberian international striker and at the time the World Footballer of the Year. From his playing days as a tough tackling midfielder who took no prisoners, Souness was not a man to be impressed by reputations, but even he had to sit up and listen when someone with the prestige of George Weah was on the other end of the line. "He said he had a relative in France," recalled Souness, "who was interested in playing in the UK. Would we have a look at him?"

Enter Ali Dia, aged 31, claiming to be a Senegal international striker. Nobody had ever heard of him, but not unreasonably Souness wasn't exactly an expert on the Senegal team so Weah's recommendation was enough to guarantee a trial. Ali Dia talked a good game and possessed sufficient glimpses of talent to encourage Souness to put him in the starting line-up against Leeds United on 23 November. Since Southampton were going through a particularly lean spell, any injection of new blood was welcome. Among those interested to read of his forthcoming debut was Peter Harrison, manager of Unibond League strugglers Blyth Spartans whose average crowd is nearer 200 than 60,000 and where the main topic of conversation during a match is the quality of the meat pies. For Ali Dia had been training with Blyth the previous week. Harrison said:

"I opened the newspaper and there was a story saying Ali Dia was going to play for Southampton, which came as a great surprise to not just me but everyone who knew him."

And so Ali Dia, the boy from nowhere, ran out in the red and white stripes of Southampton to face Leeds. His one and only appearance lasted just 43 minutes. "He didn't touch the ball too many times, as I remember," admitted Souness, "so we took him off. He didn't do so well. He was out of his depth. After that, we knew he'd never be any good to us."

The mystery of Ali Dia's playing career deepened when George Weah denied having made any call. Souness had been well and truly taken in by someone with no soccer qualifications whatsoever, someone who was just one step up from a parks player. Ali Dia's contract with Southampton was cancelled just 14 days after he had signed it.

From Southampton, Ali Dia went on to ply his trade in non-League football in the humbler surroundings of Gateshead where the handful of hard-core fans chanted a song in his honour:

"Oh Ali Dia,
Came from Senegal,
And proved to be a liar."

While at Gateshead, he also claimed to be a good friend of French international winger David Ginola who was playing at the time for Newcastle. Ginola had never heard of him either. Gateshead chairman John Gibson summed up the Ali Dia phenomenon. "He was a likeable lad and at non-League level he was OK, but the thought of him being a Premiership player, apart from in Ali's mind, are ludicrous."

David Duval: Road Hole Rage

US golfer David Duval lost a cool £173,000 in prize money after taking a calamitous eight at the penultimate hole in the 2000 British Open at St Andrews.

Duval was still in contention for second place behind runaway leader – and eventual winner – Tiger Woods when he came to the notorious 17th, also known as the Road Hole. His second shot landed in a huge pot bunker at the side of the green, perilously close to the near-vertical face of the sand trap. His first attempt to blast it out bounced back off the face of the bunker, as did his second. His ball fell back into an almost unplayable lie, forcing Duval to scoop it backwards for his fifth stroke. His sixth shot again hit the bunker face, but this time it toppled onto the green. Having taken four shots to get out of the bunker, he then two-putted for a quadruple bogey eight.

Duval's blunder saw him drop from joint second in the tournament, whereby he would have shared £630,000 with South African Ernie Els and Denmark's Thomas Bjørn, to joint 11th for which he picked up just £37,000.

Duval said wryly: "I shouldn't have put it in the bunker in the first place."

Dodgy Shorts

Watching Washington

In February 1993 boxer Virgil Hill retained his WBA light-heavyweight title by virtue of a bizarre technical decision against Adolpho Washington in Fargo, North Dakota. Washington had been troubled by a cut eye and, in his corner before the 12th and final round, he had it examined by the ringside physician. With Washington's corner man and manager also hovering anxiously, a TV cameraman tried to get a close-up of the action but as he moved in, he merely succeeded in banging Washington's eye with the camera. The collision caused Washington's eye to bleed profusely, and he was unable to continue.

Bad timing

American sprinters Eddie Hart and Rey Robinson, who were among the favourites for the men's 100 metres at the 1972 Munich Olympics, lost out on the chance of a medal because their coach misread the starting time for their second-round heats. Waiting for the team bus at the Olympic village, Robinson was watching television when he saw to his horror that the athletes on screen were lining up for the race he should have been in. Both men were eliminated for their non-show.

Bonehead Merkle

Fred Merkle, a rookie with the New York Giants' baseball team, committed a truly inspirational blunder at the end of a crucial National League game with the Chicago Cubs on 23 September 1908. With the score tied in the ninth inning, Merkle was so overjoyed at a team-mate's apparent game-winning single that he forgot to complete the formality of a run to second to touch base. Merkle's oversight meant the game ended in a tie. It also ultimately cost the Giants the National League pennant. No wonder the New York press referred to "Merkle's Bonehead Play."

A wing and a prayer

At the start of each match, Isidore Irandir, goalkeeper with Brazilian soccer club Rio Preto, went through a ritual of kneeling down in the goalmouth and praying. He went into his usual routine just as opponents Corinthians kicked off in a match at the Bahia Stadium, but had reckoned without the celebrated left foot of Roberto Rivelino. Receiving the ball on the halfway line, Rivelino, all too aware of Irandir's custom, blasted a shot towards the Rio Preto goal. It sailed into the back of the net after just three seconds' play, whistling past the ear of a startled Irandir who was still on his knees in prayer. As the Corinthians players celebrated, Irandir's brother ran onto the pitch armed with a revolver and pumped six bullets into the ball.

Dozy Dorothy

South African tennis player Abe Segal had reached match point in his 1964 Wimbledon men's singles first-round match with Clark Graebner of the United States when Graebner hit a ball which landed well beyond the baseline. Segal waited for the inevitable call of "Out!," which would mark his victory, but, to his alarm, none was forthcoming. All eyes on court number three then turned to the lineswoman, Dorothy Cavis Brown . . . who was sitting in her chair fast asleep. A kindly ball boy eventually woke her up, but it was too late to spare her blushes, and she was suspended from duty. She gave up umpiring shortly afterwards.

Irritating insect

American golfer Lloyd Mangrum missed out on winning the 1950 US Open because he inadvertently broke the rules by picking up his ball and flicking away an insect which had landed on it. Mangrum was penalised two strokes for his misde-meanour, and it also cost him the championship as at the end of 72 holes he was tied for first place with Ben Hogan, but lost the resultant play-off.

Wrong turn

Nearing the end of the marathon in the 1954 European Championships in Berne, Russian athlete Ivan Filin powered into the stadium clear of Finland's Veikko Karvonen. But once inside the stadium, the Soviet runner turned the wrong way and lost over 100 metres before realizing his error. By the time he had got back on course, he could manage only third place.

Self knock-out

Rookie American boxer Harvey Gartley had the distinction of knocking himself out in his first fight. Pitted against Dennis Outlette in a regional heat of the 1977 Saginaw Golden Gloves Championships in Michigan, Gartley sized up his opponent for the opening 47 seconds during which time neither man had thrown a punch. With the crowd growing restless, Gartley suddenly launched a wild swing in the vague direction of Outlette, missed by a mile, collapsed in a heap on the canvas and was counted out.

Tardy Scot

Scottish golfer Colin Montgomerie was left red-faced with embarrassment after a mistake over his starting time cost him a two-shot penalty at the 2000 BMW International Open in Munich. Montgomerie, the defending champion, was 20 seconds late for his scheduled tee-off time of 1.20 p.m., believing that he was not due to start until 1.30. He never recovered from the penalty blow, and went on to miss his first tournament cut in two years.

No gun, no run

The 1966 Jamaican national track championships were delayed because nobody had remembered to bring the starting pistol.

Sammy's slip

With his reputation for being a great thrower, Slingin' Sammy Baugh was expected to be a key player for the Washington Redskins in their 1945 National Football League championship play-off with Cleveland Rams. But on this occasion Sammy's expertise was to desert him in spectacular fashion. During the first quarter, finding himself under pressure near his own line, he stepped back into the end zone and prepared to deliver one of his arrow-like passes, only for his throw to hit the back of his own goalpost and drop in the end zone to give the Rams two points. Sammy's slip proved decisive as the Redskins went on to lose by one point, 15–14.

Leg of honour

Australian Kevin Magee was delighted to have finished fourth in the 1989 500cc US Motor Cycle Grand Prix at Laguna Seca,

California. But while waving to the crowds on his lap of honour, he fell off his machine and broke a leg.

Car park view

Contractors installing Bradford City Football Club's new executive boxes accidentally fitted them the wrong way round – with the windows facing the car park instead of the pitch. The mistake was discovered less than two weeks before the start of the 2000–2001 season. Following City's dismal start to the season, fans were soon begging the club to turn the boxes round again.

Header

Chasing a deep fly ball in a game with Cleveland Indians in 1993, Texas Rangers' baseball star Jose Canseco allowed it to bounce off the top of his head and over the fence for an embarrassing home run. Canseco's aberration proved decisive as the Indians went on to scalp the Rangers 7–6.

Dark at The Shay

Halifax Town Football Club had to stage their September 2000 Worthington Cup tie against Tranmere Rovers at Bradford City's Valley Parade ground because they had run out of bulbs for the floodlights at The Shay.

Crushed Czechs

Arriving in Canada to prepare for the 1976 Montreal Olympics, the Czech cycling team's medal hopes were dashed when all their wheels and spare tyres were mistakenly picked up by garbage collectors and crushed.

Tea Time

Following a magnificent run in the 1938 Natal marathon, South African athlete Johannes Coleman stormed across the finish line at Alexander Park, Pietermaritzburg, confident that he had shattered the world record. He eagerly sought out chief timekeeper Harold Sulin for confirmation, only to find Sulin and his colleagues quietly sipping tea in the park refreshment area. Apologising for their absence, they explained that they hadn't been expecting any of the runners to arrive back so soon. Consequently Coleman's record could not be ratified.

Bad finish

Having driven 3,000 miles across Europe, German rally driver Georg Etterer crashed just 100 yards from the finish after he forgot which was the right side of the road. Etterer had been competing in the 2000 Gumball Rally from England to Russia and back and had crossed 13 countries in the course of six days when his Mercedes neared the finish in Hampshire. Alas Etterer and navigator Lars Guggenburger got hopelessly lost and resorted to offering a taxi driver £25 to lead them to the finish at the Beaulieu Motor Museum. Shortly afterwards, Etterer allegedly became impatient at the taxi's slow progress and sped off into the distance. When the taxi driver gave chase to claim his £25 he found that the Mercedes had been in a head-on collision with a Peugeot whose driver was on his way home. Etterer and Guggenburger emerged unscathed, but their car was too badly damaged to complete the final 100 yards of the rally. Etterer was fined £400 and banned from driving on British roads for 18 months. His defence counsel said that his client was unused to driving on the left-hand side of the road and had simply forgotten which country he was in.

Psyched

Preparing for his bout in the New York Golden Gloves Championships in 1992, boxer Daniel Caruso was psyching himself up by pounding his gloves into his face prior to the introductions. Unfortunately he overdid it and scored a direct hit with one punch, breaking and bloodying his own nose. On examining him, doctors ruled that he was unfit to box.

Three-man bobsled

Competing in the four-man bobsled at the 1992 Winter Olympics at Albertville, Canadian number two team's Jack Pyc hesitated fatally at the start and missed the sled altogether. As his bewildered team-mates headed off down the course, Pyc slid along helplessly yards behind until he was rescued by a spectator. The Canadians were duly disqualified for arriving at the finish one man short.

Japiopian

At the medal ceremony for the 1964 Tokyo Olympics marathon, won by Abebe Bikila of Ethiopia, the stadium band played the Japanese national anthem because they didn't know the tune for the Ethiopian anthem.

Fight on the 17th

Spanish golfer Sergio Garcia stormed out of the 2000 Volvo Masters Pro-Am in Montecastillo following a major altercation with his amateur playing partner. The row broke out on the 9th hole after haulage contractor Luis Somoza had asked the 20-year-old Ryder Cup star for a yardage. When Somoza's approach shot came up short of the green, he accused Garcia of giving him the wrong yardage. According to Garcia, Somoza then threatened to hit him whereupon Garcia marched off the course. Defending his actions, Garcia said: "I don't think I was unprofessional. Do you think it would have been better to have a fight on the 17th?"

Comatose Coll

At the 1930 World Cup, the trainer of the United States soccer team had to be carried off after accidentally anaesthetizing himself. During the semi-final with Argentina, trainer Jock Coll was still angry about a disputed Argentine goal when he was required to run on to the pitch to treat an injured player. In a fit of pique, Coll threw down his medical bag, thereby breaking a bottle of chloroform. Overcome by the fumes, he then suffered the indignity of being carried off by his own team.

Hitching while hurdling

Competing in the 1950 Empire Games at Auckland, South African hurdler Tom Lavery was shocked to find that the first thing that rose from its blocks was the button on the front of his shorts. No sooner was he in motion than he could feel his shorts slipping down towards his knees, so as he cleared each hurdle he covered up his embarrassment by hastily hitching them up without breaking stride. Remarkably, he still managed to take the bronze medal.

Able athletes

The Spanish gold medallists in the men's basketball event at the 2000 Paralympics were forced to hand back their medals after the Spanish Paralympic Committee found that ten of the 12 team members had no disability.

Fish 1–Filipic 0

A keen angler at a lake in eastern Slovenia caught a fish so big that he drowned while trying to reel it in. Franc Filipic, 47, was out fishing in 1998 when he landed a bite from a sheatfish, a type of catfish. After hooking it, he walked into the lake and steadfastly refused to let go even when it pulled him under. His body was found by divers after a two-day search. A friend said Filipic's last words before he drowned were: "Now I've got him!"

Prét

American athlete Loren Murchison was left at the start of the 1920 Olympic men's 100 metres final in Antwerp because he didn't understand French. When the starter said "Prét" (French for "Get set"), Murchison thought the runners had been told to stand up and was just in the act of relaxing his body and rising to his feet when the gun went off. Left trailing by 10 yards, he finished plumb last.

Careering Carrera

Celebrating his country's shock victory over the United States in the 1967 Davis Cup, Ecuadorian captain Danny Carrera made a mess of trying to jump the net and ended up breaking an ankle.

Nice drive there

After driving 375 miles from his home in Par, Cornwall, to make his motor racing debut at Brands Hatch, John George crashed his car just three seconds after the start. His Renault Clio was shunted from behind at the first corner and he ended up stuck in the gravel and out of the race. He lamented: "It was a long way to go for just three seconds of action." His wife Susan added: "I have to say, the race wasn't what I expected. But the drive there was quite scenic."

Marshalling mayhem

Incompetent marshalling at the 1988 Liège–Bastogne–Liège cycle race sent the entire field of 200 riders speeding down a hill straight into roadworks. Over 50 of the competitors were brought down in the ensuing pile-up.

Barnsley blunder

Soccer referee Andy Hall allowed Barnsley midfielder Mitch Ward to stay on the pitch for three minutes after he should have been sent off in the game at Fulham on 9 September 2000. Ward had already been shown a yellow card in the first half, and then referee Hall showed him a second yellow for a bad tackle in the 63rd minute. This should have meant an automatic sending-off, but Hall forgot all about the first caution and allowed Ward to stay on the pitch until the fourth official spotted the blunder. Hall later explained: "I wrote the player's name down in the first half but I couldn't read my writing."

Cyclists without bikes

In the mistaken belief that machines would be provided by the games organizers, the Ugandan cycling team arrived in New Zealand for the 1974 Commonwealth Games without any bikes. They had to borrow some from local riders.

Overlap

The 3,000-metre steeplechase at the 1932 Los Angeles Olympics descended into farce when the regular lap-checker was taken ill at the last minute and his inexperienced replacement forgot to change the lap count at the end of the first circuit. First to cross what should have been the finish line at the end of the race was Volmari Iso-Hollo of Finland, but instead he found no tape and a lap counter reading one to go. Thinking he must have miscalculated, he kept on running and won comfortably, but behind him, Britain's Thomas Evenson overtook Joseph McCluskey of the United States on the extra lap to grab the silver. McCluskey was offered a re-run the next day by embarrassed officials, but he declined the offer because he was too exhausted.

Pathetic putt

Playing the par-3 14th in the third round of the 1983 British Open at Royal Birkdale, Hale Irwin left his putt no more than an inch from the hole. But as he went to tap the ball in, he took his eye off it momentarily and missed the ball completely. The one-stroke penalty which he incurred was to prove costly for at the end of the four rounds, Irwin finished joint second – just one stroke behind the winner, fellow American Tom Watson.

Not saved by the bell

When the organizers of the boxing tournament at the 1988 Seoul Olympics decided to partition the hall in half and stage two fights simultaneously, they had overlooked one small point . . . the bell. In the general commotion surrounding the fights, it became impossible for the boxers to determine whether the bell they were hearing was for their fight or for the one in the other ring. Nowhere was this better illustrated than in a light-welterweight contest between Todd Foster of the United States and Chun Jin Chul from South Korea. Towards the end of the first round, Chun heard a bell, assumed it was for his bout, and strolled back to his corner. In fact, there were 17 seconds remaining in that round, and the bell was for the other fight. The referee appeared puzzled by Chun's actions, but said nothing. However the quick-thinking Foster realized what was happening and caught the unprepared Chun with a left hook which sent the Korean reeling to the canvas. The referee started the count, but then changed his mind. As confusion reigned supreme, the judges ordered a rematch to take place the following day which Foster won fair and square.

Zig Zaag

Competing in the 1950 Tour de France, exhausted North African rider Abd-El Kader Zaag gratefully accepted the offer of a bottle of wine from a spectator. But instead of just taking a swig, he drank the entire bottle. The alcohol took almost immediate effect, causing him to fall off his bike a few yards further on. Realizing that he was in no fit state to continue, he decided to sleep it off at the roadside. Five minutes later, he was back in the saddle and sprinting off down the road . . . in the wrong direction.

Aaron's accident

Argentine golfer Roberto de Vicenzo lost out on a play-off for the 1968 US Masters because playing partner Tommy Aaron filled in his card incorrectly. In the final round, Aaron accidentally wrote de Vicenzo's score at the 17th as a 4 instead of a birdie 3. De Vicenzo left the last green convinced that his 65 had earned him a play-off against America's Bob Goalby, but he failed to spot the mistake on the card and signed for a 66. Since the carded score has to stand – even if it is wrong – he finished one shot behind Goalby.

Offside owl

Oldham Athletic Football Club mascot Chaddy the Owl was sent off during his team's 4–1 home defeat by Peterborough United on 26 August 2000 because the assistant referee mistook him for an Oldham player and flagged him offside. "Fair enough, I had a replica shirt on," said Kevin Williams who wears the outfit, "But I also had a big, furry head."

Infelicitous Apples

Despite having to run in his everyday clothes, diminutive Cuban postman Felix Carvajal would surely have finished among the medals for the 1904 Olympic marathon at St Louis had he not stopped en route to pick apples from an orchard. Not only did the detour cost him valuable time, but the unripe apples left him with severe stomach pains. In agony, he staggered on gamely towards the finish, crossing the line in fourth place.

Big-busted golf

Callers to a freephone number advertising a US amateur golf tournament in 2000 were surprised to hear instead a sultry female voice telling them they had "come to the right place for nasty talk with big-busted girls."

Cold comfort

Sixteen-year-old Romanian gymnast Andrea Raducan was stripped of her gold medal at the 2000 Sydney Olympics after testing positive for a banned substance that was in a cold remedy she took. The blundering Romanian team doctor was expelled from the Games and suspended for the 2004 Olympics.

False Prophets

Michael Fish: An Ill Wind

To a nation obsessed with the weather, Michael Fish has been the friendly face of BBC television forecasting for some 20 years. Viewers forgave him the occasional slip-up – even his appalling taste in checked jackets – but when he failed to predict the dreadful hurricane of 1987 which lashed southern England, he became the butt of jokes and jibes the length and breadth of the land.

Fish's error was compounded by the fact that he had positively dismissed the notion of a hurricane to millions less than 12 hours before it struck. In his 1.25 p.m. forecast on 15 October, he said reassuringly: "Earlier on today, apparently, a woman rang the BBC and said she had heard that there was a hurricane on the way. Well, if you are watching, don't worry, there isn't." As denials go, it was pretty emphatic, but his words would quickly return to haunt him. For that night Britain was pounded by its worst hurricane for 284 years, the violent storms leaving 20 people dead and creating an £835,000,000 trail of destruction from Cornwall to East Anglia. Michael Fish had goofed . . . big time.

The offending storm was caused by a belt of exceptionally humid air from the west of Africa meeting cold Arctic air dragged down across the Atlantic in the Bay of Biscay off the western coast of France. The subsequent depression deepened rapidly before hitting Britain in the early hours of Friday 16 October. The extreme weather came as no surprise to European forecasters. As early as the previous Sunday the European Centre for Medium Range Weather Forecasting at Reading in Berkshire had warned of severe weather conditions ahead. On Tuesday 13 October the French Meteorological Department predicted winds gusting up to 90 mph, and the following night

Dutch TV viewers were told that freak storms were expected to hit the south coast of England two days later. Yet the British Meteorological Office chose to ignore the Reading warnings because the information conflicted with that from its own computer down the road at Bracknell.

Consequently while the rest of Europe was battening down the hatches, British forecasters predicted nothing worse than "breezes." Michael Fish became the fall guy, but in truth it could have been any one of them. Even when the Bracknell computer finally predicted a depression over northern France on 15 October, the men from the Met Office remained convinced that its effect on southern England would be nothing out of the ordinary. In his fateful forecast that afternoon, Fish added, after rejecting notions of a hurricane: "Actually the weather will become very windy, but most of the strong winds will be down over Spain and across into France." England, it seemed, would escape.

But the depression had ideas of its own. Skirting France and the Channel Islands, it headed straight for England, hitting the coast at around 1 a.m. As householders slept, night workers went about their business and revellers returned from parties and clubs, all totally unprepared for what was heading across the Channel. The storms struck with devastating force. Over the next four hours, with winds reaching up to 122 mph, 15 million trees crashed to the ground, lorries and planes were overturned, ships were sunk, houses were demolished, and cars were crushed by falling trees. Homes were plunged into darkness as electricity supplies failed and 3,000 miles of telephone wires were pulled down. In London the Fire Brigade dealt with no fewer than 6,000 emergency calls in the space of 24 hours. Meanwhile the Met Office's emergency reports of extraordinary winds did not go out even to specialist customers such as airlines and the fire and ambulance services until 3 a.m. – just an hour before the storm developed into a hurricane. At that time the London Weather Centre issued a warning to the London Fire Brigade of winds expected to reach 80 mph during the next hour. It was too little, too late.

Among the first victims of the storms were two fire officers en route to an emergency call. They were killed when an 80-foot oak tree crashed on to the cab of their water tender as they drove through Dorset. Tragically, the call turned out to be a false alarm. A guest at a hotel in Windsor died when a chimney crashed through the roof and a Hastings fisherman sustained fatal injuries after being struck by a flying beach hut. In the same town a man's body was recovered from the rubble of a hotel which had blown down "like a deck of cards."

In Central London's three royal parks alone, over 1,000 trees were brought down. Sevenoaks in Kent lost six of the seven oaks which gave the town its name and Kew Gardens in London lost a third of its valuable collection of trees. The curator lamented: "It was as if a giant had walked through the gardens, kicking over everything in his path."

As Britain began the lengthy clearing-up operation, the recriminations against the Met Office raged with a force almost as strong as the actual hurricane. Conservative MP Teddy Taylor described the lack of advance warning as "incomprehensible" and the Met men were accused of ignoring warnings from foreign forecasters. The howls of outrage were so great that Defence Secretary George Younger ordered an official inquiry into the Met Office's ineptitude. A Met Office spokesman admitted ruefully: "We could have got the forecast better."

The under-fire weathermen were as unprepared for the flak as they had been for the hurricane. Michael Fish admitted that he had been "caught out" by the direction of the low pressure trough while his colleagues put on a brave face. They insisted that they had predicted the storm – it had simply been stronger than they had expected and in a different place! They blamed a shortage of data from the Bay of Biscay where the depression had formed; they blamed a computer misreading; and they blamed budget cuts. They said that since their fleet of weather ships had been reduced from six to just one, there simply weren't enough observation ships to provide them with early warning of storms crossing the Atlantic. Among the weather ships that had been axed for financial reasons was the one stationed in the Bay of Biscay. Dr John Houghton, the Director General of the Meteorological Office, went a step further, claiming that there hadn't been a hurricane at all. "There was no hurricane," he stated boldly. "A hurricane can last for hours. There were intense gusts of short duration. Given the same equipment and the same data, we would make the same forecast again." So the weathermen buried their heads in the sand – that which hadn't been blown away.

The official report was more objective. It blamed Met Office staff for failing to interpret the data properly, pointing out that French and Dutch forecasters had correctly predicted the storms using the same data available to their British counterparts. The report also criticized Met Office scientists for placing too much trust in Bracknell's seven-year-old, out-of-date computer. Ironically at the time of the hurricane, the Met Office was supposed to be getting a new computer anyway. Almost a year later it arrived, at a cost of £5 million and eight times more powerful than its obsolete predecessor.

After being subjected to so much public ridicule, the television weathermen were determined not to make the same mistake again. Since 1987, they have erred on the side of caution. Their forecasts have adopted the tone of Wagnerian operas with the mildest of sea breezes bringing doom-laden warnings of dramatic storm-force gales, and the lightest shower prompting predictions of terrible floods of the like not seen since the days of Noah. Never again would they be accused of underselling the weather.

Crystal Balls-ups

Blathering Bernard

In the year AD 960, scholar Bernard of Thuringia caused considerable consternation in Europe when he confidently predicted that the world would end in AD 992.

Wrong in Toledo

In 1179 astrologer John of Toledo circulated pamphlets announcing that an alignment of planets would bring about the end of the world in 1186. When the fateful day arrived, the Byzantine emperor walled up the windows of his palace in Constantinople, but the 24 hours passed without incident.

Dry deluge

In 1523 British astrologers predicted that the world would end on 1 February 1524 following a deluge. 20,000 people fled their homes but the appointed doomsday failed to produce a single drop of rain over London. The astrologers duly apologized, saying they had been 100 years out and had really meant 1624.

Flaming Melchior

In 1533 Melchior Hoffmann announced in Strasbourg that the world would be consumed by flames that year. Many wealthy citizens of Strasbourg gave away their money and goods to the poor in the hope of being saved.

Shoot him!

In 1591 Colonel John Smyth told the Privy Council that the bullet was no match for the arrow. “The bow is a simple weapon,” he said. “Firearms are very complicated things which get out of order in many ways.”

Mad King George

“Nothing of importance happened today.” – George III’s diary entry for 4 July 1776, American Independence Day.

Music critic

Far too noisy, my dear Mozart. Far too many notes.” – the Emperor Ferdinand at the opening night of *The Marriage of Figaro*.

Dionysian drivel

“Rail travel at high speed is not possible because passengers, unable to breathe, would die of asphyxiation,” said Dr Dionysius Lardener in the early ninteenth century.

False prophet

Prophet John Turner, leader of the Southcottian sect from England, predicted that the world would end on 14 October 1820.

“Ostrich Gizzard” Gregory

The world’s largest diamond strike, which took place in South Africa in 1868, was dismissed out of hand by eminent Professor James Gregory. He insisted that any diamonds found there must have been carried from elsewhere in the gizzards of ostriches. “The whole story of the Cape diamond discoveries is false,” he proclaimed, “and is simply one of many schemes for trying to promote the employment and expenditure of capital in searching for this precious substance in the colony.”

Still nigh
Founded in 1872, the Jehovah's Witnesses have made no fewer than eight prophecies that the end of the world was nigh – in 1874, 1878, 1910, 1914, 1918, 1925, 1975, and 1984.

Pasteur's poppycock

"Louis Pasteur's theory of germs is ridiculous fiction," theorized Pierre Pachet, Professor of Physiology at Toulouse, 1872.

Telephone schmelephone

"This 'telephone' has too many shortcomings to be seriously considered as a means of communication. The device is inherently of no value to us," read a Western Union internal memo, in 1876.

Wrong Wilson

"When the Paris Exhibition closes, electric light will close with it and no more be heard of." – Professor Erasmus Wilson, Oxford University, 1878.

Blinkered Brits

"This might be good enough for our transatlantic friends but it is unworthy of the attention of practical or scientific men." – British Parliamentary Committee dismissing Thomas Edison's light bulb, 1878.

Rudyard rejected

"I'm sorry, Mr Kipling, but you just don't know how to use the English language." – Editor of the *San Francisco Examiner* turning down the opportunity to publish further articles by Rudyard Kipling, 1889.

Prophetic poppycock I

The ordinary horseless carriage is only a luxury for the rich and although the price will probably fall in the future, it will never be as popular as the bicycle." – *Literary Digest*, 1889.

Prophetic poppycock II

"It doesn't matter; he'll never make a success of anything." – A Munich headmaster when asked by Albert Einstein's father what profession his son should adopt, 1892.

Prophetic poppycock III

"Heavier-than-air flying machines are impossible." – Royal Society president Lord Kelvin, 1895.

Prophetic poppycock IV

"Everything that can be invented has been invented." – Charles H. Duell, Commissioner of the United States Office of Patents, 1899.

Caterpillar landships

The British Admiralty was singularly unimpressed by the development of the tank in 1915: "These caterpillar landships are idiotic and useless. Those officers and men are wasting their time and not pulling their proper weight in war."

Interesting toys

French commander Marshal Ferdinand Foch, who led the Allied armies in 1918, insisted: "Aeroplanes are interesting toys but are of no military value."

Wireless music box

"The wireless music box has no imaginable commercial value. Who would pay for a message sent to nobody in particular?" – David Sarnoff's associates in response to his request for investment in the radio, 1920s.

Market saturation

"I think there is a world market for maybe five computers." – Thomas Watson, chairman of IBM, 1943.

Hose house

"The modern home of 2000 will be waterproof inside and out, so the lucky housewife can do all her cleaning with a hose." – *Popular Mechanics* magazine, 1957.

Floating air platforms

The *New York Times* of 1967 predicted that in the year 2000 "a trip to Europe will only take half an hour by rocket and people will go about their normal everyday lives, getting from place to place by floating air platforms."

Too soon, too soon

In May 1975 the World Health Organization announced that malaria had been defeated and that the campaign to fight the disease was being scaled down. That afternoon the organization's deputy general was rushed to hospital in Geneva suffering from suspected malaria.

Clairvoyant crap

Citizens of Adelaide fled for the hills after Australian house painter and self-styled clairvoyant, John Nash, predicted that the city would be destroyed by an earthquake and a tidal wave at noon on 20 January 1976. Nash's premonition of doom was supported by leading Australian astrologer Richard Sterling, prompting locals to stage pre-quake parties and car dealers to advertise "crumbling prices". In the event, the day passed off without incident, but Nash was taking no chances. He was 400 miles away in Melbourne.

Prescient president

"There is no reason anyone would want a computer in their home." – Ken Olson, president, chairman and founder of Digital Equipment Corporation, 1977.

Flexi-disc fiasco

In 1979 pop guru Jonathan King introduced the flexi-disc to revive the ailing British music industry. Made of flimsy vinyl, it sold for just 33p – a third of the price of a normal vinyl single – and prompted King to predict: "The flexi-disc revolution could be as significant commercially as the introduction of the paperback book was decades ago. They are just what the pocket-money market, the 12- to 15-year-olds, are crying out for. A disc that gives them change from 50p could soon bring them back into the record shops." It didn't. The flexi-disc was shunned by buyers and retailers alike because of its poor sound quality, and proved a resounding miss.

Moon mania

According to a NASA prediction in 1980, there would be over 1,000 people living on the moon by 2001.

Bull

"There is no scientific evidence that BSE can be transmitted or that eating beef causes it in humans." – Prime Minister John Major, 1995. Four months later, the British government finally admitted that there was evidence.